High Places in Cyberspace
Second Edition

SCHOLARS PRESS
HANDBOOK SERIES

High Places in Cyberspace
Second Edition
by
Patrick Durusau

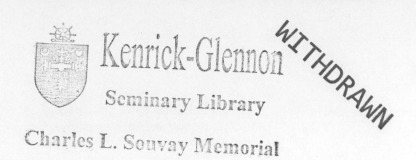

High Places in Cyberspace

*A Guide to Biblical and Religious Studies, Classics,
and Archaeological Resources on the Internet*

Second Edition

by
Patrick Durusau

Scholars Press
Atlanta, Georgia

High Places in Cyberspace
A Guide to Biblical and Religious Studies, Classics,
and Archaeological Resources on the Internet

Second Edition

by
Patrick Durusau

Library of Congress Cataloging in Publication Data
Durusau, Patrick, 1954–
    High places in cyberspace : a guide to biblical and religious
studies, classics, and archaeological resources on the Internet /
by Patrick Durusau. — 2nd ed.
      p.   cm. — (Scholars Press handbook series)
    Includes bibliographical references and index.
    ISBN 0-7885-0492-4 (alk. paper)
    1. Archaeology—Computer network resources—Handbooks, manuals,
etc. 2. Civilization, Classical—Computer network resources—
Handbooks, manuals, etc. 3. Religion—Computer network resources—
Handbooks, manuals, etc. 4. Internet (Computer network)—Handbooks,
manuals, etc. I. Title. II. Series.
CC82.9.D87 1998
930.128—dc21   98-45570
                                  CIP

Printed in the United States of America
on acid-free paper

This book is dedicated to my wife, Carol and our daughter, Elizabeth.

Table of Contents

Preface to Second Edition

Since the publication of the first edition of this work in 1996, the breadth of resources on the Internet of interest to scholars has increased dramatically. The bibliographic resources of most of the major research institutions worldwide are now available to anyone with an Internet connection. Textual databases, online journals, excavation reports, recreations of temples and archaeological sites, and other online resources cover virtually every field of scholarly endeavor.

The ability to rapidly distribute the results of scholarly research or electronic facsimiles of source materials has brought change or pressure to change on several aspects of academia. First, there is increasing dissatisfaction with traditional models of access that result in the obligatory "I was entrusted with this fragment by Prof. A" or "Museum Y has granted permission" in dissertations and publications respectively. Such restrictions are the result of personal status seeking at the expense of scholarship and are increasingly under pressure from funding agencies that are seeking the widest distribution for funded research or excavations. The culture of distribution of results or publication in the scholarly community is also changing from the unique opportunities offered by the Internet.

The Internet has offered the opportunity for distribution of scholarly research that would not be possible or would be prohibitively expensive by any other means. For example, archaeological excavation reports are typically published in limited numbers and consider only a small part of the artifacts found at even modest excavations. Electronic publication has made it possible to grant scholars access to all the artifacts found at any excavation without many of the attendant costs of hardcopy publication. High-resolution scans can provide scholars with easy access to manuscripts too fragile for routine handling or located at distant universities. The routine use of the Internet for scholarly collaboration and instruction is rapidly becoming a reality of academic life.

These changes to traditional academic practices have not been without their critics. Self-publication and the lack of traditional gatekeepers, such as academic publishers, has resulted in a large amount of substandard material on the Internet. Many of the critics of academic use of the Internet point to such materials as proof that electronic publication is not "serious" academic publication. These critics are confusing the medium of communication with the content that it delivers. There are legitimate presses in the field of biblical studies, just are there are vanity presses that publish a large number of titles each year. Yet none of the critics of electronic publishing decry print publication as a whole as failing to meet the standards of scholarship. The mechanisms of peer review and active scholars as editors have operated for years to filter and improve the content of recognized scholarly publications. These mechanisms are as applicable to electronic publication as to print. (Interested readers might want to consult Stevan Harnad's "Learned Inquiry and the Net: The Role of Peer Review, Peer Commentary and Copyright", **http://citd.scar.utoronto.ca/EPub/talks/Harnad_Snider.html**, for an examination of the role of peer review and copyright in academic publishing.)

Its critics notwithstanding, the number of scholarly resources on the Internet and its adoption by most major universities as a tool in the scholarly enterprise have made Internet literacy a requirement for modern scholars. In an effort to promote Internet literacy this work outlines the basic information needed to use the Internet and presents a selective listing of Internet resources. The resource listings are not exhaustive but are intended to provide a good starting place for exploration in a variety of subjects. Expanded coverage has been given to the effective use of search engines in finding new or updated scholarly resources on the Internet.

But finding scholarly resources is only the beginning of academic literacy, whether in traditional resources or the Internet. This work concludes with coverage of some of the techniques for creating new scholarly resources on the Internet. Questions to be answered before creating resources, techniques for delivery of primarily textual information, to the more advanced methods of presenting information are the focus of the concluding section of this work. Most of these techniques require book length treatment severally, and this guide seeks only to provide an overview of their possibilities with references for those who wish to pursue these methods.

Michael Fraser, one of the leading figures in electronic resources in the humanities, wrote in his review of the first edition of *High Places in Cyberspace* that "The title to this work may have rather unfortunate connotations given that in the Bible the term high places is invariably linked with their imminent destruction along with graven images and Asher'im." (Fraser's review can be found at: **http://info.ox.ac.uk/ctitext/publish/comtxt/ct14/fraser.html**) Yes, the title does refer to high places as found in the Hebrew Bible but I do not interpret it in quite so negative a fashion. While respecting scholars who hold traditional views of Israelite history, I think it is more likely to have been a pluralistic society that was only retrospectively portrayed as a united theocracy. The High Places in the title of this work is a recognition of the plurality of scholarly views that constitute the academic world.

Patrick Durusau

Atlanta, 1998

Preface to First Edition

The idea for this book began when Harry Gilmer, the Director of Scholars Press, was investigating the idea of using the Internet and electronic publishing to supplement our traditional publishing efforts in the fields of archaeology, classics and religion. While there are books on the Internet, both simple and advanced, there are none that seek to be a map of scholarly resources for the disciplines traditionally served by Scholars Press. That lack of a map to the Internet has left scholars to find such resources as they might, some more or less successfully than others. An analogous situation would be a Greek scholar studying the use of a word without the concordances, lexicons, and other tools associated with a critical study of the text, save as he or she could devise. This book is the first step toward providing scholars of archaeology, the classics and religion with a map to the resources for those areas on the Internet.

Maps can be viewed as merely representing the locations of physical features on the terrain and in relationship to each other. The events of the twentieth century have demonstrated rather pointedly, however, that maps are also social and political statements, whether so acknowledged by their creators or not. This map of the Internet is no different from a map of the Balkans, the Middle East or any other area where boundaries of all types are being redrawn. Yes, this map lists resources and their locations on the Internet, much as its roadmap counterpart records street addresses and intersections. But this map also seeks to demonstrate that the Internet offers avenues for scholarly communication and collaboration that have not heretofore existed, avenues that enhance teaching, research and collaboration by and among scholars. In that regard, this work argues by example for a redrawing of the map that defines the tools and methods of scholars.

This book does not seek to be a manual for setting up your computer or software for access to the Internet. There are a number of good manuals listed in Further Reading that cover the variety of computers and software with far more completeness and competence that would be possible here. In addition to those manuals, the reader might consider finding a colleague or graduate student who is interested the Internet and exploring it together. One of the nicer aspects of the early Internet culture was the willingness of the more experienced to help others learn the highways and byways of the Internet.

In terms of audiences, this book is addressed to the scholar who needs a quick source of information concerning resources currently available on the Internet, scholars who are contemplating the use of the Internet for teaching or publishing, and scholars who wish to demonstrate the need for Internet access for themselves and their students. For the scholar looking for particular resources, this is not a comprehensive listing of all resources in any given subject area for several reasons. First and foremost, the number of resources available on the Internet is increasing faster than any print-bound medium can possibly mirror. For that reason, ideas for finding new resources are listed in the Staying Current section of this book. Updates to the resources listed in this work can also be found on TELA, the WWW site maintained by Scholars Press, at **http://shemesh.scholar.emory.edu/scripts/highplaces.html**. Secondly, there approaches to the subject matter under consideration. This is not meant as any denigration of those sites. Denominational resources, for example, are excellent resources for their intended audiences but do not meet the academic orientation necessary for inclusion here. Lastly, and hopefully the smallest category, sites may have been overlooked that deserved inclusion in this work. If you maintain a site or know of a site not included that should have appeared, please contact the author at pdurusau@emory.edu so that oversight can be corrected on the updates posted to TELA and in any subsequent editions of this work.

The scholar who is contemplating the use of the Internet for teaching or publishing will find many examples of such uses. As in more traditional scholarly activities, you will find a great deal of support and advice from are a number of resources that were intentionally omitted as not representing scholarly those who are currently using these new tools in your area. It is not necessary to understand the complexity of computer transmission protocols to use the Internet any more than it is necessary to understand digital switching theory to use your office telephone. Successful presentation of information over the Internet requires new skills and knowledge, but none that is beyond the average scholar in archaeology, classics and religion. All of these fields assume a degree of multilingual ability and the ability to learn and integrate new information into successful research. Those same skills will serve scholars who wish to make use of the Internet in their scholarly activities.

The third audience of this book is scholars who wish to demonstrate the importance of the Internet for their scholarly activities to their institutions and their colleagues. The use of the Internet for dissemination of scholarly information has been given strong and consistent institutional support at many academic institutions, as attested by the resources listed in this work. Unfortunately, many institutions does not equal all institutions, just as the originators of the resources listed do not equal the number of scholars who contribute to scholarly publications each year. In each of the areas covered by this work, archaeology, classics, and religious studies, there are contributions by acknowledged leaders in their respective areas of expertise. Those contributions range from new translations, bibliographies, book reviews, articles, excavations reports, images of important texts and artifacts, to, in some cases, entire monographs. I hope the resources listed in this work will assist scholars in demonstrating the importance of the Internet for their field while soliciting institutional support for their activities.

The Internet offers myriad possibilities for the dissemination of scholarly information and collaboration with other scholars. It is now possible to make available images of artifacts found at an archaeological excavation, create hypertexts demonstrating multiple textual traditions, publish hyperlinked texts and translations, teach a class to students across multiple continents, or prepare a virtual tour of an ancient temple that has not survived the ravages of time. Scholars can collaborate with colleagues based upon similar interests and strengths, sharing resources and ideas, without regard to physical location. The integration of these resources and collaborative possibilities into traditional scholarship will not always be easy or universally acclaimed. But then, neither was the invention of the movable type printing press.

Patrick Durusau

Atlanta, 1996

Acknowledgements

Since the first edition of this work there has been an explosion of academic resources on the Internet as scholars discover new ways to use the Internet as part of the academic enterprise. Many projects have moved from the seeds planted by pioneering scholars into the institutional framework of universities and research centers, gaining mainstream academic status and concurrently increased institutional support. This work is both an honor roll of some of the leading projects on the Internet and a call to scholars to increase their use and awareness of Internet technology. Without the continuing efforts of both longtime computing humanists and newly arrived Internet-aware scholars, this work would not be possible or necessary. Scholars Press and its director, Dr. Harry Gilmer, have provided continuing support for both this work and my interest in electronic publishing for scholars. It was at their urging that I have composed this work in TEILite markup and provided Scholars Press with an SGML document instance and a typeset manuscript created using James Clark's **Jade** program with Richard Light's TEILite DSSSL stylesheet.

1. Introduction

The Internet, controversies about it's content (or lack thereof), new resources or software for it and its impact upon society and scholarship are now topics of daily conversation. In the past few years, what was once only the domain of computer scientists and a limited number of research institutions has become a daily presence in the lives of many academics. The history of the Internet has been told more fully by authors who participated in its origins and rise and need not be repeated here (see the Further Reading section, below). This work has a limited goal of acting as a resource guide for academics who seek to take advantage of the resources to be found on the Internet for the fields of religious studies, archaeology and classics. Before turning to those portions of this work that detail such resources, some basic questions about the Internet, such as the quality of its resources how to obtain access, are addressed.

What is the Internet

It may come as a surprise to learn that the term Internet does not properly refer to a single network or even group of networks. Terms such as the Net or Cyberspace also lack any referent that can clearly be defined as the object of those terms. The Internet is actually a vast collection of individual computer networks which all communicate with each other by means of a commonly defined means of communication, known as a protocol. The scope and limitations of what may be made available to others on this collection of networks is actually the decision and responsibility of each separate computer network that comprises the Internet. It is perhaps an example of what political philosophers would call a state of anarchy.

To refer to the Internet as anarchy does not mean that there are no rules for its use but rather indicates that there is no central authority which governs the uses to which this vast collection of inter-connected computers are put. Many of the rules of the Internet are more of the nature of customary usage and practice than actual rules codified by some authority. An example of one such rule, it is generally considered to be unacceptable practice to post messages to dozens or hundreds of email discussion lists, which are not in keeping with the topic of the list. For example, it is considered a serious *faux pas* to send email advertising legal services for immigrants to a mailing list on Pauline Studies. When that occurs, the person sending such messages is usually overwhelmed at the response of the online community, which usually consists of sending so many protesting messages to the offender that the mail service at their site ceases to function. Such users are generally invited by their service provider to seek access to the Internet elsewhere. The most common examples of such mailing are from commercial ventures that are seeking to sell services unrelated to any topic under discussion.

Users who have what is called a SLIP/PPP connection to the Internet are also part of the collection of computers that comprise the Internet, at least while their computers are connected. Those users are free to decide what, if any, material they would like to offer to others, just as are larger computer sites on the Internet. This ability to offer materials to a wide audience has led to what has been decried as self-publication by some academic commentators. The quality of the materials found on the Internet is the focus of the next general question about using the Internet.

Whither Quality with Internet Publishing?

Questions concerning the quality of information available on the Internet are of serious concern both for those who seek to publish in this new medium and those who must judge the contribution of such publications. In any discussion concerning the quality of materials on the Internet, it is important to note that quality is more closely related to the efforts of the author than to the means chosen to make that work available. Consider, for example, *Cassiodorus*, the standard treatment of the life and work of Flavius Magnus Arurelius Cassiodorus by James J. O'Donnell. This work was first published in 1979 by the University of California Press and now can be found in its entirety on the Internet at **http://ccat.sas.upenn.edu/jod/cassiodorus.html**. The availability of this work on the Internet has not lessened its quality and may have enhanced its usefulness by making it available to a larger scholarly community.

That is not to say that there is no material on the Internet in the subject areas covered by this work that is of far lesser quality than the cited work by O'Donnell, but that lack of quality cannot be attributed to the medium over which such works are made available. Traditionally, the quality of scholarly publishing has been the province of editors and editorial boards of academic presses and journals. Some of those same mechanisms have been adapted by electronic journals found herein, such as *the Journal of Buddhist Ethics*, *the Journal of Hebrew Scriptures* and *TC: A Journal of Biblical Textual Criticism*. If an active board of editors can assure quality in the publication of a print journal, there is no reason to expect a different outcome with the publication of an electronic one.

Few resources on the Internet are guided by a board of editors, although that number is increasing in academic areas. For the vast majority of resources, the individual users must make their own judgments as to the quality of the work presented. Academics can all recall articles, even books, published by respected publishers or journals that were scarcely worth their weight as waste paper. The simple fact of publication is no guarantee of quality, either on paper or on the Internet. The same tools used to judge works published by more traditional means, the reputation of the author, evidence cited for the positions advanced, and reliable citation of prior work in the field, are all part of that process of judgment.

Another way to describe the function of academic presses and journals, as suggested by Harry Gilmer, is to consider them as "gatekeepers." To some degree on the Internet, that role of "gate keeper" has been fulfilled by sites such as **ABZU**, by Charles Jones of the University of Chicago; **CLASSICS**, by Linda Wright of the University of Washington; and **TELA**, by James R. Adair of Scholars Press. New sites and sources are not added to these sites simply because it has the proper words in the site name or upon request. Each of these sites reviews the material for its relevance to the users of that site and accept or reject materials accordingly. In the final stages of proofing this manuscript for publication, a search was run on one of the WWW indexes for the term "biblical," finding some 20,000 documents with that term as part of the document. A quick review of the top thirty documents returned revealed that they ranged from materials cited in this resource guide to the simply banal.

Publishers, libraries, and Internet sites will recreate the traditional role of gatekeepers to filter the virtually unlimited scope of electronic resources. This new role will focus on the creation and dicovery of useful resources rather than limiting the number of total resources available. Given the vast reach of the Internet and the growing number of resources to be found there, it would be unwise to ignore the respective strengths of both libraries and publishers in assisting scholars in the use of this tool.

Why Should I Use the Internet?

It is taken as a given in some circles that all academics should want to flock to the Internet, and it comes as a surprise that not all academics are interested in online access. Academics have mastered the tools of their field of study and need no other projects to fill their already tight schedules, filled with classes and other research obligations. For the most part, scholars reluctant to use the Internet are neither closet Luddites nor simply technophobes. They have not been shown the usefulness of the Internet to their teaching and research needs and hence see no need to learn the skills necessary to use a tool that produces no results of interest to them.

One of the more obvious benefits of access to the Internet is the ability to use email for routine communications with other scholars and on electronic discussion lists. Email is particularly useful when collaborating with scholars located at other universities or overseas, as it avoids the uncertainties and delays of regular mail communications. Email currently allows electronic journals to have a functioning editorial board with members on several different continents. Email discussion lists offer the possibility for the informal exchange of ideas and information among scholars who would rarely have the opportunity to meet in a physical conference setting. Email and discussion lists do not have the same spontaneity or give and take of traditional academic society meetings, but they can establish contacts between scholars who might otherwise not meet in the current climate of limited academic budgets.

Along more traditional lines, the Internet offers access to some of the premier research libraries of the world from the office computer. The excellent Egyptology collection at the Griffith Institute is a good example of a reference collection that is in the process of placing its catalog of holdings on the Internet. Library access primarily is to the catalog of holdings, although many libraries are working with publishers to provide greater access to actual contents of items in a library collection. Scholars Press, for example, is currently working with the Emory University libraries to bring the 1996-1998 issues of the *Journal of the American Academy of Religion*, *Critical Review of Books in Religion*, *Semeia* and *Biblical Archaeologist* (now, *Near Eastern Archaeology*) to the Internet. More monographs and rare materials will increasingly become available as a part of library collections accessible over the Internet. Online catalogs for libraries are an excellent way to check bibliographic sources, look for recent additions to major research collections, and build research bibliographies. The use of computer access allows the scholar to cut and paste the information found in the card catalog into a word processing or other program, without the tedious necessity of copying and then entering the information by hand.

A wide variety of textual materials and artifacts have been or are becoming available as more scholars seek to explore the use of the Internet for low cost distribution of information. The Cobb Institute of Archaeology's **Lahav DigMaster Digital Archaeology Archives** is an illustration of how a larger number of artifacts can be made available for examination than by the traditional means of publishing excavation reports for archaeological sites (**http://www.sarc.msstate.edu**). Other sites also offer virtual representations of archaeological sites with images of the sites as excavated and as reconstructed. This is not to mention the growing amount of textual information that has been made available by the leading scholars in various areas of study.

The Internet is and should be viewed as a tool to advance the traditional activities of scholars. All scholars seek to consult and collaborate with others, use libraries as a part of their professional lives and communicate the results of their work to other scholars and students. This new means of electronic communication has created tools which can make the pursuit of those activities more timely, effective and wide ranging than previously thought possible. In order for these tools to be effective, however, they need the capable hands of scholars as their masters.

Getting Online

There are any number of options available for the scholar who wishes to connect to the Internet, and the number of ways that such connections can be made is increasing on almost a daily basis. It is not the purpose of this section to recommend a particular service provider, software or computer platform for use with your Internet connection. There are too many variations in the types of services, software and computers for such advice to be practical in a work that primarily seeks to record what is available to scholars from the Internet. Rather what follows is a general description of the various options generally available to scholars seeking to access to the Internet. The specifics of how to set up and use software for such access are best resolved in conjunction with the Internet Service Provider chosen for access.

Access Options

There are several means of connecting a personal computer to the Internet. The first, and until recently the most common means, is through a standard dial-up connection. After securing a phone number and password from an access provider, the user calls over the telephone to establish a connection to the Internet. The primary limitation of this method is the speed of the connection offered, which is generally limited by the speed of the modems used by the scholar and the service provider. At present, the fastest connection generally available by this method is 56.6 kilobaud, which is a measurement of the speed at which the modem can transmit and receive information. Unfortunately, the speed at which such connections actually operate is limited by the quality of the phone line connecting the two computers. The sole advantage of dial-up access is that you can use your account from any computer with a modem, an important factor for those who need portability. Of the methods for connecting to the Internet, the dial-up account should be chosen only if other options are unavailable or too expensive to be of practical use.

As the demand for Internet access has grown, so have the number of options to obtain high-speed connections to the Internet. The options for any given user vary widely both in terms of availability and costs. There are several technologies currently competing to become the standard method for access to the Internet. One of the oldest of these has been offered by telephone companies for a number of years and is known by the acronym ISDN. (Integrated Services Digital Network) Unfortunately, ISDN connections tend to be rather expensive and are available only to users who live within specified distances from local telephone substations. The emerging market for Internet services has lead other technologies such as ASDL (Asymmetric Digital Subscriber Line) over traditional phone lines and cable modems that permit access over the optical cable used by cable TV companies. Users should check the types of access offered in their local community and compare prices before choosing a method of accessing the Internet. These competing technologies are incompatible with each other and special hardware from one type of connection cannot be reused should the user switch to another type of access.

A direct connection to the Internet over existing university network systems is the preferred means of access for scholars at such locations. This type of connection avoids the impact of changing technology on the individual scholar and may provide greater access to the Internet than can be justified for a personal connection. It may also provide more reliable Internet access with greater support from the local university computer support service. Access information should be obtained from the university-computing center, which probably will have advice and software to be used with such a connection.

Service Providers

As noted above, the method of access to be preferred is to use an existing university network connection for Internet access. In the happy event of such a connection being available, the university is your Internet service provider and you or your department can make arrangements with the university for the access account. For a number of scholars, however, that type of arrangement will not be an option at present, and they will have to rely upon commercial access providers for their access to the Internet.

Commercial providers of access to the Internet are a relatively recent phenomenon, being the result of the rapid growth of both the Internet and its commercialization. There are a large number of such providers, offering a wide range of services and types of accounts, at widely varying prices. As is often the case with material concerning the Internet, listings of such providers are available on the Internet, but that is of little use to someone not yet using the Internet. Most of the resources cited in the Further Reading section contain listings for some of the better known service providers, usually with a brief description of the type of access offered. Unfortunately, those listings become quickly dated due to the delay between the recording of the information and its appearance in printed form. Anyone who already has access to an Internet connection can obtain a more current listing of service providers from the following source. Celestin Company, Inc. maintains a very comprehensive and updated list of Internet Service Providers, both for the U.S. and for other countries. The list can be obtained by email by sending a blank message to info@celestine.com, with the subject line: SEND POCIA.TXT. POCIA is an abbreviation of Providers of Commercial Internet Access, and the message you will receive in response to your query contains a listing of service providers and telephone contact information (WWW at **http://www.celestin.com/pocia** or by FTP at **ftp://ftp.celestin.com/biz/celestin/pocia/pocia.txt**). Whether a service provider is found in a printed source, in the Celestin listings or by recommendation of a fellow scholar, there are several questions that should be addressed to any contemplated service provider.

The basic questions that should be addressed to any Internet Service Provider are as follows, in no particular order of importance:

1.   What are the rates for access?

2.   Is there a local number for dialup access to this service?

3.   What type of technical support is available?

4.   Does it offer SLIP/PPP?

Most Internet service providers offer basic Internet service at a flat monthly rate for an unlimited number of hours online. This is not always the case, and it is best to resolve questions about billing and what services are provided before accepting a particular service provider. It can be very inconvenient to change service providers because of billing disputes once the software has been setup and the user's email address has been given to colleagues. There are enough service providers available in most areas for users to avoid having to accept one with billing practices or policies that they find objectionable.

A local access number for an Internet Service Provider is essential if the user contemplates spending any amount of time connected to the Internet. One of the service connections used in the preparation of this work was actually based in California, but it had a local access number in Atlanta, Georgia. A local access number is called a POP, which stands for Point of Presence. It is difficult to overestimate the amount of time that will be spent using the Internet, particularly as the user tries new sites and resources, so a service provider that offers a local access number is highly recommended.

Technical support for university based connections is usually handled by the university computer services department. The amount of service offered by commercial providers varies from support only for connection difficulties to broader support for problems encountered in using Internet access software and Internet resources. The best source of information about the type of support offered by a particular service provider is another user of that particular service. With the large number of academics online, it should not be too difficult to find a colleague who is using the same service provider and who can offer his or her opinion of the type of support provided.

Types of Service

In discussing the basic rates for services with an Internet Service Provider, the user should be aware that there are two main types of connections offered by most providers. The first, and now largely disappearing, type of service is called a shell account. With the shell account, the user logs into the service provider's computer and is confronted with a Unix prompt. This type of account, while very useful, requires some knowledge of Unix commands in order to be fully utilized by the user. There are programs, which can provide a graphical interface for access to WWW resources over such an account, but they are not as useful as those found for the other main type of connection offered to the Internet. With the shell account your local computer is acting as a terminal of the provider's computer which is connected to the Internet. There are other connections that make your computer, for the time it is connected, an active member of the computers that collectively comprise the Internet.

The rapidly growing type of connection that makes a user's computer an active part of the Internet is known as a SLIP/PPP connection. SLIP and PPP refer to the means by which your computer talks to the computer used to access the Internet. As part of such a connection, your computer is assigned a unique Internet address that is different from any other computer on the Internet. In order to use any of the WWW browsers, such as Mosaic or Netscape, it is necessary to have a SLIP/PPP connection. WWW browsers provide a graphical interface for most, if not all, of the usual tasks faced by users of the Internet. It is definitely the preferred means of accessing the Internet via a dialup connection, and if one local service provider does not offer this type of connection, it is definitely in the user's interest to seek out one that does offer SLIP/PPP connections to the Internet.

Online Services

There is one other way to access the Internet, which was not covered in the foregoing summary. Online services are providers that generally charge a monthly fee for an account plus per minute charges for use of their services. Such providers typically generate their own content for subscribers, which is usually not available to people who are not subscribers to that service, in addition to providing some type of access to the Internet. The scope of that access has generally increased as online services have been faced with increasing calls for the ability to connect to the wider range of information and services available on the Internet.

Examples of online services include Compuserve, America Online, and Delphi. Online services have traditionally provided access to fee-based information services, such as the Chemical Abstracts, RLIN and other information services which require payment for use. At this point in time, no online service provides the type of access to the Internet that can be found with a traditional Internet Service Provider. If budgetary constraints allow, it is probably best to have a SLIP/PPP connection with an Internet Service Provider for regular use and an account with an online service provider only for those services not otherwise available on the Internet.

2. Email Discussion Lists

One of the earliest experiences most scholars have with the Internet is that of using email. One important source of information for scholars on the Internet are the many discussion lists which address topics of interest to scholars. Discussion lists are mailing lists on the Internet that accept messages from subscribers and then forward those messages to all the subscribers on that discussion list. There are several types of discussion list software used on the Internet, and each responds to a slightly different set of commands. The major types of mailing list software discussed in this chapter are: **listserv**, **listproc**, **mailbase** and **majordomo**. Examples of the various commands are shown by reproducing the actual screen. Your screen may not appear the same as this mail program, known as Pine, but the addresses used and commands used for the mailing lists are entered the same way in all mail programs.

There are other types of software that are used for the management of mailing lists that are not covered in this guide to discussion lists. If the user encounters a mailing list that does not appear to follow the rules for the major types of mailing list software set forth below, it will be necessary to use the instructions that accompany the announcement of such a list. Most such software responds to a message that contains the word "help" in the body of a message by sending instructions for that particular type of mailing list software. If a list owner is named for the list and the user is unable to obtain satisfactory responses using the instructions returned by the "help" request, write to the list owner for assistance. The vast majority of list owners are operating their discussion lists on their own time and to advance the discussion of an area of study in which they have a great deal of interest. Please allow sufficient time for the list owner to respond to your request before sending your request for assistance a second time.

Before turning to the commands peculiar to each separate type of mailing list software, it is important to note a few basic rules for courteous and effective use of email discussion lists. Some of the rules are the application of common courtesy in a new setting, while others reflect the mores and usage of the online community. These rules, to some degree, also reflect the author's view of email discussion lists as a means of conducting academic discussions without regard to geographic distance or departmental travel allowances. As with all rules of conduct, they should be applied in the light of the circumstances at hand and are a poor substitute for good taste and judgment.

Rules for Email Discussion Lists

1. Never send private or confidential information to an email discussion list.

While no one would intentionally send private or confidential information to an email discussion list read by hundreds if not thousands of other academics, it does occur. One of the main reasons for this type of posting is a lack of familiarity with the email software being used to read the discussion list. What begins as an attempt to forward a message to a colleague with some private remark about the originator of the message or the message itself, does indeed go to the colleague, but a copy also is sent back to the discussion list! One defense against this type of embarrassment is to learn how to properly reply to a discussion list using the email software at hand.

The other defense against this type of Internet faux pas is to follow a related rule, which the author first learned as a practicing attorney: Do not put anything in writing or say anything in front of witnesses that you would not want to see on the front page of the newspaper or read to a federal grand jury. That may seem harsh or even paranoid, but in these litigious times, a chance, even humorous remark at the time, may surface years later to be seen as evidence of intent to discriminate, harass, or commit some other wrongdoing. It is impossible to reconstruct the overall context of the remark in an ongoing email discussion and viewed on its own, the questioned remark may indeed seem outrageous. It is also important to note that any email message, whether sent to an email discussion list or not, may be forwarded to anyone or group with an email address. A posting critical of individuals or policies may receive far more public distribution than was originally intended by the sender of the message.

2. Always address administrative requests to the proper address.

The instructions for the various types of email discussion lists set forth below detail what address should receive request to subscribe, unsubscribe and other administrative requests. The people who are already on an email list for the discussion of religious ethics, for example, are not really interested in your desire to subscribe to or unsubscribe from the list and have no ability to answer your request. At best, such posts demonstrate an unwillingness to master the fundamentals of email discussion lists to avoid the inconveniencing of other members of the list.

3. Always quote appropriately.

In answering a prior post to an email discussion list, it is appropriate to quote only those portions of the prior message that you are addressing. It is not necessary to quote the entire post and wastes the time of readers of the list, who must wade through the prior post to find your comments. By quoting appropriately, you should quote enough of the prior message to fairly set forth the position of the person sending the prior message.

4. Avoid ad hominem attacks.

It would seem unnecessary to state this as a rule for academic discussion lists, but the immediacy of the email medium seems to invite quick, often ill-considered remarks that would not be made in the course of normal academic channels. For example, on one discussion list there arose a discussion that included a statement to the effect, "A majority of scholars of X concur that ..., including Prof. A and Prof. B ...." The quick response to that statement was: "Prof. A and a student of Prof. A equals one opinion ...." (The names and topic were omitted to protect the innocent/guilty, depending upon one's view of that discussion.) Suffice it to say that this exchange did little to advance the discussion of the subject matter under discussion. Continued abuse of a list through frequent *ad hominem* attacks or other breaches of netiquette may result in a person being permanently banned from the list.

5. Offer messages that advance the topic under discussion.

In the course of some discussions, scholars will indicate that they are willing to share copies of programs they have written or data sets. In such cases it is more appropriate to reply to that individual indicating an interest in those materials instead of posting a statement of your interest with a copy of the original post to the discussion list. In the same category of posting falls the quoting of an entire post with the message "I agree" and the new poster's signature line appended to the bottom of the original post. No doubt the original poster and the members of the discussion list are delighted to learn of your agreement but would be even more pleased to learn of any original thoughts you have on the subject at hand.

6. Always cite relevant resources in postings.

Whether answering requests for information or in the course of discussion, it is helpful if reference can be made to resources relevant to the topic under discussion. For example, in the course of discussing Hebrew verb forms it would not be necessary to refer to standard references known to those in the field, but it would be useful if new or recent books/articles were cited as appropriate. The amount of available information in all fields is growing at a rate that makes it difficult to be aware of all the relevant resources even in narrow areas of specialization. Citing of new resources can advance both the discussions on the email list and make other scholars aware of material they may not have seen.

7. Remember not to SHOUT.

One very obvious clue to a person's experience with email is a posting that is written IN ALL CAPITAL LETTERS. Using all capital letters is known as shouting and can be rather difficult to read in most email programs. Postings should follow the normal course of upper and lower case letters save for those instances where material is capitalized for emphasis.

8. Remember that members of discussion lists are people.

This final rule, if followed, would obviate the need to state the prior seven in such detail. All of the participants in email discussion lists have hopes, dreams, aspirations and job responsibilities. They should not be confused with the positions they may advocate in academic discussion, nor should they be abused simply because at the moment another member of the list has a mistaken belief in a different position. As a contracts law professor once told his first year law school class, "If you take any lesson from this past year of contracts law, let it be this: The plaintiff had a name, and the defendant had a face." Abstract positions, whether in law or other academic debates, should not overshadow the real participants in these discussions.

There are other listings of suggested rules for the use of email discussion lists and even for the Internet in general. One of the better guides to courtesy on the Internet can be found at **ftp://ftp.lib.berkeley.edu/pub/net.training/FAU/netiquette.txt**. Arlene H. Rinaldi of Florida Atlantic University authored this document, "The Net, User Guidelines and Netiquette," for use at Florida Atlantic University, but it is a useful document for all users of the Internet.

LISTSERV

One of the earliest and still widely used type of mailing list software is the listserv. It was most often seen on the Bitnet network and offered a range of commands that has not been fully duplicated by any subsequent software. Unfortunately, true listserv software runs only on VMS platforms, and its Unix cousin is a pale imitation of the original program. The commands discussed below work on the original VMS version of the software and are not guaranteed to work with the Unix version of that software.

Subscribe/Unsubscribe

The most important thing to remember about listserv discussion lists is that all commands, in order to be effective, must be mailed to the listserv@somewhere.edu address. The resource listing for mailing lists has the subscription address for each listserv in that format. Commands sent to the mailinglist@somewhere.edu are sent to all the subscribers and do not accomplish anything other than annoying the members of that discussion list. To join the AIBI-L discussion list, which is a discussion forum for l'Association Internationale Bible et Informatique, consult the resource guide for mailing list and send the subscription request to listserv@listserv.uottawa.ca. Open your email program to address and compose the message as follows: (The comments following the "#" sign and the "#" sign itself should not be reproduced in your mail message. Those comments are included for purposes of illustration only.)

```
To: listserv@listserv.uottawa.ca          #Note, sent to listserv address
Cc:
Attchmnt:
Subject:                                  #Subject left blank
----- Message Text -----
subscribe AIBI-L Patrick Durusau #Substitute your name

//EOJ                                     #Tells LISTSERV software it is at the
                                          #end of the commands in the message.
                                          #Useful for lines automatically added to
                                          #your mail messages. Signature lines may
                                          #confuse the listserv #software if //EOJ
                                          #is not included in the message.
```

Then send the message to the listserv, and within a short time, the length depending upon network traffic, you will be sent an acknowledgment of your subscription to the AIBI-L discussion list. It will also forward a file detailing various options and commands for use with the list. Please print out a copy of that file for future reference. Unless you use listserv commands on a daily basis it is quite easy to forget the very one you will need six months from subscribing to the list.

To unsubscribe from a listserv mailing list, either of the following messages can be sent to the listserv@somewhere.edu address:

```
UNSUBscribe <listname>
SIGNOFF <listname>
```

If a user wanted to unsubscribe from the AIBI-L list, with the listserv address of listserv@listserv.uottawa.ca, the following message could be sent to that address.

```
To: listserv@listserv.uottawa.ca      #Addressed to listserv address
Cc:
Attchmnt:
Subject:                              #Subject left blank
----- Message Text -----
unsubscribe AIBI-L                    #No name required to unsubscribe

//EOJ                                 #//EOJ to avoid confusion from a signature line
```

Note that it is not necessary to put your name in the message for the unsubscribe command. The message could have also used the command signoff followed by the listname.

Digest and Nomail Commands

The novelty of being on an email discussion lists lasts until a long train of messages are on topics of no interest to the user or the time consumed by reviewing all of the daily postings begins to interfere with non-Internet tasks and responsibilities. Some lists have a large number of postings every day, while others may not have twenty messages a week. With lists that have a large number of messages daily, the question also arises about how to deal with those messages during holidays or vacations when no one will be present to delete the messages for the account. The LISTSERV software offers two practical options to deal with both problems of volume and with the user being on vacation.

If the volume of a mailing list is simply overwhelming on a daily basis, simply convert the subscription to the digest version of the list. The digest contains a certain number of postings, based on the length of the postings or their number, and is one message that contains all the others. Digests usually begin with a listing of the messages and their subjects in the digest. Once you are subscribed to a list, to convert to receiving the posts in a digest format, send the following message to the appropriate listserv:

```
To: listserv@listserv.uottawa.ca
Cc:
Attchmnt:
Subject :
----- Message Text -----
set AIBI-L digests
```

```
//EOJ
```

This would set the AIBI-L list to sending the digest form of posts rather than the individual messages as they are received. Once the digests of messages have been received, the messages can be reviewed, stored or deleted as one packet of messages. This is particularly useful for those who wish to keep several days of postings for review and analysis or who plan to edit the digest to store all messages on given topics for later use.

Another problem, particularly with high traffic lists, is what to do about messages that arrive on holidays or during vacation periods. Space on the computers that handle email messages is not unlimited, and after some period of time, your mailbox will begin to "bounce" or send back messages sent to your mailbox to the listserv. This creates several problems for list owners, not the least of which is removing participants from the lists because their mailboxes are full. Since their mailbox is full, it is impossible to even notify them that they are no longer on the discussion list! To avoid both this problem and inconveniencing other list participants, set your listserv discussion groups to forward no mail during your absence. The no mail option can be set as follows:

```
To: listserv@tamvm1.tamu.edu
Cc:
Attchmnt:
Subject :
----- Message Text -----
set ARCH-L nomail
```

```
//EOJ
```

Upon your return from the holidays or vacation, you will not be facing several hundred email messages generated from various discussion groups in your absence. It is also easier to find personal messages that were sent during your absence without all the clutter of automatically generated messages. To restart your mail service from the discussion list, simply reset the mail option to mail as follows:

```
To: listserv@tamvm1.tamu.edu
Cc:
Attchmnt:
Subject :
----- Message Text -----
set ARCH-L mail


//EOJ
```

That will restart your mail service from the time that it is received and processed by the listserv. It does not obtain all the messages that were sent in your absence, although if message archives are maintained by the listserv for that list, it is possible to access the postings from that period with the database functions of listservs detailed below.

Requesting Information from the List

Scholars often are interested in writing to particular colleagues, or they may simply be curious as to who else is a member of a particular discussion list. It is possible to discover the email addresses and names of those participants on an email discussion list by use of the review command. The following example demonstrates the use of that command to retrieve a listing of all the participants on the ecclesiastical history list, ECCHST-L:

```
To: listserv@bgu.edu
Cc:
Attchmnt:
Subject :
----- Message Text -----
review ECCHST-L


//EOJ
```

It is also possible to sort the information concerning subscribers to the list in a number of useful ways, including by country of origin or by name. There are other less commonly used options, and the reader should consult the reference card for listservs to explore other options.

Some scholars may wish, for reasons known only to themselves, to conceal their presence on email discussion lists. Concealment of one's presence from the review command is possible with listserv commands. Even with conceal in place all postings will bear the email address of the list member who has posted the message. The concealment option only prevents those who are trying to obtain a list of subscribers to an email discussion list from seeing your name and address. The concealment option is set by a message as follows:

```
To: listserv@listserv.uottawa.ca
Cc:
Attchmnt:
Subject :
----- Message Text -----
set ELENCHUS conceal
```

```
//EOJ
```

This message will prevent your name and email address from being displayed to anyone doing a review on the ELENCHUS discussion list. Should you wish to change that option in the future, simply replace the command conceal with noconceal.

In the event that a user has lost or misplaced the information sent upon subscribing to a listserv managed mailing list; there are commands that will send that information back to the user. That information contains a listing of all the commands for using listserv software, many of which have been omitted from this treatment as of little or specialized interest. One of the most useful informational commands is simply "help." In order to obtain basic information about the listserv and what commands are available; send the following message to any listserv:

```
To: listserv@listserv.uottawa.ca
Cc:
Attchmnt:
Subject :
----- Message Text -----
help
```

```
//EOJ
```

The listserv will respond listserv by mailing a list of listserv commands to the user. If more complete information is desired, send the command "INFO REFCARD" to the listserv as follows:

```
To: listserv@listserv.uottawa.ca
Cc:
Attchmnt:
Subject :
----- Message Text -----
INFO REFCARD
```

```
//EOJ
```

The listserv will send a complete list of all the available commands and not simply the set forwarded in response to the help command.

If you are certain of the list name and the listserv address where it resides, you can obtain information about the list and the types of files, usually archives of prior postings, available from the listserv. To obtain information about a particular list, it is necessary to know the proper address for the list. Armed with that information, the user can send the following message:

```
To: listserv@listserv.uottawa.ca
Cc:
Attchmnt:
Subject :
----- Message Text -----
lists detail


//EOJ
```

The listserv will return a message detailing all of the local lists served by that listserv. In response to this query the following message was sent by the listserv@listserv.uottawa.ca (edited for space considerations):

```
Subject: File: "LISTSERV LISTS"
From: "L-Soft list server at UOttawa (1.8b)" <LISTSERV@mercury.cc.uottawa.ca>
To: pdurusau@EMORY.EDU


(Other lists edited from the response)


>>> List: AIBI-L
*
* The Computerised Analysis of Biblical Texts Discussion Group
*
* Review = Private Subscription = Open,Confirm
* Send = Private Notify = Yes
* Reply-to = List,Respect Files = No
* Confidential = No Validate = Store Only
* X-Tags = Yes Stats = Normal,Private
* Ack = No
* Mail-Via = Distribute
* default-options=repro
* Notebook = Yes,C,Weekly,Private
* Errors-To= Owner
* Digest = Yes,Same,Daily
*
* Owner = GBLOOMQ@Acadvm1.uottawa.ca (Gregory Bloomquist)
* Owner = quiet:,GBLOOMQ@UOTTAWA (Gregory Bloomquist)
```

From this information it has been confirmed that this is the proper location to subscribe to this list. The line Subscription = Open, Confirm states that the list is open to subscriptions from any valid email address and that a confirmation message will be sent to each person who sends a subscription message to the listserv. The notation Notebook = Yes, C, Weekly, Private denotes that archives are kept for this list and may be accessed only by members of the list. The line

Digest = Yes, Same, Daily indicates that the digest option is available for this lists and is sent on a daily basis. Finally, the owner of the list, Gregory Bloomquist and his email address are given as the final information for the list.

While it is most often limited to actual members of the list, it is also possible to discover what types of files are held by the listserv. These files are generally archives of prior discussions on the list. It is possible to search and retrieve particular messages from those discussions, but that is covered in the following section on listserv database searches. As a member of the AIBI-L list, one can send the following message to the listserv to see if what, if any, files are maintained by the listserv.

```
To: listserv@listserv.uottawa.ca
Cc:
Attchmnt:
Subject :
----- Message Text -----
index AIBI-L


//EOJ
```

The listserv returns the following message (edited for space considerations):

```
Subject: File: "AIBI-L FILELIST"
Date: Wed, 21 Aug 1996 10:47:34 -0400
From: "L-Soft list server at UOttawa (1.8b)" <:LISTSERV@mercury.cc.uottawa.ca>:
To: pdurusau@EMORY.EDU


* AIBI-L FILELIST for LISTSERV@UOTTAWA.
*
(Material omitted)


* NOTEBOOK archives for the list
* (Weekly notebook)
* rec last - change
* filename filetype GET PUT -fm lrecl nrecs date time Remarks

AIBI-L LOG9405B PRV OWN V 74 16  94/05/11 06:25:44
AIBI-L LOG9405C PRV OWN V 78 154 94/05/19 12:43:09
AIBI-L LOG9405D PRV OWN V 79 129 94/05/27 16:11:43


(Material omitted)


AIBI-L LOG9512C LOG OWN V 80 235 96/03/13 11:17:54
```

The index of weekly notebooks indicates that the archive has postings to the AIBI-L list from May of 1994 until present for retrieval or searching. For the moment, it is assumed that the all the posting between December 15, 1995 until January 1, 1996 are of interest. The weekly notebook known to the listserv as AIBI-L LOG9512C covers the time period in question. That file can be obtained from the listserv in the following manner:

```
To: listserv@listserv.uottawa.ca
Cc:
Attchmnt:
Subject :
----- Message Text -----
get AIBI-L LOG9512C


//EOJ
```

The listserv responds to this request by forwarding the requested file to the user. Note that you must be a subscriber to the AIBI-L list for this request to be honored by the listserv software. That is not always the case, but use of the "lists detailed" command will list whether archives are kept at all and who may access the archives. Note that in responding to this request, the listserv simply sends a message containing all the messages for the time period in question, with no index or listing of topics. The user may simply read through the message or use other software to search for items of interest. This manual searching for topics is not a burden for one or two archive periods but would quickly become tiresome if any extended time period were to be covered with some degree of reliability. Fortunately, the listserv software provides for database searching functions to be used with archives of mailing lists that make such searches both reasonable in terms of time spent and reliable in terms of results.

Database functions of listservs

One of the most helpful features of listserv is the ability to search archives maintained for different mailing lists and to obtain only those messages of interest. It is unfortunate those capabilities have not been extended to the other forms of mailing list software covered in this guide. The instructions for the database functions were originally written for users who would access such database functions interactively, i.e., over a direct BITNET connection. Users who are not on a BITNET connection must use what is called "batch" processing to submit their searches. In this context, "batch" processing simply means that all requests must be submitted by email, and the user must then await the results. It is somewhat less flexible than the original interactive searching was reported to be, but it does have the advantage of being able to submit searches to several archives in succession, without waiting for a response.

The database functions of listserv software allow for complex searching of the archives of discussion lists maintained by the listserv. The examples of proper formatted search requests below can be used as templates for new searches. The only lines that should be changed until the user is comfortable with listserv database searching are those listed as command 1 and command 2 in the first database search example. The command "index" has been added to this basic example on the assumption that most users will be submitting listserv database searches by email and not in an interactive mode over a BITNET connection.

Database Search Template

```
// JOB Echo=No
Database Search DD=Rules
//Rules DD *
command 1
command 2
index

/*
```

To use this template to search the JOHNLITR discussion list, which focuses on the Gospel of John, the user should first verify that archives are kept for that list with the "lists detail" command shown above. The output of that command shows that archives may only be accessed by members of the list so joining the list is a prerequisite to using the database search function. As a first search of the JOHNLITR database, the following query was submitted:

```
To: listserv@vm.sc.edu
Cc:
Attchmnt:
Subject :
----- Message Text -----
 // JOB Echo=No
Database Search DD=Rules
//Rules DD *
search eschatological in JOHNLITR
index

/*
//EOJ
```

The command line is composed of the command "search," followed by the term sought "eschatological," the keyword "in," and concludes with the database to be searched "JOHNLITR." On the next line, the command "index" appears and the result of that search and index command produced the following result:

```
From: "L-Soft list server at UNIVSCVM (1.8b)"
 <LISTSERV@VM.SC.EDU>
To: Patrick Durusau <pdurusau@EMORY.EDU>
Subject: File: "DATABASE OUTPUT"


> Search eschatological in JOHNLITR
--> Database JOHNLITR, 9 hits.


> Index
Item # Date Time Recs Subject
------ ---- ---- ---- -------
000070 94/10/09 23:02 50 Synonymity
000257 95/02/21 08:32 93 Re: Historical Jesus?
000262 95/02/21 15:52 61 Historical Jesus
000272 95/02/22 13:33 33 jesus seminar
000277 95/02/22 14:35 97 Re: Historical Jesus
000290 95/03/01 23:46 170 Historical Jesus/Sayings of John?
000822 96/01/09 14:52 35 Signs in John
000823 96/01/09 13:26 41 Re: Signs in John
000828 96/01/10 07:01 55 Re: Signs in John
```

Unless the searcher is very certain that the amount of output from the search will be small, it is best to always use the index command to gain some idea of how many records will be returned by a given search command. Since all these commands must be submitted as "batches" of commands, it is necessary to resubmit the search command in order to obtain a copy of all the records found by the first search. To have all the records found by the first search printed in a file sent to the user, use the following template:

```
To: listserv@vm.sc.edu
Cc:
Attchmnt:
Subject :
----- Message Text -----
 // JOB Echo=No
Database Search DD=Rules
//Rules DD *
search eschatological in JOHNLITR
print
...
/*
//EOJ
```

In response, the listserv will send all the messages listed in response to the first search request in a single file.

If only certain records can be identified as of interest from the subject headings-for example, 000822 96/01/09 14:52 35 Signs in John, 000823 96/01/09 13:26 41 Re: Signs in John 000828 96/01/10 07:01 55 Re: Signs in John, the database search can be modified to print only those records:

```
To: listserv@vm.sc.scarolina.edu
Cc:
Attchmnt:
Subject :
----- Message Text -----
 // JOB Echo=No
Database Search DD=Rules
//Rules DD *
search eschatological in JOHNLITR
print 822-823, 828
/*
//EOJ
```

In response to this search plus print command, the listserv only prints out the particular messages specified by message number. Note that the leading zeros were removed from the message numbers prior to placing them in the print request.

Another listserv database search option that is often useful is the ability to limit searches by date of posting. If you have been unable to see the list posting for the last three months but are unwilling to read all the postings from that time period, this makes an excellent way to search for recent postings on topics of interest. The basic search structure is the same as seen in the first example, with the addition of the time limitation.

```
To: listserv@vm.sc.edu
Cc:
Attchmnt:
Subject :
----- Message Text -----
 // JOB Echo=No
Database Search DD=Rules
//Rules DD *
search eschatological in JOHNLITR since 96/01/01
index
/*
//EOJ
```

The result of this search shows the three messages from 1996 shown in the first search for "eschatological."

```
> search eschatological in JOHNLITR since 96/01/01
--> Database JOHNLITR, 3 hits.

> index
Item # Date Time Recs Subject
------ ---- ---- ---- -------
000822 96/01/09 14:52 35 Signs in John
000823 96/01/09 13:26 41 Re: Signs in John
000828 96/01/10 07:01 55 Re: Signs in John
```

The limitation of searches by posting date reduces the drain on the computer resources necessary to process the request and produces a manageable number of records for consideration.

This does not exhaust by any means the various database searching options available for listserv archives. It is possible to restrict searches by the name of the sender, subject line and in other ways similar to traditional database functions. Further information on listserv databases can be found by sending email to any of the listserv addresses in the resource section with the only text in the message body being: "get listdb memo." As a result of that message, you will be sent a file detailing all the capabilities of the listserv database functions.

LISTPROC

Listproc software runs primarily on Unix platforms and duplicates some of the features found on the listserv software which originated on the BITNET network. The basic commands simply use different commands for similar functions of listserv mailing list. The most significant differences are in the search facilities, but those are covered only to the extent necessary to perform simple searches of archives. The manner of entering commands differs for each particular type of mailing list software, and those differences are illustrated by the examples of the basic commands for a listproc managed mailing list below.

Subscribe/Unsubscribe

The most important thing to remember about Listproc discussion lists is that all commands, in order to be effective, must be mailed to the listproc@somewhere.edu address. The resource listing for mailing lists has the subscription address for each listproc in that format. Commands sent to the mailinglist@somewhere.edu, are sent to all the subscribers and do not accomplish anything other than annoying the members of that discussion list. To join the CLASSICS discussion list, which is a discussion list managed by Linda Wright, consult the resource guide for mailing list and note that its address is listproc@u.washington.edu. Open your email program to address and compose the message as follows:

(The comments following the "#" sign and the "#" sign should not be reproduced in your mail message. Those comments are included for purposes of illustration only.)

```
To: listproc@u.washington.edu #Note, sent to listproc address
Cc :
Attchmnt:
Subject :                            #Subject left blank
----- Message Text -----
subscribe classics Patrick Durusau       #Substitute the proper list name


--                                   #Serves the same function as //EOJ for
                                     #a listserv list. Prevents the listproc
                                     #software from being confused by
                                     #signature lines
```

The lisproc software will return a message advising users of their subscription to the mailing list with a short summary of the most common commands. As is noted for all mailing lists, the user should save or preferably print out a copy of these instructions. It is difficult to remember the precise commands needed for a particular mailing list some five or six months after originally joining the list.

If a user decides to unsubscribe from a listproc list, there are two commands which work equally well to end his subscription. Like the original subscription message, the unsubscribe message is addressed to the listproc address, not the mailing list, as shown in this example.

```
To: listproc@u.washington.edu #Note, sent to listproc address
Cc :
Attchmnt:
Subject :                                #Subject left blank
----- Message Text -----
unsubscribe classics                     #Substitute the proper list name,
                                         #the other command to leave the
                                         #mailing list is "signoff." To use that
                                         #command, simply substitute it for the
                                         #"unsubscribe" command in the example.


--
```

Mail Options, Including digests, vacation

Listproc uses a set command to control all the subscription settings for a subscriber. The most common settings are used to request that mail posting be sent in digest format, to postpone mail message deliveries, and to resume mail messages after they have been suspended. A complete list of these commands and others can be obtained by following the instructions in the Help and Information Commands section below.

With high traffic lists it is not uncommon for thirty or forty messages to arrive each day, and it is sometimes more convenient to have all the messages from one list set forth in the digest format. For the listproc mailing list, a digest setting is requested in the following manner.

```
To: listproc@u.washington.edu        #Note, sent to listproc address
Cc:
Attchmnt:
Subject :                            #Subject left blank
----- Message Text -----
set classics mail digest             #Substitute the proper list name


--
```

When the user desires to return to a normal delivery of messages as they are posted, the "set" command is used to change this setting.

```
To: listproc@u.washington.edu          #Note, sent to listproc address
Cc:
Attchmnt:
Subject :                              #Subject left blank
----- Message Text -----
set classics mail                      #Substitute the proper list name


--
```

Like the listserv software, it is possible to suspend the mailing of postings from a mailing list using the listproc software in order to avoid email arriving during holiday or vacation periods. Note that once such mailings have been suspended, the user must reactivate the account upon his return. To suspend mail deliveries from the Classics list, the following message should be sent to the listproc address.

```
To: listproc@u.washington.edu          #Note, sent to listproc address
Cc:
Attchmnt:
Subject :                              #Subject left blank
----- Message Text -----
set classics mail postpone             #Substitute the proper list name


--
```

In order to resume mail deliveries, send the same message detailed above to resume non-digest delivery of mail messages(i.e., "set classics mail" to the listproc address).

Help and Information Commands

Listproc offers a basic help command as well as several others that will send details concerning lists managed by that particular Listproc site. The most basic command is "help," which returns a short list of the available commands for use with the Listproc software. A related command is "information" which is followed by the list name for which further information is requested. The information returned in response to the "information" command is dependent upon the owner of that particular list having prepared a description of the list and its appropriate topics. It is also possible to review the list of subscribers to the list in order to obtain email addresses for others interested in the subject area of the list.

The "help" command will return general information on the Listproc software and its basic commands. For information on any particular command, simply follow the word "help" with the name of the command, and further information will be sent on that particular command. For a listing of all the available topics for which help is available, send what is called a "bogus" message in the documentation (e.g., send "help me") to the Listproc address. The software will respond that there is no help on "me" and will also return a list of valid help topics.

The "information" command is used to obtain basic information about a list managed by the Listproc software. It is particularly helpful in the case of new list that may or may not be of interest and for which further information is desired. Sending the information command to the Listproc for the Classics list would take the following form:

```
To: listproc@u.washington.edu          #Note, sent to listproc #address
Cc:
Attchmnt:
Subject :                              #Subject left blank
----- Message Text -----
information classics                   #Substitute the proper list #name
--
```

The Listproc software responds by returning the following information, abbreviated for presentation, concerning the Classics list:

```
Subject: INFORMATION classics


CLASSICS@U.WASHINGTON.EDU (Internet address only)
An unmoderated list for discussing ancient Greek and Latin subjects. This list is open
to everyone interested in Classics, and prospective members are warmly welcomed. The
discussions assume a background in ancient Greek and/or Latin and postings are expected
to remain within the confines of these subjects. Only list-members are able to post or
reply to CLASSICS messages, and this list does not appear on Usenet. As of 09/95 the
membership numbers over 1,100 subscribers.

The CLASSICS list is neither run by nor directly affiliated with the University of
Washington Classics Department.


(material omitted)
```

In order to find others who are also subscribers to the Classics list, there are two commands that can be used with the Listproc software to generate such a listing. The review command returns more information about the list settings and a description of the list as well as a list of all the current subscribers. If the only interest is in the actual listing of recipients, the recipients command followed by the list name will generate such a listing. To use the more informative command for a list of the subscribers to the Classics list, which number some 1,100 strong send the following message.

```
To: listproc@u.washington.edu        #Note, sent to listproc address
Cc :
Attchmnt:
Subject :                            #Subject left blank
----- Message Text -----
review classics                      #Substitute the proper list name,
                                     #could also use the command
                                     #"recipients" in place of "review"
                                     #if object was a list of recipients.


--
```

In response to either the review or recipients command, followed by the name of a list, the mailing list will return a listing of all the current subscribers who have not set their subscriptions to be concealed from these commands.

Archives, Database Functions

It is possible to maintain searchable archives of prior postings to mailing lists managed by Listproc software. To discover if a list maintains archives and the extent of those archives, the user first issues the "index" command followed by the name of the mailing list.

```
To: listproc@u.washington.edu        #Note, sent to listproc address
Cc:
Attchmnt:
Subject :                            #Subject left blank
----- Message Text -----
index classics                       #Substitute the proper list name


--
```

In response to this example, classicists will be pleased to learn that the archives of the Classics discussion list are available from the spring of 1992 until the latest postings. Of perhaps greater importance, however, those archive files are searchable by email, although not in the same manner as the searches detailed for listservs.

The basic search request for a list archive managed by the Listproc software takes the form of "search <archive> <pattern>" and like all commands it is sent to the Listproc address. The Listproc documentation offers the following helpful advice on the formulation of the pattern portion of the search request: "The pattern can be an egrep(1)-style regular expression with support for the following additional operators: '~' (negation), '|' and '&' (logical OR and AND), '<' '>' (group regular expressions). The pattern may be enclosed in single or double quotes. Note: "." matches any character including new line."

For those scholars who have not committed to memory the nuances of egrep style regular expressions (egrep is a rather useful Unix search tool), the following examples demonstrate the basic search capabilities of the Listproc search request.

Example: Find all postings concerning or by Theodore Brunner to the Classics discussion list.

```
search classics "brunner"        #Note the pattern brunner has been
                                 #enclosed in double quotation marks.
                                 #Single quotations marks can be used as
                                 #well. The search software ignores
                                 #case in its search.
```

Example: Find all postings concerning or by Theodore Brunner and containing the term TLG on the Classics discussion list.

```
search classics "brunner & TLG"        #Posting must contain both
                                       #"brunner" and "TLG"
```

Example: Find all posting concerning or by Theodore Brunner and not containing the item TLG on the Classics discussion list.

```
search classics "brunner & ~TLG"        #Posting must contain "brunner"
                                        #but not contain TLG
```

Unlike the listserv software, the listproc software does not return the posting that match the search request. The user is returned a listing of the matching messages with a notation of the archive file that contains the matching post. It is then the responsibility of the user to manually retrieve that particular archive file and search it locally for the information requested.

In order to obtain the archive file(s) containing the material which, matched the search pattern, the user sends a "get" command in the following format to retrieve the archive file.

```
To: listproc@u.washington.edu          #Note, sent to listproc address
Cc :
Attchmnt:
Subject :                              #Subject left blank
----- Message Text -----
get classics classics.log9204          #Substitute the proper list and file name


--
```

The Listproc will return the entire archive file, and it is then up to the user to extract the information requested in the original search request.

MAILBASE

Mailbase is a mailing list program that is primarily found for lists originating in the U.K. A number of important lists, such as RELIGION-ALL, mailbase@mailbase.ac.uk, maintained by Michael Fraser, use this software. It does not maintain searchable archives but does provide the usual functions associated with mailing list programs. The basic commands for use with a mailing list that uses the Mailbase software are set forth below.

Subscribe/Unsubscribe

As is the case with all other mailing lists, commands should be sent to the proper address in order to them to be properly executed. In the case of the Religion-All list, commands should be addressed to mailbase@mailbase.ac.uk. The resource listing for mailing lists sets forth the subscription address for each mailbase list in that format. Commands sent to the mailinglist@somewhere.edu, are sent to all the subscribers and do not accomplish anything other than annoying the members of that discussion list. To join the Religion-All discussion list, which is a super list that includes the lists for ecotheol, liturgy, postmodern-christian and religious-studies-uk, consult the list of mailing lists and note that its address is: mailbase@mailbase.ac.uk. Open your email program to address and compose the message as follows (the comments following the "#" sign and the "#" sign should not be reproduced in your mail message, these comments are included for purposes of illustration only.)

```
To: mailbase@mailbase.ac.uk          #Note, sent to mailbase address
Cc:
Attchmnt:
Subject :                            #Subject left blank
----- Message Text -----
JOIN religion-all Patrick Durusau #Substitute the proper list name.

stop                                 #Tells mailbase software it is at
                                     #the end of the commands in the
                                     #message. Useful if your signature
                                     #line is automatically added to your
                                     #mail messages. Signature lines may
                                     #confuse the mailbase software if
                                     #"stop" is not included at the end
                                     #of the commands.
```

Send the message to the mailbase address, and within a short time, the length depending upon network traffic, you will be sent an acknowledgement of your subscription to the Religion-All mailing list. It will also forward a file detailing various options and commands for use with the list. Please print out a copy of that file for future reference. Unless you use mailbase commands on a daily basis it is quite easy to forget the very one you will need six months from subscribing to the list.

To unsubscribe from a mailbase mailing list, the following message can be sent to the mailbase@somewhere.edu address:

```
unsubscribe <listname>
```

If a user wanted to unsubscribe from the Religion-All, mailbase@mailbase.ac.uk, the following message could be sent.

```
To: mailbase@mailbase.ac.uk        #Note, sent to mailbase address
Cc:
Attchmnt:
Subject :                          #Subject left blank
----- Message Text -----
LEAVE religion-all                 #Substitute the proper list name.

  stop
```

Mail Options, Including Digests, Vacation

The Mailbase software does not offer an automatic digest option for posts to the discussion list but does offer the other common commands for handling the starting and stopping of messages from the lists for vacations or other absences from email access. It is also possible to obtain files containing prior postings or other files contained in the archives for any particular mailing list. Mailbase does not have the capability of searching the archived files, so the user must request the file by name, as detailed below.

In order to suspend the delivery of messages from a mailbase mailing list, the user should use the "SUSPEND MAIL" command as follows:

```
To: mailbase@mailbase.ac.uk        #Note, sent to mailbase address
Cc:
Attchmnt:
Subject :                          #Subject left blank
----- Message Text -----
SUSPEND MAIL religion-all          #Substitute the proper list name.

  stop
```

When the delivery of mail messages is to be resumed, the user should issue the "RESUME MAIL" command and the delivery of mail messages will be resumed.

```
To: mailbase@mailbase.ac.uk        #Note, sent to mailbase address
Cc:
Attchmnt:
Subject :                          #Subject left blank
----- Message Text -----
RESUME MAIL religion-all           #Substitute the proper list name.

  stop
```

Help and Information Commands

Mailbase offers a basic help command as well as several others that will send details concerning lists managed by that particular mailbase site. The most basic command is "help," which returns a short list of the available commands for use with the mailbase software. A related command is "REVIEW," which is followed by the list name for which further information is requested. The information returned in response to the "REVIEW" command is dependent upon the owner of that particular list having prepared a short (hopefully) explanation of the list and its appropriate topics.

If a user was without their copy of this guide or simply wanted to obtain a full list of all the mailbase commands, the "help" command could be forwarded as shown in the following message.

```
To: mailbase@mailbase.ac.uk              #Note, sent to mailbase address
Cc:
Attchmnt:
Subject :                                #Subject left blank
----- Message Text -----
help
```

If more information is desired concerning a particular list, the "REVIEW" command will return a description of the list in question and a list of its subscribers in response to the following message.

```
To: mailbase@mailbase.ac.uk           #Note, sent to mailbase address
Cc:
Attchmnt:
Subject : #Subject left blank
----- Message Text -----
REVIEW RELIGION-ALL
```

The mailbase program would respond to this request with the following information:

```
Review of the religion-all list:


Current Attributes
------------------


For this list non-members may:
Subscribe direct: yes Contribute mail: yes
Request review: yes Request files: yes



This list is moderated: yes

Contributions to this list are archived: yes

Replies to a message in this list are sent to
the list rather than to the message-sender: no
```

```
Description
-----------


Religion-all is a moderated superlist intended to make available
files  and  items  of  interest  to  religion-relevant  lists  on  Mailbase.  At  present
Religion-all  acts  as  an  umbrella  for  EcoTheol,  Liturgy,  and  Religious-Studies-UK.
Subscriptions are welcome from users who are not members of these lists.


(material omitted)
```

The "review" command also lists all the current subscribers to the list by name with the email address for each subscriber.

Archives, Database Functions

Other commands that may prove useful are the commands to find the names of files held in the archives of the mailing list and to retrieve those files by email. This is particularly relevant in cases where mail has been suspended for some period of time and the user wishes to review posts that were made in his absence. The "INDEX" and "SEND" commands form the basis for the retrieval of such files. The "INDEX" command takes the following format:

```
To: mailbase@mailbase.ac.uk            #Note, sent to mailbase address
Cc:
Attchmnt:
Subject :                              #Subject left blank
----- Message Text -----
INDEX religion-all                     #Substitute the proper list name.
```

The mailbase program will reply with a listing of the files held in its archives that will appear substantially in the following form:

```
From: mailbase-admin@mailbase.ac.uk
Subject: Index of religion-all
Status: RO
X-Status:


 The files associated with religion-all:


(material omitted, several other archive files are actually available)



SHORTLIST.TXT


A shortlist of electronic mail discussion groups broadly relevant to religious studies.
Last updated: 06/08/95
```

```
Size in characters: 137715
File type: ASCII text
Last Updated: 25/09/95 Last Retrieved by Email: 26/01/96


Source: Michael Fraser (m.a.fraser@durham.ac.uk or mike.fraser@oucs.ox.ac.uk)
```

The returned information describes the file name, in this case SHORTLIST.TXT, and other information concerning the file, such as the last time it was updated or obtained by email. In order to retrieve Michael Fraser's Shortlist, the user would issue the following commands:

```
To: mailbase@mailbase.ac.uk          #Note, sent to mailbase address
Cc:
Attchmnt:
Subject :                            #Subject left blank
----- Message Text -----
SEND religion-all SHORTLIST.TXT      #Substitute the proper list name
                                     #and the file name as listed in
                                     #the listing of the #archive files.
```

Majordomo

Majordomo is a mailing list program that consists of a series of Perl (programming language) scripts that provide the various functions seen for other types of mailing lists. It is a fairly popular program for Unix platforms, although it can be used on any computer with a working copy of Perl installed. It is not the most sophisticated mailing program available, but it is relatively easy to install, configure and maintain. The basic commands for use with a mailing list that uses the Majordomo software are set forth below.

Subscribe/Unsubscribe

The most important thing to remember about Majordomo discussion lists is that all commands, in order to be effective, must be mailed to the majordomo@somewhere.edu address. The resource listing for mailing lists sets forth the subscription address for each majordomo list in that format. Commands sent to the mailinglist@somewhere.edu are sent to all the subscribers and do not accomplish anything other than annoying the members of that discussion list. To join the tc-list discussion list, which is a discussion forum for *TC: A Journal of Biblical Textual Criticism*, consult the resource guide for mailing lists and note that its address is majordomo@shemesh.scholar.emory.edu. Open your email program to address and compose the message as follows (the comments following the "#" sign and the "#" sign should not be reproduced in your mail message, these comments are included for purposes of illustration only).

```
To: majordomo@shemesh.scholar.emory.edu      #Note, send to majordomo address
Cc:
Attchmnt:
Subject :                                     #Subject left blank
----- Message Text -----
subscribe tc-list                             #Substitute the proper list name.
                                              #Often also seen as subscribe
                                              #tc-list <your-address>.
                                              #Either is proper.


end                                           #Tells Majordomo software it is
                                              #at the end of the commands in the
                                              #message. Useful if your signature
                                              #line is automatically added to
                                              #your mail messages. Signature lines
                                              #may confuse the Majordomo software
                                              #if "end" is not included at the
                                              #end of the commands.
```

Send the message to Majordomo, and within a short time, the length depending upon network traffic, you will be sent an acknowledgment of your subscription to the TC-list mailing list. It will also forward a file detailing various options and commands for use with the list. Please print out a copy of that file for future reference. Unless you use Majordomo commands on a daily basis it is quite easy to forget the very one you will need six months from subscribing to the list.

To unsubscribe from a Majordomo mailing list, the following message can be sent to the majordomo@somewhere.edu address:

```
unsubscribe <listname>
```

If a user wanted to unsubscribe from the tc-list, the following message could be sent to that address:

```
To: majordomo@shemesh.scholar.emory.edu    #Addressed to majordomo address
Cc:
Attchmnt:
Subject :                                  #Subject left blank
----- Message Text -----
unsubscribe tc-list pdurusau@emory.edu     #The documentation for Majordomo
                                           #states that an unsubscribe message
                                           #may contain only your name. Under
                                           #Majordomo release 1.93, your name
                                           #must be followed by your email address,
                                           #as that is how Majordomo tracks
                                           #subscribers. The better course is to
                                           #use your email address for subscribe
                                           #and unsubscribe commands.


end
```

Mail Options, Including Digests, Vacation

The careful reader will recall that with a listserv managed mailing list, it was possible to change the mail settings of a subscription from being forwarded each message as it was posted to receiving all the messages in a digest format. Majordomo mailing lists do not allow the resetting of a current mail subscription to a digest mode as with the listserv software. In order to obtain digests of postings, the mailing list must be set up to offer the digest option, and the user must subscribe to a different list in order to obtain the digest format. The messages that compose the digest are identical to those sent out by the regular list, but they are sent out periodically rather than as they are posted to the list. Majordomo also offers options to look for files that are available from the discussion list and to review the lists of subscribers to the list.

In order to subscribe to the tc-list in digest format, it is necessary to send the subscribe command with a different list name than that in the first example. The following message would start a subscription to the tc-list in digest format.

```
To: majordomo@shemesh.scholar.emory.edu
Cc:
Attchmnt:
Subject :
----- Message Text -----
subscribe tc-list-digest              #Note list name difference,
                                      #email address is optional
```

```
end
```

This subscription will be acknowledged as a separate subscription request, and the user is once again sent the introductory information file and a confirmation of his subscription. If all the user wants is the digest edition, he should unsubscribe from the original list after he has successfully subscribed to the digest version of the list. Otherwise, he will continue to be sent all postings as they occur and a digest of all the messages as well. In this respect, the Majordomo software does not offer the flexibility of the original listserv software for the BITNET network.

Majordomo does not support the vacation commands found for listserv lists, so if a user is going to be absence from email access for an extended period of time, it is necessary to unsubscribe from the list until a regular reading of email messages can be resumed. It also does not support any of the database functions noted for the listserv software, although, as noted below, it is possible to retrieve files and archives from mailing lists managed with Majordomo software.

Help and Information Commands

Majordomo offers a basic help command as well as several others that will send details concerning lists managed by that particular Majordomo site. The most basic command is "help," which returns a short list of the available commands for use with the Majordomo software. A related command is "info" which is followed by the list name for which further information is requested. The information returned in response to the "info" command is dependent upon the owner of that particular list having prepared a short (hopefully) explanation of the list and its appropriate topics. To use the "info" command for the tc-list, the request would read as follows:

```
To: majordomo@shemesh.scholar.emory.edu
Cc:
Attchmnt:
Subject :
----- Message Text -----
info tc-list
```

```
end
```

The Majordomo software would answer this command by returning a mail message that contains a description of the tc-list prepared by James R. Adair, which is also sent to each new subscriber.

It is an excellent way of gathering information on a discussion list in order to determine if a user is interested in subscribing.

If the user is interested in who else is a subscriber to the mailing list, there is an equivalent to the review command found for listservs, namely, "who." The "who" command must be directed to the majordomo@somewhere.edu address and is followed by the name of the list in question. For the tc-list, the "who" command would be issued by the following message.

```
To: majordomo@shemesh.scholar.emory.edu
Cc:
Attchmnt:
Subject :
----- Message Text -----
who tc-list

end
```

Archives, Database Functions

If a majordomo mailing list maintains an archive of postings or of other files, these can also be listed and obtained by commands addressed to the majordomo address. The "index" command, directed to the majordomo address for B-Hebrew, majordomo@virginia.edu, would be addressed as follows:

```
To: majordomo@virginia.edu
Cc:
Attchmnt:
Subject :
----- Message Text -----
index B-Hebrew

end
```

In response to that command, the majordomo program returns an email message with the following information:

```
>>>> index b-hebrew
total 408
-rw-rw---- 1 domo 130452 Nov 28 22:06 b-hebrew.9511
-rw-rw---- 1 domo 147720 Dec 31 16:23 b-hebrew.9512
-rw-rw---- 1 domo 103465 Jan 26 18:18 b-hebrew.9601
```

To obtain one of the digests for the B-Hebrew list, simply use the "get" command as set forth in the following example.

```
To: majordomo@virginia.edu
Cc:
Attchmnt:
Subject :
----- Message Text -----
get B-Hebrew b-hebrew.9511          #Note that the "get" command is
                                    #followed by the list name and
                                    #then the name of the file.


end
```

This command will return all of the messages archived in the file hebrew.9511, namely, all those messages posted to the B-Hebrew list in November of 1995.

3. World Wide Web Browsers

WWW browsers are clients that connect to servers on the Internet using a mutually agreed upon computer language and which interpret the content found there for display on the user's screen. The server sends the client one or more pages of information which can contain text, images or even interactive forms for the user to complete. These pages are written in what is known as HyperText Markup Language, HTML, a simplified derivative of Standard Generalized Markup Language, or SGML. The use of HTML allows the author to construct a page that may include hypertext links to other portions of the page, such as footnotes or links to other relevant resources on that server or a server located on another continent.

HTML is a derivative of SGML but unfortunately it remains even in HTML 4.0 something of a presentational markup language. However, HTML 4.0 has an extensive specification for cascading stylesheets (CSS) and is a vast improvement over preceding versions of the HTML standard. The presentational aspects of HTML are made worse by the continued incorporation into browsers of features that are not specified by the HTML standard. Non-standard HTML extensions force sites to either choose a preferred browser or create pages that meet the lowest common denominator among web browsers.

There are literally dozens of free or shareware browsers available for use on the WWW. One popular editor for Unix platforms, Emacs, has a WWW mode that allows users to surf the web while using the editor. (In all fairness to lesser editors it should be noted that Emacs is perhaps the most versatile and extensible editing program ever created.) Most users will choose either the Netscape Navigator (version 4.1 or higher) or Microsoft's Internet Explorer (version 4.1 or higher) as their main browsing program. Users who are concerned with following the latest advances in WWW standards work should consider obtaining a copy of the W3C's Amaya browser.

The Netscape Navigator browser is available from **http://www.netscape.com** at no charge. Netscape has released all the source code for version 5 of the Netscape Navigator to public inspection on the condition that any improvements be shared with Netscape for incorporation into the next release of version 5 code. This is very similar to the basis on which Linux (a Unix operating system) and the GNU Project software have been developing for a period of years. It would be difficult to find any Unix shop that does not use some tools that were developed by one or more such public participation projects. Whether this will be the case with the release of the source code for the next generation Netscape browser remains to be seen.

The Microsoft Internet Explorer browser is available from **http://www.microsoft.com** at no charge. First time users should be aware that Internet Explorer will take over the desktop of any Windows 95 computer on which it is installed. There is an option in the installation to defeat the desktop takeover features but it will still install itself as the default browser and will reset any downloaded HTML files to recognize Internet Explorer as the default application for opening these files. Microsoft has advanced the use of XML as a data transfer standard and does include an XML parser as part of the latest Internet Explorer release.

The choice between Netscape Navigator and Internet Explorer is largely one of personal preference unless the user is serious about working with the standards for the WWW. In that case, the Amaya browser, which can be downloaded from **http://www.w3c.org** is the only real option. The W3C maintains the current release of Amaya so that it is compatible with the standards of the WWW as written and it does not incorporate extensions by either Netscape or Microsoft. Amaya makes an excellent second browser for users who are developing pages for viewing by more than one type of browser.

4. FTP-File Transfer Protocol

Most WWW browsers currently in use will perform FTP file transfers without any special intervention of the user. It will be necessary to consult the documentation or help files for any particular browser to learn how it handles ftp transfers and how to use it. Occasions may arise when a WWW browser is not available or a user may only have access to use of the ftp commands themselves, such as on an ordinary dial-up access account. This section does not cover all the possible ftp commands and is meant as a brief guide and ready reference for situations where the user is using the ftp commands at the command prompt.

FTP Addresses

The ftp addresses listed in the resource section of this guide are written as they would be used with WWW browser software. In order to use these addresses at the command prompt, the user must separate the address as given into several component parts. The address of one of the documents from the Leiden Ur III Project at the University of Pennsylvania, List of Transliteration Conventions, is the following:

```
ftp://enlil.museum.upenn.edu/pub/Ur3/convntns.txt
```

This address works properly for a WWW browser, because the browser automatically recognizes that it is composed of four separate parts. First, the manner of accessing the desired file is specified by the beginning ftp://. Second, the address of the site is specified as enlil.museum.upenn.edu. Third, the directory where the file can be found is listed as /pub/Ur3. Last, the name of the file is given: convntns.txt. All of the ftp addresses shown in the resource guide follow this four-element form, which is formally known as a **URL**, Uniform Resource Locator.

FTP By Example

Logging In

1. At the Unix prompt (yours may be a %, $, or other symbol), enter the command ftp followed by a space and then the address of the site you wish to access. If a connection is successfully made with the ftp server, you will see a message similar to the one reproduced below asking for a Name. Please note that for all anonymous ftp sessions, you must enter anonymous and not your login name or other name. If you enter any name other than anonymous the server will expect a password recorded for a user on that system. Some systems do not request entry of a password for access to ftp files, while others do, primarily for record keeping purposes. The first example shows a login at the University of Pennsylvania ftp site, which does not request a password, and the second, a login at the SimTel archive, which does request a password.

Example with no password requested

```
% ftp enlil.museum.upenn.edu
Connected to enlil.museum.upenn.edu
220 enlil FTP server (IBM OS/2 TCP/IP FTP Version 1.2) ready
Name (enlil.museum.upenn.edu:pdurusau): anonymous
230 User anonymous logged in.
ftp>
```

Note that the FTP server did not ask for an email address, but simply logged the user in as anonymous. The anonymous login restricts the directories that can be entered and the files that can be retrieved. In this case, but not always, the anonymous login results in the user being in the /pub directory immediately after login.

Example with password requested

Many sites require a password after you type anonymous at the name prompt. Note that you should never; never enter the password for your system account in response to an anonymous ftp password prompt. All the ftp server is asking for in this case is your email address, which in this example was pdurusau@crl.com. It is not shown in the example because the ftp server does not echo passwords in case you are a user on that system and are logging into your actual account.

```
crl1% ftp oak.oakland.edu
Connected to oak.oakland.edu.
220 oak.oakland.edu FTP server (Version wu-2.4(9) Wed May 3 15:02:49 EDT 1995) ready.
Name (oak.oakland.edu:pdurusau): anonymous
331 Guest login ok, send your complete e-mail address as password.
Password:
230-
*****Welcome messages omitted*****
230 Guest login ok, access restrictions apply.
```

Navigating around an FTP Site

Once you have logged into the ftp server, you will need to change directories and list its contents in order to see the file(s) of interest. The basic commands are not difficult to learn. Let's return to the example where we have logged into the University of Pennsylvania ftp site to obtain some of the Leiden Ur III Project files. This example assumes that we have already logged in as user anonymous and are in the default directory of the ftp site. (A default directory is the place the user is placed after being accepted by the ftp server as user anonymous.)

In the following examples please note that where the user sees the prompt ftp>, that indicates a place where a valid command can be issued by the user. All commands issued at that prompt will be executed by the ftp server and the results of those commands displayed to the ftp user. (It is possible to issue commands that are executed on your local computer, but it is not necessary to use such commands to take advantage of any ftp facility.)

Where am I?

We know that the file convntns.txt is located in the pub/Ur3 directory of the University of Pennsylvania site from its address. After having logged into the ftp server, however, how do we know where we are on the site? A very useful command in many Unix situations is pwd, or present working directory. It is rather difficult to move from one location to another unless you know where you are at present, or so I have been told by the proponents of the analytic philosophy school. This seems to be the case in Unix, whatever its validity in other realms of existence.

Since we are already logged into the ftp server, in order to discover our present location, we issue the pwd command at the Unix prompt. Note that Unix is case sensitive both for file names and commands, so PWD does not equal pwd. On the Pennsylvania server, issuing the pwd command yields the following result:

```
ftp>pwd
257 "E:\pub" is current directory.
ftp>
```

You will not always be placed in the pub directory after logging into an ftp site and sometimes must change to the pub directory. The pwd command will always give you the present directory location and provide the information you need to change directories to the one you are seeking. (N.B.: the results of a pwd command are determined by the operating system of the ftp server. The Enlil server in this example is running IBM's OS/2 and lists directories with a beginning backslash \. A Unix-based ftp server would list directories with a beginning forward slash /.)

Moving Around the FTP Site

We now know that we are in the pub directory, but the file we are seeking in located in the Ur3 directory. The Unix command to change directories is cd followed by the name of the directory you are seeking. At the Unix prompt, we would issue the follow command and see the response of the server as:

```
ftp> cd Ur3
250 CWD command successful.
ftp>
```

Now if we issue the pwd command, we will see the following response:

```
ftp>pwd
257 "E:\pub\Ur3" is current directory.
ftp>
```

Please note that cd followed only by the name of the directory is effective in changing directories only to those located within your present working directory. The cd Ur3 worked because the Ur3 directory is contained within the pub directory. If the user wants to change to the uploads directory, which is found at pub/uploads, from the Ur3 directory, then the full path of the directory must follow the cd command. To change to the pub/uploads directory from the Ur3 directory, the command line would read cd /pub/uploads. The first forward slash / indicates to the server that the first required directory is at the root of the directory structure.

Following the cd command with the full path of a directory is an easy way to avoid issuing separate cd commands for each step of the way. In an example to be discussed below to show how to transfer binary files, the URL reads ftp://ftp.coast.net/SimTel/win3/educate/wlatin45.zip. After logging into this ftp server, the user can simply issue the command cd SimTel/win3/educate to move to the desired directory. When changing more than one directory level, make sure to use the forward slash or backslash (whichever is used by the ftp server to display your current location) to separate directories and file names from one another.

In order to change directories up to a higher directory use the cdup command, and you will be returned to the directory immediately above your present directory. The cd directory and cdup commands form the basis for moving about in the file directories of the ftp server. If you get an unexpected response from a cd command, simply issue the pwd command to find your present location, and check the name of the directory you are seeking.

Listing Files (and Directories)

Once the user has changed to the appropriate directory, there are two common Unix commands to list the files and directories contained in that directory. The one that is probably most often used is the dir command. An example of it being used on the University of Pennsylvania directory pub\Ur3 is as follows:

```
ftp>dir
200 PORT command successful.
150 Opening ASCII mode data connection for E:\pub\Ur3.
0 DIR 08-25-93 14:48
0 DIR 08-25-93 14:48
129648 RA 09-24-93 12:07 aleppo.txt
55764  RA 10-17-93 11:12 bct_1.txt
193069 RA 11-10-94 11:19 bin_09.txt
122641 RA 11-10-94 11:20 bin_10.txt
3216   RA 09-24-93 12:10 convntns.txt
70121  RA 10-10-94 12:01 ct_01.txt
51342  RA 09-24-93 12:09 ct_32.txt
95711  RA 10-24-94 12:12 hirose.txt
10578  RA 08-13-94 03:41 ligabue.txt
231026 RA 10-10-94 12:01 mvn_02.txt
140478 RA 08-13-94 03:42 mvn_07.txt
```

```
123680 RA 08-13-94 03:42 mvn_11.txt
187860 RA 11-10-94 11:18 mvn_12.txt
168338 RA 10-10-94 12:02 mvn_14.txt
219963 RA 08-13-94 03:42 mvn_15.txt
119892 RA 10-10-94 12:02 mvn_17.txt
216677 RA 11-10-94 11:21 pdt_2.txt
832    RA 08-17-94 13:59 readme
67122  RA 12-12-93 07:12 sact_1.txt
96965  RA 12-12-93 07:12 tcnd.txt
87212  RA 10-24-94 12:11 tlb_3.txt
8284   RA 10-24-94 12:11 tlb_5.txt
11833  RA 10-17-93 11:12 uchitel.txt
76507  RA 09-24-93 12:08 unt.txt
227905 RA 10-24-94 12:11 utami_3.txt
226 Transfer complete.
1728 bytes received in 0.23 seconds (7.3 Kbytes/s)
ftp>
```

The dir command lists several pieces of information that are of interest to anyone who wishes to obtain a copy of the file. It generally lists information in the following format:

```
permissions size owner date time name
```

File permissions are omitted from this listing, but the remaining information for the file convntns.txt are as follows:

```
size owner date time name
```

```
3216 RA 09-24-93 12:10 convntns.txt
```

From this listing, the ftp user discovers that the file size of *convntns.txt* is 3,216 bytes, that it was placed in this directory on 09-24-93 and that the file is known to the ftp server as *convntns.txt*. Bear in mind that sometimes file names change due to updates, or you may only have a partial or incorrect name for the file. In these cases it is necessary to use the file name as shown by the dir command.

Some ftp servers respond to the dir command by not only listing the information shown above but also include the file permissions for the files listed. File permissions are the method by which Unix determines who may read, write or execute a file. Here is an example of this type of directory listing from the SimTel site:

```
ftp> dir a*
200 PORT command successful.
150 Opening ASCII mode data connection for /bin/ls.
-rw-r--r-- 1 djgruber OAK 514575 Sep 15 17:40 am_so40.zip
-rw-r--r-- 1 djgruber OAK 789468 Apr 9  1995 annie14.zip
-rw-r--r-- 1 djgruber OAK 650640 Nov 29 1994 arith12.zip
-rw-r--r-- 1 djgruber OAK 232651 Mar 5  1995 ayli12.zip
226 Transfer complete.
remote: a*
267 bytes received in 0.0056 seconds (46 Kbytes/s)
ftp>
```

The information in the far left column are the Unix file permissions for the listed files. For the casual ftp users, it is sufficient to note that any file that has r-- in positions 8 through 10 of the line can be obtained by using ftp. In order to get a listing short enough to warrant use as an example, note the use of what is known as a wild card character, i.e., the * with the dir command. If the user is only certain about part of the name of a file, such as the first letter, it is possible to issue the dir command, followed by a space, then the letter that begins the file name, and then * to get a listing of only those files beginning with that letter. The other typical command for obtaining a listing of files and directories in a directory is ls. It does not return as much information as dir but may be useful at times when the files names are too long to display properly on your screen. An example of ls on the SimTel site, using the wild card character, produced the following listing:

```
ftp> ls a*
200 PORT command successful.
150 Opening ASCII mode data connection for file list.
am_so40.zip
annie14.zip
arith12.zip
ayli12.zip
226 Transfer complete.
remote: a*
51 bytes received in 2.8 seconds (0.018 Kbytes/s)
ftp>
```

Note that the ls command requires the return of a smaller amount of information, which may be important if you have a slow connection to the Internet or between your personal computer and the University system that is actually connected to the Internet.

It will not take very many ftp sessions until you will discover one rather glaring problem with both the dir and ls commands. Both commands will list all of the files and directories found in your present directory location, but often at a speed that would defeat a speed reader. Some communication programs provide the ability to scroll back to text that has already appeared on your screen, but that may not be an option with your software. Fortunately, there is a solution to this problem that works with either the dir or ls commands. This solution involves what is known as "piping," which simply means sending the results of one command to another command. In this case, we need to send the result of the dir or ls command to a command that will not allow the text to scroll off the screen until the user has had time to read it. Preferably, it will not scroll until told to do so by the user. Unix provides that ability by piping the results of the dir or ls command into the Unix command "more." The following example illustrates the usage of this command sequence:

```
ftp>dir * |more
200 PORT command successful.
150 Opening ASCII mode data connection for /bin/ls.
-rw-r--r-- 1 djgruber OAK 9529    Jan 14 09:15 00_index.txt
-rw-r--r-- 1 djgruber OAK 278600  Mar 21 1995 2dflow.zip
-rw-r--r-- 1 djgruber OAK 514575 Sep 15 17:40 am_so40.zip
-rw-r--r-- 1 djgruber OAK 789468   Apr 9 1995 annie14.zip
-rw-r--r-- 1 djgruber OAK 650640  Nov 29 1994 arith12.zip
-rw-r--r-- 1 djgruber OAK 232651   Mar 5 1995 ayli12.zip
-rw-r--r-- 1 djgruber OAK 205464   Jul 2 1993 bear_bee.zip
-rw-r--r-- 1 djgruber OAK 1240492 Oct 13 15:10 boxes52.zip
-rw-r--r-- 1 djgruber OAK 1342791 Aug 18 23:07 bxword11.zip
-rw-r--r-- 1 djgruber OAK 240581 Jul 31 23:52 calmem10.zip
-rw-r--r-- 1 djgruber OAK 83264    May 13 1993 cbmath15.zip
-rw-r--r-- 1 djgruber OAK 426649 Nov 17 01:15 ccwin31.zip
-rw-r--r-- 1 djgruber OAK 139733  Dec 15 1994 cnetd101.zip
-rw-r--r-- 1 djgruber OAK 40147    Aug 23 1993 color12.zip
-rw-r--r-- 1 djgruber OAK 173505 Oct 21 01:59 const1_3.zip
-rw-r--r-- 1 djgruber OAK 190892 Nov 20 22:53 corner1.zip
-rw-r--r-- 1 djgruber OAK 592944 Aug 17 23:14 cpix11.zip
-rw-r--r-- 1 djgruber OAK 146364 Nov 11 03:42 cross10.zip
-rw-r--r-- 1 djgruber OAK 142093   Nov 5 1994 crypto15.zip
-rw-r--r-- 1 djgruber OAK 170992   Jul 5 1995 crypto20.zip
-rw-r--r-- 1 djgruber OAK 11268    Apr 3 1994 cscat11.zip
-rw-r--r-- 1 djgruber OAK 227536   Jul 1 1995 cwkit120.zip
--More--
```

In this example, the dir command was entered, followed by a space, then the wild card character *, followed by the vertical bar and the command more with no space between the vertical bar and the command. The results of the dir command will scroll up on the screen. After you have viewed that section of the text, simply press the space bar and it will scroll up another screen of text until the entire output has been shown. If you wish to quit the listing of files, simply press q for quit, and you will be returned to the ftp prompt. One limitation of the more command is that you cannot scroll back up to an earlier portion of the text, but it does provide the ability to read long directory listings without their scrolling off the screen.

Once the desired files have been found, the user then transfers them either to his local computer, if he has a direct connection to the Internet, or to the computer he is using to access the Internet for later transfer to his computer. In either case, the user must recognize the type of file that is to be obtained in order to have a usable file once it arrives at his computer. A brief digression on the types of files found on ftp sites and the appropriate transfer methods for those file is our next topic.

File Types and Getting Files

File Types

File types found on ftp sites fall into two basic categories, ASCII and BINARY. If the user transfers a binary file, typically a compressed or program file, with the wrong transfer mechanism, the resulting file on his local computer will be corrupt and unusable. Fortunately, it is possible to recognize the type of file, either ASCII or BINARY, from its file extension and to proceed accordingly. The file extension is the last portion of a file name, found after the last period found in the file name. The file from the University of Pennsylvania archive, convntns.txt, has a file extension of .txt and is an ASCII file. The Latin file from the SimTel archive, wlatin45.zip, has a .zip extension, which refers to a popular DOS compression program, and must be transferred as a BINARY file. The critical difference is that an ASCII file can lose or gain a few bytes in transfer and not suffer any ill effects. The BINARY file, however, must be transferred in such a way that is does not lose or gain any bytes and is identical on your machine to the one found on the ftp site. The following brief listing of file types and the transfer method for each will assist you in choosing the proper method for obtaining a copy of the file.

Extension	Means	Use
.exe	Executable program file	BINARY
.gif	Image file format	Binary
.gz	Gzip file (Unix)	BINARY
.hqx	Mac BINHEX compression	ASCII
.jpeg	Image file format	BINARY
.pdf	Adobe Acrobat format	BINARY
.ps	Postscript files	ASCII
.rtf	Rich Text Format	ASCII
.shar	Unix file transfer format	BINARY
.sit	Mac STUFFIT compression	BINARY
.tar	Unix file transfer format	BINARY
.tex	TeX or LaTeX files	ASCII
.txt	Text file	ASCII
.uue	Uuencoded file	ASCII
.zip	PC compression program	BINARY
.zoo	PC compression program	BINARY
.Z	Compressed file (Unix)	BINARY

Getting Files

Once the desired file has been found and its type identified, the user can then proceed to obtain a copy of the file. Whether an ASCII or BINARY file, the general file transfer command is get followed by the file name. In order to set the proper method for transfer, the user must issue the binary command prior to transferring a BINARY file. The normal means of transmission is ASCII, so no special command is needed when obtaining ASCII files.

In order to obtain a copy of the convntns.txt file mentioned above, the user issues the following commands after changing to the proper directory:

```
ftp> get convntns.txt
200 PORT command successful.
150 Opening ASCII mode data connection for convntns.txt (3216 bytes).
226 Transfer complete.
local: convntns.txt remote: convntns.txt
3215 bytes received in 0.43 seconds (7.3 Kbytes/s)
ftp>
```

The file *convntns.txt* is now located on the local hard drive of the user or on the computer being used to access the Internet. It is important to note that the original directory listing showed that this file had 3216 bytes, but the file as transferred only arrived with 3215 bytes. This difference will not affect the usefulness of an ASCII file but would prevent a binary file from being of any use at all.

Since a binary command is required to obtain a binary file, it requires one more step than a plain ASCII file. Using the SimTel example listed earlier, the user must issue a binary command at the ftp prompt before using the get command to obtain a copy of the file. The following example shows the proper sequence of commands:

```
ftp> binary
200 Type set to I.
ftp> get wlatin45.zip
200 PORT command successful.
150 Opening BINARY mode data connection for wlatin45.zip (359480 bytes).
226 Transfer complete.
local: wlatin45.zip remote: wlatin45.zip
359480 bytes received in 2.2e+02 seconds (1.6 Kbytes/s)
ftp>
```

Note that in this example, the number of bytes listed for the file wlatin45.zip matches that shown in the directory listing. This file can now be successfully decompressed with the appropriate software on a DOS computer.

Users can obtain as many files as desired, or to the limits of their disk space allowance, with the methods outlined above. It would be tiresome, however, if one wanted to obtain all of the Leiden project's texts, to have to name and "get" each separate file. After one becomes comfortable with the basic ftp commands, there are other commands that will allow multiple file transfers with single commands. First, in order to use these commands, it is necessary to turn off the interactive prompting from the ftp server. Otherwise, the server will ask if the user wishes to transfer each and every file, and the user must respond for the transfer to occur. To turn off the interactive prompting of the ftp server, issue the following command:

```
ftp>
ftp>prompt
Interactive mode off.
ftp>
```

Once the interactive command has been turned off, the user can then use what is known as the mget (multiple get) command. With the mget command, the user can use a wild card character to obtain all of the files with certain names or extensions in a given directory. For example, at the SimTel site, assume that the user wants all the files whose names start with the letter r. To obtain those files using mget, the user would issue the following commands:

```
ftp>
ftp>binary
200 Type set to I.
ftp>prompt
Interactive mode off.
ftp>mget r*

200 PORT command successful.
150 Opening BINARY mode data connection for raytr207.zip (317585 bytes).
226 Transfer complete.
local: raytr207.zip remote: raytr207.zip
317585 bytes received in 3.2 seconds (97 Kbytes/s)
200 PORT command successful.
150 Opening BINARY mode data connection for rockcy14.zip (144016 bytes).
226 Transfer complete.
local: rockcy14.zip remote: rockcy14.zip
144016 bytes received in 1.4 seconds (1e+02 Kbytes/s)
200 PORT command successful.
150 Opening BINARY mode data connection for rsistn62.zip (127436 bytes).
226 Transfer complete.
local: rsistn62.zip remote: rsistn62.zip
127436 bytes received in 1.3 seconds (98 Kbytes/s)
200 PORT command successful.
150 Opening BINARY mode data connection for rtg13.zip (236183 bytes).
226 Transfer complete.
local: rtg13.zip remote: rtg13.zip
236183 bytes received in 2.3 seconds (1e+02 Kbytes/s)
ftp>
```

Special Unix File Types

In the listing of file types above, there are several that may be unfamiliar to most users and are only applicable to people who are on a Unix platform. Those files have the extensions .gz, .Z, and .tar followed by .gz or .Z. Software is available for both DOS and Mac platforms to process these files types, but some users may not have this software available. In that event, the user should seek advice from other Internet users on obtaining the appropriate software, and in the meantime he or she can use the following techniques to process the files.

.gz files

Files which end with the .gz extension, sometimes preceded by .tar, are files compressed with a program known as gzip. Most Unix platforms have a software program known as gunzip to process files with this extension. In order to decompress these files, issue the following command at the Unix prompt:

```
% gunzip somefile.gz
```
This will decompress the original file, and it will now appear in a listing of your directory without the .gz extension. If your system does not have the gunzip program-that is you get the message command not found-try the following variant on that command:

```
% gzip -x somefile.gz
```
The -x following the gzip command is an indication to the gzip program to extract the file from its compressed state.

.Z files

Files which end with the file extension .Z have been compressed with the Unix command compress. To uncompress such files, issue the uncompress command (a rare instance of a rational name in Unix).

```
% uncompress somefile.Z
```
This will uncompress the file, and then you may perform any other operations, such as using the tar command on the resulting file if necessary.

.tar files

Files which have .tar as part of the file name have been generated with a Unix utility known as tar. It is important to note that .tar files can contain not only multiple files but also directories and sub-directories containing files. Please check with your system administrator if you are uncertain whether you have enough space to unpack a .tar file in your directory. Files with the .tar extension are most often seen combined with the .Z or .gz extensions as well, such as somefile.tar.gz or somefile.tar.Z. In either case, just use the commands for .gz or .Z detailed above and then apply the instructions for unpacking the resulting file, which after uncompressing will read somefile.tar.

To extract a .tar file, you should be at the Unix prompt in the directory where the file is located and have enough room for the extraction. Then issue the tar command as follows:

```
% tar -xf somefile.tar
```

This will extract the file from the .tar format and write the directory and/or files into your present directory. You should also consult a good Unix reference manual to learn how to safely use the rm command to remove the file somefile.tar after you have extracted the contents.

5. Telnet

Telnet is used to connect one computer to another over the Internet. Unlike WWW browsers and FTP, telnet allows users to use the computer accessed by telnet just as if they were logged into the computer as local users. One primary use for telnet on the Internet is to connect to library catalogues at other universities for bibliographic research. Telnet allows the user to search a library catalogue with the same commands that are available from a local terminal located in the library itself. A growing number of libraries have WWW interfaces to their collections, but telnet remains an important tool for scholars using the Internet for scholarly research.

Telnet Addresses

The telnet addresses listed in the resource section of this guide are written as they would be used with WWW browser software. In order to use these addresses at the command prompt, the user must separate the address as given into several component parts. The telnet address of the National Archaeology Database reads as follows:

```
telnet://cast.uark.edu or telnet://130.184.71.44, log in as "nadb"
```

That address is correct and works properly for a WWW browser, because the browser automatically recognizes that it is composed of two separate parts. First, the manner of accessing the site is specified by the beginning telnet://. In order for this to work properly, a telnet helper application must be specified for the WWW browser. Consult browser documentation for specific instructions. Second, the address of the site is specified as: **cast.uarch.edu** or **130.184.71.44**. Both forms of the telnet address are given here, but only one is actually used with the telnet command. Either address will work to connect to the site. Third, the login password is given for the site, which should be entered after a connection has been established. Public telnet sites have well known passwords and are often listed in the text which acknowledges the connection. Some telnet sites require connections to a particular port, which is usually shown as a colon followed by a number and is appended to the telnet address.

Telnet Commands

Telnet itself is a command, and it lacks the complexity found in dealing with FTP. An example of a session with the Emory University library computer illustrates the basic commands needed to make effective use of telnet.

```
scholar% telnet euclid.cc.emory.edu
Trying 170.140.110.129 ...
Connected to euclid.cc.emory.edu.
Escape character is '^]'.


AIX telnet (libcat1.cc.emory.edu)


     ----------------------------------------------------------------
        E m o r y   U n i v e r s i t y   C o m p u t i n g   a n d
     ----------------------------------------------------------------


    EEEEEEEE   UU      UU     CCCCCCC  LL          IIIIII  DDDDDDDD
    EE         UU      UU     CC    CC LL            II    DD     D
    EE         UU      UU     CC       LL            II    DD    DD
    EEEEE      UU      UU     CC       LL            II    DD    DD
    EE         UU      UU     CC       LL            II    DD    DD
    EE         UU      UU     CC    CC LL      LL    II    DD     D
    EEEEEEEE    UUUUUUU        CCCCCCC  LLLLLLLLL  IIIIII  DDDDDDDD


     ----------------------------------------------------------------
     L i b r a r y   I n f o r m a t i o n  D e l i v e r y  S y s t e m
     ----------------------------------------------------------------


AIX Version 3
(C) Copyrights by IBM and by others 1982, 1993.
Enter euclid or your login: euclid
```

By pressing return after entering the username, the user is logged onto the library computer at Emory University. From that point forward, all of the commands are determined by the program that is located on the remote computer. If you want to access several library catalogues in succession, simply type telnet at the Unix prompt and there will appear a telnet prompt as follows:

```
telnet>
```

At this prompt, you can enter the same address as before, but the telnet command "open" must precede the actual address of the computer to be accessed.

Example

```
telnet> open euclid.cc.emory.edu
```
The resulting screens for access to the Emory library catalogue will be identical to those shown earlier. The user should note all help and other informational commands for the computer system or library catalogue that has been accessed by the use of telnet. Most systems have preferred methods for users to terminate their use of the remote computer. There is no requirement that these resources be made freely available over the Internet, and users should attempt to follow the instructions given for proper use. In the unlikely event that the remote system will not let you exit the telnet program, hold down the control key and press the "]" (right bracket) key. This is a universal telnet escape sequence that will terminate your connection to the remote computer. It should only be used as a last resort after having tried to exit the remote program properly.

6. Internet Resources for Biblical and Religious Studies, Archaeology and Classics

The resource listing is divided into one section for discussion lists and another for other types of Internet resources. In part this was due to the original division in the first edition but it also reflects the different audiences that use the Internet. There are some users who have only email access and they will find the gathering of all email resources together more convenient than interspersing these items within the larger Internet listing.

Discussion Lists

Mailing lists, which allow email discussions, were the first arena of scholarly communication on the Internet. Even with the advent of World Wide Web software and other tools on the horizon, they still play an important role in academic discussions. Although this is not a comprehensive listing of every mailing list related to archaeology, classics, and religious studies, those included herein are primarily oriented towards scholars working in these fields.

A broader compilation of mailing lists for religious studies, and one consulted in the preparation of this listing, can be found at A Shortlist of Email Forums for Theologians (**http://info.ox.ac.uk/ctitext/theology/email.html**). This listing by Michael Fraser includes denominational resources and general discussion lists for religious subjects. It is somewhat dated now but remains a very useful guide to religious studies discussion lists, including those of a scholarly nature mentioned herein, along with a number of other lists.

The mailing lists found below are listed by the name of the list, followed by a subscription address and a brief description of the list. Subscription addresses are printed in uppercase for ease of reading and because email on the Internet ignores case in addresses. Addresses listed for other Internet resources are case sensitive and must be entered as they appear. The descriptions for the lists are based upon announcements by the list owners or descriptions of the list found in other online resources.

A-Z ANNOUNCE
MAJORDOMO@ORT.ORG

A-Z Announce is a companion to the A - Z of Jewish & Israel Related Resources WWW page. This list sends a notice as new resources are added to the new resources section.

ACTS-L
LISTSERV@LISTSERV.UOTTAWA.CA

ACTS-L is a forum for discussion of the Acts of the Apostles and critical issues surrounding that work. It is used as a service to members of the Saint Paul University's course THO 2151 "Acts of the Apostles" to expose them to the ongoing scholarly discussion of the Book of Acts.

AEGEANET
Majordomo@acpub.duke.edu

Aegeanet is a discussion list on the pre-classical Aegean world.

Aegyptian-L
Listerver@rostau.demon.co.uk

This is a list on Ancient Egyptian language. List members exchange ideas and proposed translations of texts ranging from the Old Kingdom to the New Kingdom.

AIBI-L
LISTSERV@LISTSERV.UOTTAWA.CA

AIBI-L is a discussion forum for l'Association internationale bible et informatique. AIBI-L is an on-going forum and meeting place for AIBI members and others who wish to join the discussion of issues related to the computerized-analysis of Biblical and related texts.

ALEXANDRIA
MAJORDOMO@WORLD.STD.COM

ALEXANDRIA is a mailing list for the discussion of the Western cosmological traditions.

AMERCATH
LISTSERV@LSV.UKY.EDU

An electronic discussion group for those interested in the history of American Catholicism.

ANAHITA
LISTSERV@LSV.UKY.EDU

An unmoderated list focusing on the scholarly study of women and gender throughout the ancient Mediterranean world. A companion to the WWW site Diotima.

ANGLICAN
LISTSERV@AMERICAN.EDU

The Anglican mailing list provides a forum for discussion of items of interest to the worldwide Anglican community and the Episcopal Church.

ANCIEN-L
LISTSERV@ULKYVM.LOUISVILLE.EDU

ANCIEN-L is a forum for debate, discussion, and the exchange of information by students and scholars of the Ancient Mediterranean.

ANE
MAJORDOMO@OI.UCHICAGO.EDU

ANE is the companion mailing list to the ABZU WWW site maintained by the Oriental Institute at the University of Chicago. It is the first and foremost discussion list for all topics related to the Ancient Near East. Archives of the site can be found at **http://www-oi.uchicago.edu/OI/ANE/OI_ANE.html** or with a more sophisticated searching interface at: **http://www.findmail.com/list/ane/**

ARCH-L
LISTSERV@TAMVM1.TAMU.EDU

ARCH-L focuses on discussion of archaeological problems, especially those concerned with research, excavations, etc. Also, relevant conferences, job announcements, calls for papers, publications, bibliographies and the like should be publicized. Discussions of new techniques and the significance of new discoveries are welcome.

ARCH-THEORY
MAILBASE@MAILBASE.AC.UK

This is a list for discussion of archaeological theory, social theory, material culture, cultural identity, and perspectives from anthropology and history.

ARIL-L
LISTSERV@UCSBVM.UCSB.EDU

ARIL-L is the on-line forum for the Association for Religion and Intellectual Life, publishers of the journal Cross Currents. It is intended to provide opportunities for members to discuss issues raised in the journal and at ARIL's annual consultations, as well as other issues of concern to ARIL members.

ARTIFACT
LISTSERV@UMDD.UMD.EDU

ARTIFACT serves scholars interested in material culture, artifacts and their cultural context. Topics of interest may include current research, methods of artifact study, teaching material culture, and employment opportunities. Its focus is primarily North American.

ASOR-L
MAJORDOMO@SHEMESH.SCHOLAR.EMORY.EDU

The ASOR-L list hosts discussions of interest to members of the American Schools of Oriental Research.

ASREL-L: The Asian Religions Discussion List
(N.B.: Closed List, No Automatic Subscription)

John McRae formed this list as a discussion forum for introductory courses on Asian religions. Only faculty teaching such courses, students enrolled in those courses and authors of texts on such materials are allowed to participate. Please contact John McRae, jrm5@cornell.edu, directly for further information on this list.

ATLANTIS
LISTSERV@HARVADA.BITNET

ATLANTIS serves as a medium of exchange and communication among members of the American Theological Library Association, hence the name, ATLA Networked Theological Information Service. It is not, however, exclusively for ATLA members. It is requested that ATLA members identify themselves when subscribing to the list.

B-ARAMAIC
MAJORDOMO@NAZARENE.NET

B-ARAMAIC is an electronic conference focusing on study of the Aramaic Bible and related Aramaic texts.

B-GREEK (formerly NT-GREEK)
MAJORDOMO@VIRGINIA.EDU

B-GREEK is an electronic conference designed to foster communication concerning the scholarly study of the Greek Bible. Anyone interested in New Testament Studies is invited to subscribe, but the list will assume at least a working knowledge of Biblical Greek.

B-HEBREW (formerly OT-HEBREW)
MAJORDOMO@VIRGINIA.EDU

B-HEBREW is an electronic conference designed to foster communication concerning the scholarly study of the Hebrew Bible. Anyone interested in Biblical Hebrew Studies is invited to subscribe, but the list will assume at least a working knowledge of Biblical Hebrew and Aramaic.

BIBLE
MAJORDOMO@VIRGINIA.EDU

Bible is a general discussion list for topics relating to the Bible. Scholars interested in a more traditional academic approach to biblical studies should consider the B-Hebrew or B-Greek lists as alternatives to Bible.

BMCR-L
MAJORDOMO@BRYNMAWR.EDU

The Bryn Mawr Classical Review is an electronic journal devoted to reviews of current books in Greek and Latin literature and Greek and Roman history. The journal is published in both paper and electronic form (ISSN for paper: 1055-7660, ISSN for e-version: 1063-2948).

BMMR-L
MAJORDOMO@BRYNMAWR.EDU

The Bryn Mawr Medieval Review, is a sister publication of the Bryn Mawr Classical Review (BMCR). BMMR will publishes timely reviews of current work in all areas of medieval studies.

BONHOF-L
listproc2@bgu.edu

Bonhof-L is dedicated to the study of the life and thought of Dietrich Bonhoeffer. Appropriate topics would include close readings of key texts, assessments of Bonhoeffer's place in modern theology, analysis of Bonhoeffer's activism in light of his theology, and evaluation of Bonhoeffer's impact on post-modern theology

BUDDHA-L
LISTSERV@ULKYVM.LOUISVILLE.EDU or LISTSERV@ULKYVM.BITNET

BUDDHA-L provides a forum for serious academic discussion of Buddhism and Buddhist studies. It is open to all persons inside and outside the academic context who wish to engage in substantial discussion of topics relating to Buddhism and Buddhist studies.

BUDDHIST
LISTSERV@VM1.MCGILL.CA

BUDDHIST is an unmoderated list for the discussion of any and all aspects of Buddhism: academic scholarship, questions of practice, and inquiries from beginners. Topics have included history, philosophy, text study, culture, practice methods, reference sources, and the meaning of Buddhist teachings. Subscribers include professional scholars, practitioners of various accomplishments and traditions, students of religion, and the general public.

BYTETORAH
LISTPROC@SHAMASH.ORG

Weekly mailing of discussion for Torah portion for each week.

C14-L
LISTSERV@LISTSERV.ARIZONA.EDU

Radiocarbon dating issues discussion list.

CAAL
CAAL-OWNER@FF.CUNI.CZ

CAAL (Computers and ancient languages) is focused mainly on the languages of the Ancient Near East (Indo-European, Semitic and others). The interests of the list include: computer databases of ancient Indo-European, Afro-Asiatic (Hamito-Semitic) and other languages, the use of hypertexts for the texts and secondary sources, especially on the Ancient Near East, linguistic and philological analysis of ancient languages based on electronic text corpora, and the problems of encoding of the texts of ancient languages. (N.B.: Subscription requests are handled by the owner and not automatic subscription software.)

CALVIN-L
LISTSERV@LISTSERV.UCALGARY.CA

CALVIN-L is a distribution list for the study of Reformation thought. The central focus of the list is the Neo-Calvinist tradition developed by Groen van Prinsterer, Abraham Kuyper and Herman Dooyeweerd.

CATHOLIC
CATHOLIC-REQUEST@SARTO.GAITHERSBURG.MD.US

CATHOLIC is a list for the orthodox discussions of the Catholic religion. Most participants are Roman rite, but all Catholic rites are welcome. This is a moderated list and is shaped by the moderator's criterion for orthodoxy, which is primarily based upon traditional Catholic works, such as Papal encyclical letters, the Summa of St. Thomas Aquinas, the (original) Catholic

Encyclopaedia and other such works. (N.B.: No automatic subscription, your request is being read by a person. Actually, this list is using software written by the moderator, so it may not respond to other commands as expected to usual mailing list commands.)

CHRISTLIT
LISTSERV@BETHEL.EDU

CHRISTLIT is an open, moderated discussion list featuring the interrelations between Christianity and Literature. The list will maintain a relationship with the Conference on Christianity and Literature and has among its purposes increasing a sense of community among subscribers. It is not intended for theological dispute.

CLASSICS
LISTPROC@U.WASHINGTON.EDU

CLASSICS is an unmoderated list for discussing ancient Greek and Latin subjects. This list is open to everyone interested in Classics, and prospective members are warmly welcomed. The discussions assume a background in ancient Greek and/or Latin and postings are expected to remain within the confines of these subjects. Only list-members are permitted to post or reply to CLASSICS messages, and this list does not appear on Usenet. There are searchable archives for this discussion list beginning in the spring of 1992 and continuing to present. Linda Wright maintains the last thirty (30) days of digests at the following location: **http://weber.u.washington.edu/~lwright/classics.html**.

CLASSICS-M
LISTPROC@U.WASHINGTON.EDU or contact Linda Wright: lwright@cac.washington.edu

Moderated version of the Classics list. The moderated list carries all of the job postings, conference announcements, and resource information that appear on the full Classics list. The moderated list also receives an occasional request for assistance on research matters. All postings are forwarded by Linda Wright from the full list and do not exceed six per day.

CLASSICSLGB
MAJORDOMO@ACPUB.DUKE.EDU

A forum for lesbian, gay, and bisexual academics (faculty and students) and gay-friendly academics in the broad field of Classical Studies (Greek and Latin literature), Greek and Roman history, art, archaeology) to discuss and apply queer studies in classical studies. ClassicsLGB is sponsored by the Lesbian, Gay, and Bisexual Classical Caucus, an independent affiliate of the American Philological Association (APA) and associated with the Archaeological Institute of America (AIA), and by the Department of Classical Studies, Duke University.

COE
COE-REQUEST@USIS.COM

COE, Circles of Exchange, is a discussion list that focuses on women's spirituality.

COPTIST
MAJORDOMO@CISADU2.LET.UNIROMA1.IT

The Coptist list is a forum for all scholarly discussion on the Coptic language and relevant texts.

DERRIDA
LISTSERV@CFRVM.CFR.USF.EDU

A list focused on discussing the philosophical, literary and political importance of deconstruction and specifically the work of the French philosopher Jacques Derrida (in such works as Of Grammatology, Glas, etc.). Other writers who use a deconstructive approach to philosophy or literature, J. Hillis Miller, Paul de Man, etc., are appropriate subjects. The effects of deconstruction, its applications and criticisms of deconstruction are likely topics.

ECCHST-L
LISTSERV@BGU.EDU

ECCHST-L is a discussion list for scholars, students and others interested in Church History, History of Christianity, and/or Historical Theology. Comparative dialogue across time and traditions is encouraged.

ECOLE-READERS
MAJORDOMO@EVANSVILLE.EDU

A forum for those who are interested in following the development of the Early Church On-Line Encyclopedia Initiative (ECOLE) which can be found at **http://www.evansville.edu/~ecoleweb**. Regular updates about the Encyclopedia will be sent to the list. It is hoped that conversation about the articles in the Encyclopedia will develop here as well.

ECOTHEOL
MAILBASE@MAILBASE.AC.UK

ECOTHEOL has been established to provide a forum for discussion of ecological or environmental issues from a theological and ethical perspective. The list welcomes contributions from those in other disciplines, including philosophy and the social sciences.

EEF - The Egyptologist's Electronic Forum

EEF is a broad ranging discussion list on Egyptian culture, broadly defined to include religion, history, literature, archaeology, art, etc., from the fourth millennium BCE until 622 CE. The application form for scholars and students who are interested in discussions of Egyptology can be found at: **http://www.bosagate.demon.co.uk/appform.htm**.

ELECTRONIC ANTIQUITY: COMMUNICATING THE CLASSICS
ANTIQUITY-EDITOR@CLASSICS.UTAS.EDU.AU

A monthly journal for the classics edited by Peter Toohey (founding editor) and Ian Worthington which began in June 1993. Electronic Antiquity aims to act as a medium through which scholars (and graduate students) may exchange scholarly and general views and be kept informed of developments and items of interest affecting classics and the classics community as a whole. Subscribers will receive notification of each issue including a table of contents. (N.B.: Subscription requests are handled by the editor and not automatic subscription software.)

ELENCHUS
LISTSERV@LISTSERV.UOTTAWA.CA

ELENCHUS is devoted to discussions of the thought and literature of Christianity during the period 100 to 500 AD (CE).

ENTMP-WORK
MAJORDOMO@CYNUS.UWA.EDU.AU

ENTMP-WORK is a discussion list for the ongoing work of the Electronic New Testament Manuscripts Project, which is seeking to make available electronic versions of New Testament manuscripts.

EXPLORATOR
dmeadows@idirect.com

Irregular newsletter from David Meadows that advises of news articles on the Web or new resources relating to the ancient world (prior to 1700, approximately). Note that subscription requests are made directly to David Meadows, with the subject line: Explorator Request.

FEMREL-L
LISTSERV@LISTSERV.AOL.COM

FEMREL-L is a discussion and resource group concerning women and religion and feminist theology. All religions, creeds, beliefs, and opinions are welcome. Send a message to the listserv with "info" in the message body for a fuller description of the list.

FEMINIST-THEOLOGY
MAILBASE@MAILBASE.AC.UK

Feminist-Theology is a forum for the academic discussion of Jewish and Christian feminist theology. Topics discussed on this list include a feminist critique of traditional ways of doing theology and may cover all aspects of theological study. It is also meant for the exchange of information about publications and research in this area.

GRAPHAI

Graphai is a discussion list dedicated to the academic study of the New Testament. The list is being conducted under the auspices of the Society of Biblical Literature and seeks to assist scholars in their professional study of the New Testament. A form for subscribing to the list can be found at: **http://ccat.sas.upenn.edu/graphai/sub.html**.

GREEKARCH
MAJORDOMO@ROME.CLASSICS.LSA.UMICH.EDU

GreekArch is a general discussion list on the archaeology of ancient Greece.

GREEK-GRAMMAR
JTAUBER@TARTARUS.UWA.EDU.AU

The Greek-Grammar list is designed for discussion about the Reference Grammar Project in particular and Hellenistic Greek linguistics in general. The Reference Grammar Project is an effort by the Greek Grammar Seminar of the Westar Institute to produce a successor the Blass-Debrunner-Funk grammar, A Greek Grammar of the New Testament and Other Early Christian Literature, University of Chicago, 1961. All of the archives for the list are located on the WWW. Please see the entry for Hellenistic Greek Linguistics Page under Internet Resources. (N.B.: your subscription request is being sent to James K. Tauber, not an automatic subscription program)

GROMARCH
MAJORDOMO@ROME.CLASSICS.LSA.UMICH.EDU

A joint subscription list that delivers posts from both the GreekArch and RomanArch lists under one subscription.

H-CLC
H-CLC@MSU.EDU

H-CLC is a moderated list focusing on the use of computers in literary studies. This list is both a place of collaboration and for discussion of issues, methodological and technical, in this rapidly developing field. An archive of bibliographies, reviews, preprints, and other resources is also maintained. Subscription requests should be addressed to the address above or to one of the co-moderators of H-CLC: Barbara Diederichs: bdiederi@artsci.wustl.edu, Craig Branham: branhacc@scuvca.slu.edu, and Randolph Pope: rpope@artsci.wustl.edu.

H-RHETOR
LISTSERV@UICVM.UIC.EDU

H-RHETOR is devoted to the history of rhetoric and communication. Since rhetoric was for a long time part of the formal training of the clergy, it may be of interest to religion scholars.

HA-SAFRAN
LISTSERVER@LISTS.ACS.OHIO-STATE.EDU

This list focuses on issues of interest to Jewish librarians.

HEBLANG
LISTPROC@SHAMASH.ORG

HEBLANG is a discussion list for the Hebrew language at any historical stage of development, but there is some focus on biblical Hebrew.

HEGEL
LISTSERV@BUCKNELL.EDU

This is an unmoderated Internet electronic discussion forum dealing with the thought and influence of the philosopher G. W. F. Hegel (1770-1831).

HOLOCAUS
LISTSERV@UICVM.UIC.EDU or LISTSERV@UICVM.BITNET

This list is primarily geared toward those who do research on the Holocaust and teach courses on it.

HCS-L

HCS is a private list designed for the use of members of the Society for Hindu-Christian Studies and subscribers to Society's journal, the Hindu-Christian Studies Bulletin. Subscription requests should be directed to lnelson@acusd.edu.

HUMCAN-L
LISTPROC@CC.UMONTREAL.CA

A companion to the Humanities Canada WWW site, HumCan-L was formed to provide a place for discussion of issues of interest to Canadian humanists.

H-XY
P-NUGENT@UCHICAGO.EDU

H-Xy is a mailing list treating the history of Christianity in every period except that of the New Testament itself, and covering every geographical area. This list is sponsored by the American Society of Church History. (N.B.: Your subscription request is sent to a person, not automatic subscription software.)

INDOLOGY
LISTSERV@LIVERPOOL.AC.UK

This list is chiefly aimed at academics interested in the study of classical India. The group might be expected to discuss topics such as the history of linguistics, Indo-European philology and grammar, issues of character set encoding, the location of citations, and the exchange of e-texts.

INTRO_GREEK
MAJORDOMO@PERSEUS.TUFTS.EDU

A mailing list for beginning students in the study of introductory Greek.

IOUDAIOS-L
LISTPROC@LEHIGH.EDU

This is an electronic seminar devoted to the exploration of early Judaism and Christian origins; its special interest is in the writings of Philo of Alexandria and Flavius Josephus. It is an international forum, with participants in North America, Europe, Australia, and the Middle East.

IOUDAIOS-REVIEW
LISTPROC@LEHIGH.EDU

This is an electronic serial that offers reviews of new scholarship in the area of early Judaism and Christian origins. Subscriptions are usually limited to members of the IOUDAIOS-L discussion list.

ISLAM-L
LISTSERV@ULKYVM.LOUISVILLE.EDU or LISTSERV@ULKYVM.BITNET

This is a non-sectarian forum for discussion, debate, and the exchange of information by students and scholars of the history of Islam.

J-SEMINAR
LISTPROC@SHAMASH.ORG

The Judaic Seminar has been formed to provide a forum in which Tanach will be discussed on an advanced level by researchers and serious students of the Bible. This is a moderated forum, led by a group of Bible instructors that will be of value to those pursuing a better understanding of the Biblical text.

JAIN-L
JAIN-REQUEST@INDIRECT.COM

A discussion list for Jainism, a non-Vedic religion of India. (N.B.: subscribe by sending mail to jain-request@indirect.com, with subscribe jain-l as the subject line (not in the body of the message.)

JOHNLITR
LISTSERV@VM.SC.EDU

A discussion forum focusing on the Gospel of John and related issues.

JTS-CAGSALUM
LISTSERV@JTSA.EDU

The Alumni Association of the Albert A. List College of Jewish Studies and Graduate School of the Jewish Theological Seminary of America presents an unmoderated discussion list available ONLY to Alumni. The discussion list was created to disseminate information, announcements, and requests for resources; share divrei torah and articles by distinguished alumni and, most importantly, as an informal area for networking and maintaining contacts. (N.B.: Open only to alumni of JTSA)

JTS-WEBNEWS
LISTSERV@JTSA.EDU

JTS-WebNews is a low traffic announcement list concerning new developments on the Jewish Theological Seminary of America website. Events such as library exhibits, online events, distance learning courses and new departments online are the subjects of this list.

JUDAICA
LISTSERV@TAUNIVM.TAU.AC.IL or LISTSERV@TAUNIVM.BITNET

This list is interested in information, work-in-progress, electronic applications, and, especially, new approaches, which relate to Judaic Studies. Questions are welcome, and participation of the broadest possible audience is encouraged.

KANT-L
LISTSERV@CORAL.BUCKNELL.EDU

KANT-L seeks to enable and encourage thoughtful, sustained, and competent discussion of issues involved in the understanding of the thought of Immanuel Kant. The list is open to anyone, from any discipline, having a serious interest in this area of study. The Listmanagers have a particular concern to encourage close critical discussions and "slow readings" of the Kantian texts and of secondary sources (commentaries, biographies, etc.) pertaining to these works, but the activities of the List will not be restricted to such discussions.

KIERKEGAARD
KIERKEGAARD-REQUEST@STOLAF.EDU

KIERKEGAARD is sponsored by the Howard and Edna Hong Kierkegaard Library at St. Olaf College, Northfield, Minnesota, USA, to promote the exchange of information regarding the 19th century Danish philosopher, Soren Kierkegaard. Discussion or questions concerning thinkers related to Kierkegaard are also welcome.

LARELS-L
LISTSERV@UCSBVM.UCSB.EDU

LARELS-L is designed to support the work of scholars studying the multiplicity of religions in Los Angeles and Southern California. It is sponsored by the Center for the Study of Religion at the University of California, Santa Barbara, which is conducting a number of research projects relating to religion, politics, and ethnicity in Los Angeles. (N.B.: Subscription is not automatic. List membership is generally limited to those doing religious research in Los Angeles or similar research elsewhere. After sending the usual subscribe message, the list owner will contact potential subscribers regarding the list.)

LATIN-L
LISTSERV@PSUVM.PSU.EDU or LISTSERV@PSUVM.BITNET

A forum for people interested in classical Latin, Medieval Latin, and Neo-Latin.

LEXI
LISTSERV@UCI.EDU

LEXI is intended to provide a forum for the presentation and discussion of issues related to the Greek and Latin languages and lexicography. In addition, the list server can constitute a vehicle for obtaining information and responding to inquiries about the progress of work on both TLG and the electronic version of TLL. The University of California at Irvine (UCI) is the home of both the Thesaurus Linguae Graecae project (TLG) since 1972 and now the Thesaurus Linguae Latinae project (TLL). It is expected that, in long-range terms, UCI will become a major focal point of lexicographic and linguistic research in ancient Greek and Latin.

LITURGY
MAILBASE@MAILBASE.AC.UK

LITURGY provides an academic forum for discussion of all aspects of Christian liturgy. The list does not confine itself to any one historical period, geographical area or Christian tradition. Therefore contributions are welcome from all historical and theological fields. Those involved in other disciplines such as literary analysis, comparative religions and sociology of religion are also invited to participate.

LT-ANTIQ
LISTSERV@UNIVSCVM.CSD.SCAROLINA.EDU

LT-ANTIQ is an unmoderated list that provides a discussion forum for topics relating to Late Antiquity (c. AD 260-640). For the purposes of this discussion list, "Late Antiquity" includes the Late Roman, Early Byzantine, Early Medieval, and Early Islamic periods. Geographical coverage extends from Western Europe to the Middle East and from the Sahara to Russia. Cross-disciplinary interaction is particularly encouraged. Along with the usual scholarly interchange, users also are invited to post notices relating to upcoming conferences, new and on-going projects, and job openings.

MANTOVANO
MAJORDOMO@VIRGIL.ORG

Mantovano is a mailing list that focuses on Virgil and his influence. Subscription to the list is handled by a form at: **http://www.virgil.org/mantovano/**.

MASORTI
LISTSERV@JTSA.EDU

MASORTI is a broadcast list formed by the Rabbinical Assembly of Israel and by the Masorti (Conservative) Movement of Israel. Only the Rabbinical Assembly of Israel will post to this list weekly Torah, news, information and opinion from the Masorti Movement.

MDVLPHIL
LISTSERV@LSUVM.SNCC.LSU.EDU or LISTSERV@LSUVM.BITNET

MDVLPHIL is for academic discussion of medieval philosophy and political thought; essentially, the membership supports each other through discussion and commentary on their research in progress. In addition, conference and fellowship announcements in any area of medieval studies are welcome.

MEDITATION
LISTSERV@UTMB.EDU

MEDITATION is a forum for discussion of all topics related to meditation and Eastern philosophy.

MEDTEXTL
LISTSERV@VMD.CSO.UIUC.EDU or LISTSERV@UIUCVMD.BITNET

MEDTEXTL is an international academic list concerned with the study of medieval texts. It is especially interested to hear from all scholars working in the philology, codicology, and technology of manuscripts. Discussions on the list also cover items of a more general historical nature.

METHODIST
LISTSERV@SERVANTNET.ORG

METHODIST is an open, unmoderated discussion list for United Methodists.

MIKRA

Mikra is a German language discussion list for all aspects of biblical studies. A subscription form can be found at: **http://www.phil.uni-passau.de/cgi-bin/majordomo.cgi/subscribe/mikra**.

MIQRA

Miqra is a discussion list dedicated to the academic study of the Hebrew Bible. The list is being conducted under the auspices of the Society of Biblical Literature and seeks to assist scholars in their professional study of the Hebrew Bible. A form for subscription to this list can be found at: **http://shemesh.scholar.emory.edu/cgi-bin/miqra-app.pl**.

NIETZSCH
LISTSERV@DARTMOUTH.EDU

NIETZSCH is a discussion list, hosted by Dartmouth College, as a forum for scholarly and interdisciplinary discussions of the philosophy and literature of Friedrich Nietzsche (1844-1900). Topics include all aspects of Nietzsche studies, including discussion of subjects closely related to Nietzsche (such as Schopenhauer and Wagner). Scholarly societies concerned with Nietzsche's thought are encouraged to post announcements here.

NEWBOOKS
LISTSERV@JTSA.EDU

NEWBOOKS is a bibliography of books recently cataloged at the Library of the Jewish Theological Seminary of America. The list will primarily announce recently published books but will also include older books recently added to the database of the library of JTSA. The online catalog of the library can be reached at **http://www.jtsa.edu/library**.

OLDCTH-L
LISTPROC@BGU.EDU

OLDCTH-L is a discussion list on the independent catholic movement in general and in particular the Old Catholic Communion (descendant churches of the ancient Catholic Church of Holland).

ORION
MAJORDOMO@PLUTO.MSCC.HUJI.IL

The Orion mailing list is associated with the new Orion Web site and the Orion Center for the Study of the Dead Sea Scrolls at the Hebrew University in Jerusalem. It is devoted to the study of the Dead Sea Scrolls and Associated Literature, including Jewish Literature of the Second Temple period and other fields as they bear on this literature.

PAPY
LISTSERV@IGL.KU.DK

PAPY provides a discussion forum for all interested in papyrology and the history, epigraphy and archaeology of Graeco-Roman Egypt.

PERSEUS
LISTSERV@BROWNVM.BROWN.EDU

PERSEUS is a mailing list that acts as an informal users forum for scholars using the Perseus Project. The list emphasizes the use of Perseus in teaching and research.

PESHITTA
LISTSERV@NIC.SURFNET.NL

The Leiden Peshitta Institute is sponsoring this list for topics relating to the Peshitta.

PHIL-LIT
LISTSERV@TAMVM1.TAMU.EDU or LISTSERV@TAMVM1.BITNET

PHIL-LIT is a discussion list sponsored by the Johns Hopkins University Press for philosophers and literary critics, scholars and theorists. It offers news, job and book announcements, calls for papers, and conference plans. Subscribers post queries, trade inside information and advice, preview drafts of articles and reviews, dispute, praise, congratulate, insult, refute, and defend one another. The list owes allegiance to no particular school or style of criticism and is open to anyone who takes a serious interest in philosophical interpretations of literature, literary investigations of classic works of philosophy, philosophy of language, and literary theory.

PJC-STUDIES
MAJORDOMO@EVANSVILLE.EDU

PJC-STUDIES (Postmodern Judeo-Christian Studies) explores the use of recent developments in the study of history, philosophy, cultural anthropology, religion, textual analysis and interpretation in understanding cultural transformations in Judaism and Christianity (primarily) from 600 BCE to 600 CE.

POSTMODERN-CHRISTIAN
MAILBASE@MAILBASE.AC.UK

POSTMODERN-CHRISTIAN, an emerging community of researchers and practitioners, is exploring cultural and theological issues raised by postmodern society and Christian faith. Theology, culture, technology, the arts and church history are all relevant to discussions on how theology, worship and community should respond.

PROCESS-PHILOSOPHY
MAILBASE@MAILBASE.AC.UK

PROCESS-PHILOSOPHY provides an open forum for the discussion of all topics pertaining to Process Thought. Along with the expected emphasis on Alfred North Whitehead' metaphysics and Charles Hartshorne's theology, the discussion examines the writings of historically influential thinkers such as Peirce, Bergson, James, and the work of any number of contemporary contributors to Process Philosophy.

RAMBAM
(Not Active. Archives: http://www.shamash.com/listarchives/rambam/)

RAMBAM is a discussion list for the study of Maimonides' Mishneh Torah, or "Review" of Jewish law. The instructor is Rabbi Yitzchak Etshalom (rebyitz@netcom.com), who is the principal of SAJS (the School of Advanced Jewish Studies) in Pittsburgh, PA.

RELIGION-ALL
MAILBASE@MAILBASE.AC.UK

RELIGION-ALL in part provides a means of distributing information of mutual interest to religion-related lists on Mailbase without necessitating the need for "cross-posting." RELIGION-ALL does, however, have a wider purpose. It is not intended as a discussion list (all messages sent to the list are forwarded to the moderators rather than immediately to the groups concerned) but as a center of information relating to job vacancies, conferences, and general database for religious studies in the UK. Therefore the list welcomes subscriptions from UK members who are not members of the above groups. Subscribers from other nationalities are, of course, also welcome to RELIGION-ALL.

RELIGIONLAW
LISTSERV@GRIZZLY.UCLA.EDU

RELIGIONLAW is a list for discussion of religion and the law. It addresses free exercise, Establishment Clause, Religious Freedom Restoration Act, equal protection, religious discrimination and religious harassment under Title VII, and other law and religion related topics.

RELIGIOUS-STUDIES-UK
MAILBASE@MAILBASE.AC.UK

RELIGIOUS-STUDIES-UK is a list primarily for UK academics, graduates and librarians working within the field of religious studies. Focusing on the current representation and development of the subject, it encourages the discussion of problems and opportunities regarding teaching, research, resources, etc.

RISA-L

The RISA list is for academic discussions of religion in South East Asia. The list is an outgrowth of a section by the same name in the American Academy of Religion and is generally restricted to professional scholars in this area of study. Requests for subscriptions to this list should be directed to lnelson@pwa.acusd.edu.

ROMANSITES-L
PETWORTH@SUBA.COM

Bill Thayer is the owner of this new list for announcing resources of interest to classicists. Please note that the list is not handled by software but by Bill Thayer personally.

ROMARCH
MAJORDOMO@ROME.CLASSICS.LSA.UMICH.EDU

ROMARCH is a discussion list focusing on Roman art and archaeology, including the material culture of ancient Italy from ca. 1000 B.C. to 600 A.D., including Etruscans, Samnites, Romans, Greeks, and the material cultures of all Roman provinces (including Roman interaction with local populations and cultures.)

SAMARITAN
LISTSERVER@MAIL1.GANNON.EDU

The Samaritan Studies list is designed to encourage discussion on all aspects of Samaritan history, literature, culture, and more.

SANSKRIT
MAJORDOMO@HINDUNET.ORG

Sanskrit is a mailing list for people interested in learning conversational Sanskrit. The mailing list sends out several short sentences in Sanskrit along with answers to any questions submitted by list members.

SCHLEIERMACHER
LISTSERV@LISTSERV.ARIZONA.EDU

SCHLEIERMACHER is a list for those interested in all subjects concerned with the theologian, theorist, philosopher, and author, Friedrich Daniel Ernst Schleiermacher (1768-1834).

SYNOPTIC-L
MAJORDOMO@BHAM.AC.UK

Synoptic-L is a discussion forum for scholars interested in the Synoptic Gospel problem.

SPIRIT-L
LISTSERV@AMERICAN.EDU

SPIRIT-L is a forum on spirituality in secular life in the context of the Roman Catholic faith.

SSREL-L
LISTSERV@UTKVM1.UTK.EDU

SCIENTIFIC STUDY OF RELIGION - LIST provides a forum for discussion of issues relevant to scientific study of religion similar to content of journals like Journal for the Scientific Study of Religion, Sociology of Religion, Review of Religious Research, Social Compass. The primary audience is researchers and teachers in this specialty, although any interested persons may subscribe.

TALAROS
LISTSERV@LISTSERV.ACNS.NWU.EDU

Hellenistic issues discussion list.

TANTRA-L
LISTSERV@UNCG.EDU

Tantra-L is a discussion list created to support the five-year Tantric Studies Seminar of the American Academy of Religion, to facilitate discussions among members of the Society for Tantric Studies and as a general forum for scholarly discussion of the tantras.

TAOISM-STYDIES-L
MAJORDOMO@COOMBS.ANU.EDU.AU

TAOISM-STYDIES-L was established by the Australian National University to provide a world-wide communications vehicle and a central electronic archive for anyone working on or interested in the scholarly study of the Taoism, Taoist practices and traditions and relevant aspects of other Asian religions. The Forum was established on 17 April 1994 as a replacement for an earlier open-access and unmoderated forum Taoism-L (active 30 Jul 93 - 17 Apr 94). The forum is maintained by the Coombs Computing Unit, Research Schools of Social Sciences & Pacific and Asian Studies, Australian National University, Canberra, ACT 0200 AUSTRALIA.

TC-LIST
MAJORDOMO@SHEMESH.SCHOLAR.EMORY.EDU

TC-LIST is loosely associated with the electronic journal TC: A Journal of Biblical Textual Criticism, and it is intended for a discussion of any matters relating to biblical textual criticism, broadly defined. It is hoped that subscribers to the tc-list will reflect on and respond to material from articles in TC, will deal with issues that arise in the context of text-critical study in the community of biblical scholars at large, and will use the list to suggest new ideas and methodologies. Notes on any aspect of the textual criticism of the Jewish and Christian scriptures (including extracanonical and related literature) are welcome, and threads that transcend the traditional boundary between textual criticism of the Hebrew Bible/Old Testament and New

Testament textual criticism are especially encouraged. We would also like to see threads that discuss the relationship between textual criticism and other disciplines.

THEOLOGOS
MXSERVER@ALPHA.AUGUSTANA.EDU

THEOLOGOS is a forum for the academic discussion, dialogue and research in the fields of systematic and constructive theology. This list is open to students, faculty and parties with an academic interest in these fields and to all traditions. Topics for discussion are open, but might include: faith-reason relationship, Christology, the concept of God/Goddess, eschatology, methodology, soteriology, liberation theology, feminist theology, ecotheology, etc. The list can also serve as a forum for the discussion of the constructing and/or reconstructing of theological concepts/traditions for contemporary contexts.

TIAMAT-L
LISTSERV@NETCOM.COM

TIAMAT-L is a mailing list dedicated to the discussion of the Internet as a tool to those involved in magick and the occult. Topics discussed can include software issues, theoretical material on the nature of information and infomagick, and the planning of on-line group workings, as well as others.

WITTENBERG
MAILSERV@CRF.CUIS.EDU

The Wittenberg list is a forum for the discipline of Lutheran Church History, where discussion of issues in the discipline may take place, where news may be posted, where announcements of theses, dissertations and other research may be made, where book reviews may be circulated and discussed and where news about Project Wittenberg documents will be distributed. Project Wittenberg invites anyone interested in the history of Lutheranism to subscribe.

WOMENRAB
LISTSERV@JTSA.EDU

WOMENRAB is an international discussion group for and by women rabbis and women rabbinical students. (N.B.: Subscription to this list limited to women rabbis and women rabbinical students.)

ZENBUDDHISM-L
MAJORDOMO@COOMBS.ANU.EDU.AU

ZENBUDDHISM-L is a forum for world-wide communications and a central electronic archive for exchange of scholarly and factual information dealing with the Zen Buddhism, its history, lore, scholarship, writings, and forms of meditation practice as well as its organizational forms, concerns, and activities. Subscribers are asked to note that the ZenBuddhism-L is not a usual discussion list, as all types of arguments, viewpoints, personal opinions and intellectual predilections are to be resolutely avoided by the subscribers to the list.

Internet Resources

This listing of resources can never be complete or entirely accurate given the rapidly changing nature of the WWW. Any errors, additions or updates to this resource listing should be forwarded to Patrick Durusau, pdurusau@emory.edu.

A - Z of Jewish & Israel Related Resources
http://www.ort.org/anjy/resource/a-z.htm

An alphabetical listing of Jewish and Israel related resources on the Internet.

Abila of the Decapolis, Jordan
http://198.209.222.15/mfuller/aia/aia.abila.htm

A brief information page with contact information and a short summary of activity at the site. Unfortunately no images of finds, bibliographic material, preliminary dig reports or other materials are available for this excavation at this web site.

Abu Simbel
http://www.ccer.ggl.ruu.nl/abu_simbel/abu_simbel1.html

The temple of Abu Simbel, dedicated to the glory of Pharaoh Ramses II. Through the use of image maps, the user can view the outside or can enter the temple and view images of the hallway and innermost chamber.

ABZU
http://www-oi.uchicago.edu/OI/DEPT/RA/ABZU/ABZU.HTML

Abzu, based at the Oriental Institute of the University of Chicago, is the first site to check for new resources in the area of the ancient Near Eastern. Abzu offers multiple points of access (i.e., author, project, geographic area and others) to the growing number of resources located on the Internet.

Academic Map of Israel
http://www.ac.il/

A map of Israel with links to all Israeli universities and colleges and other indexes of sites. Permits users to explore academic resources by geographic location or in locating programs in particular areas.

Accessing the Ancient World: The Bible, Antiquity, and the World Wide Web
http://www.stolaf.edu/people/kchanson/webart.html

An excellent essay to answer the question, "Why should biblical scholars should care about the World Wide Web?" In addition to covering the basics of Internet access and terminology, this essay sets forth criteria for evaluating the use of the World Wide Web for classroom use and has numerous references to useful resources. This essay should be in the first semester reading schedule of every graduate student in biblical or ancient Near Eastern studies (including divinity students).

Achaemerid Royal Inscriptions
http://www-oi.uchicago.edu/OI/PROJ/ARI/ARI.html

The Achaemerid Royal Inscriptions site is another impressive use of technology by the Oriental Institute at the University of Chicago to share resources with the wider academic community. This project is designed to "create an electronic study edition of the inscriptions of the Achaemenid Persian kings in all of their versions--Old Persian, Elamite, Akkadian, and, where appropriate, Aramaic and Egyptian." This study edition will include "translations, glossaries, grammatical indexes, basic bibliographic apparatus, basic text critical apparatus, and some graphic apparatus" and will be available for viewing and printing over the Web. Inscriptions from Persepolis and nearby Naqsh-i Rustam, sites of excavations between 1931 and 1939 by the Oriental Institute will appear first on this site.

AcqWeb
http://www.library.vanderbilt.edu/law/acqs/acqs.html

AcqWeb is a WWW site for librarians interested in acquisitions or collection development. It is also an excellent resource for scholars seeking contact information for publishers, libraries on the Internet and a host of other bibliographic information. As is befitting a site managed by practicing librarians, the site is current, well organized and a pleasure to search or browse. As of June 30, 1996, some 1,454 publishers were listed with e-mail or WWW addresses. Pointers to collections of library links provide a similar level of international coverage for libraries found on the Internet.

Adapa Films
http://www.lightlink.com/offline/Adapa.html

The homepage for Adapa Films offers information on its current release, "The Descent of Ishtar" and its upcoming release of "The Epic of Gilgamesh Tablet XI: The Deluge." Both films use the Babylonian text with English sub-titles and adaptations of Hurrian musical scores to set the tone for the re-enactment of these stories. Favorable comments have been posted at the site by leading scholars in ANE studies concerning the Ishtar video and it should be a welcome break from recitation of verbal paradigms.

Addenda and Corrigenda to the TLG Canon, 3rd edition
http://www.tlg.uci.edu/~tlg/A&C.html

This is an online source for addenda and corrigenda to the TLG Canon.

Advanced Book Exchange
http://www.abebooks.com

Scholars rarely miss the opportunity to visit bookstores when traveling, particularly those that carry out-of-print, used, rare, or antiquarian books. The Advanced Book Exchange makes it possible to search 188 such bookstores and to post wants for nightly searching, all at no cost to the user. When a want is matched, an email message is sent to the person requesting the book with contact information for the bookseller who has that item.

Aegeanet Archive
ftp://ftp.duke.edu/pub/archive/lists/aegeanet

This archive includes materials of interest to scholars of the Aegean area. It includes past issues of GreekNews, a summary of archaeological news published in Greek newspapers from 1994 to present, listings of discussion lists and other Internet resources of interest to archaeologists, and other materials relevant to the region.

Aerial Photographic Archive for Archaeology in the Middle East
http://www.arts.uwa.edu.au/Classics/archeology/rsame.html

Supported by Crown Prince Hassan bin Talal of Jordan, this project has amassed approximately 5,000 aerial photographs and hundreds of maps, primarily of Jordan. Focused on both creating a methodology and researching settlement history in the Near East, the project has identified some 20,000 sites on the photographs and transparent overlays have been prepared. The Remote Sensing for Archaeology in the Middle East project grew out of this project and has approximately 4,000 photographs taken by the Hunting Aerial Survey of Jordan in 1953. A bibliography of publications from these projects and other information for interested scholars can be found at this site.

Age, Gender, and Status Division at Mealtime in the Roman House
http://www-personal.umich.edu/~pfoss/hgender.html

An excerpt from the Ph.D. thesis of Pedar W. Foss "Kitchens and Dining Rooms at Pompeii: the spatial and social relationship of cooking to eating in the Roman household." This is a summary of literary evidence concerning the roles played by age, gender and status in Roman households.

Aiolos
http://www.uba.uva.nl/nl/e-diensten/aicweb/klassiek/index.html

Aiolus is an excellent resource for classicists with a strong emphasis on links to libraries, publishers and booksellers, specific publications and academic departments. The site has approximately 460 links at present and is well maintained.

The Akkadian Language
http://www.sron.ruu.nl/~jheise/akkadian/index.html#index

A rapidly evolving site devoted to the Akkadian language, offering such items as the Enuma Elish tablet 1 (Babylonian Creation Epic) as cuneiform text with transliteration and images, cuneiform sign lists, and cuneiform fonts for TeX and LaTeX word processing programs. The cuneiform sign list contains over 300 signs at this time, and there appears for each sign its number from Borger's Assyrische-babylonische Zeichenliste, the sign in New Assyrian orthography and the name or one of the values of the sign. This is an excellent site for all scholars interested in the Akkadian language.

Alex Catalogue of Electronic Texts
http://www.lib.ncsu.edu/stacks/alex-index.html

Alex is a catalog of electronic texts which includes works from Project Gutenberg, Wiretap, the On-line Book Initiative, the Eris system at Virginia Tech, the English Server at Carnegie Mellon University, Project Bartlesby, CCAT, the on-line portion of the Oxford Text Archive, and others. Currently, there are over 2000 works listed in this catalog.

Alexander and Darius at the Battle of Issus
http://www.tulane.edu/pompeii/text/pompeii.html

This is the first part of a Hypercard stack on Pompeii by Professor Barbette Spaeth of Tulane University. The entire stack will eventually be converted for delivery over the Tulane network to students enrolled in the Pompeii Roman Society and Culture class. This document offers a cutaway view of the House of Faun and images of some of the artwork found therein, including a depiction of a battle between Alexander and Darius in 333 BC.

Alexander and the Growth of Hellenism
http://ccat.sas.upenn.edu/rrice/clas190.html

Rob S. Rice has placed course notes (in outline form), past quizzes, other course materials, and links to other sites that would be relevant to his general studies class on Alexander and the Growth of Hellenism at this location. A map of Greece and related geographic areas with place names heads this document.

All About Mormons
http://www.mormons.org/

While not an "official" site of the Mormon Church this site is one of the more complete resources on the web for any topic or issue concerning the Mormon Church or its members. Divided into a number of useful categories the site offers access to statements concerning the beliefs of the Mormon Church, the application of those beliefs in daily life and a host of other resources.

Allen and Greenough's Latin Grammar: An On-line Reference Grammar
http://ccat.sas.upenn.edu/jod/AG/allgre.contents.html
 or
http://osman.classics.washington.edu/libellus/aides/allgre

A hypertext edition of Allen and Greenough's Latin grammar.

American Academy of Religion
http://www.aar-site.org

Home page for the American Academy of Religion. Offers societal information such as regional/annual meeting program materials and abstracts as well as other organizational type material.

American Classical League
http://www.umich.edu/~knudsvig/ACL.html

The official WWW homepage of the American Classical League offers electronic access to ACL documents and a wide range of other resources of interest to scholars in classical studies.

American Journal of Archaeology
http://classics.lsa.umich.edu/AJA.html

The website for the Archaeological Institute of American offers access to several important resources. While the contents of the journal are not available online, the tables of contents from recent and forthcoming issues can be reviewed. Of particular interest for scholars researching emerging topics are the listings of books received for review from 1990 to present.

American Oriental Society
http://www.umich.edu/~jrodgers

In addition to the newsletter of the AOS, there are links to the program for the 207th Annual Meeting (1996) and abstracts of the papers presented at that meeting. A separate page of links to other sites of interest to Oriental scholars is also maintained at this site.

American Philological Association
http://www.apaclassics.org

Home page of the American Philological Association. Links to information on Fellowships and Scholarships offered by the society as well as current deadline information. Of particular interest to classicists will be the link to Preprints, providing preliminary material from upcoming issues of *Transactions of the American Philological Association* (TAPA).

Americian Research Center in Egypt (ARCE)
http://www.arce.org/home.html

The homepage for the American Research Center in Egypt (ARCE) offers information on events, research opportunities, conservation projects, resources and membership in the ARCE.

American Research Institute in Turkey (ARIT)
http://arit.dartmouth.edu/arit/

A provisional catalog of the holdings of the library at the Istanbul Branch of the American Research Institute in Turkey (ARIT). The library in Istanbul focuses on Turkey from the Byzantine period to present. This catalog is not completely current but is intended to give scholars an opportunity to see what works are available in the Istanbul collection.

American Schools of Oriental Research
http://www.asor.org/

The ASOR home page has pointers to the current ASOR calendar and the email directory that appears in each ASOR Newsletter. Abstracts from BASOR (#298 to date), excerpts and whole articles from Biblical Archaeologist and the ASOR Newsletter are found under Books and Journals. Emphasis is given to organizational information and not to providing full text content to the publications of the society.

The American Society of Greek and Latin Epigraphy
http://asgle.classics.unc.edu/

The website of the American Society of Greek and Latin Epigraphy offers information on membership in the society and links to other information of interest to epigraphers. Of particular note is the collection of links to epigraphic resources on the WWW and the "epigrapher's bookshelf" which has the potential to become a primary starting point for students interested in epigraphic studies.

American Society of Papyrologists
http://shemesh.scholar.emory.edu/scripts/ASP/ASP-MENU.html

Contains indexes to the Bulletin of the American Society of Papyrologists, information on the society, and links to resources at other sites in the area of papyrology.

American University of Beruit, Digital Documentation Center
http://almashriq.hiof.no/ddc/

The Digital Documentation Center at the American University of Beruit has a number of projects that will be of interest to scholars of the Ancient Near East. Several issues of Berytus are available at the site including articles from Berytus, volume 1. VRML reproductions of glass and pottery is another important technique that is documented at this site.

Amphoras Project
http://www.epas.utoronto.ca/amphoras/project.html

Based on finds collected at Agora at Athens, this project seeks to make available information on ceramic storage containers used in the ancient Mediterranean to transport a variety of goods. Resources include English translations of ancient Greek literature passages remarking on the use of amphoras, a bibliography on amphoras, a searchable database of descriptions and stamp readings of Greek (and some Roman) amphoras, and links to other Web resources on amphoras.

Anathemas of the 2nd Council of Constantinople (533 AD)
http://www.iclnet.org/pub/resources/text/history/council.2constan.txt

English translation of the Anathemas of the Second Council of Constantinople.

Analyse syntaxique locale pour le reperage de termes complexes dans un texte
http://silicon.montaigne.u-bordeaux.fr:8001/HTML/ONLINE/IE10/Bourigault.html

A paper by Didier Bourigault that describes local syntactic parsing techniques used to isolate complex terms in a text.

Anchor Bible Dictionary Index
ftp://oi.uchicago.edu/pub/oi/resarch

An index to the Anchor Bible dictionary available as plain ASCII file or in compressed Mac format. Look for the files ABD.INDEX.txt.ascii and ABD.INDEX.txt.mac.sea, respectively.

Anciens documents sur l'Egypte
http://silicon.montaigne.u-bordeaux.fr:8001/HTML/EGYPTE/CPA/Catal.html

This site offers an extensive collection of photographs of Egyptian sites and artifacts. Full references to the original place of publication and numbering make this a very useful resource.

The Ancient City of Athens
http://www.indiana.edu/~kglowack/Athens/Athens.html

This site offers a tour of Athens following the writings of the traveler Pausanias who visited the city in the 2nd century C.E. Numerous images are linked to an account by Pausanias of his travels to a city considered to be ancient at this early period.

Ancient Economies
http://members.tripod.com/~sondmor/index.html

Edited by Morris Silver (Economic Structures of Antiquity (1995), Taking Ancient Mythology Economically (1992)), this site focuses on a number of disputed or unsettled areas of ancient economies. Topics currently addressed include: "TOPIC I: Did the Ancient Mediterranean World Know Nonroyal Merchants?," "TOPIC II: Business Agent as Image: Example and Broader Implications."

Ancient Egypt
http://weblifac.ens-cachan.fr:80/Portraits/S.ROSMORDUC /AEgypt.html

Most notably this site has a package of fonts and macros for typing hieroglyphics in LaTeX. It also offers a short introduction to hieroglyphics and an evolving database of hieroglyphic texts.

Ancient Egyptian Art: Introduction
http://www.emory.edu/CARLOS/egypt.gal.html

An introduction to Egyptian art illustrated by objects drawn from the Egyptian collection at the Carlos Museum, Emory University. This essay provides a brief cultural and social context for Egyptian art in general and specific comments on the objects used to illustrate this essay.

Ancient Greek Literature
http://www.hol.gr/greece/ancwords.htm

English translations of some of the more popular works from ancient Greek literature, including Aesop's Fables, Aeschylus, Aristophanes, Euripides, Herodotus, Homer, Sophocles, and Thucydides.

Ancient History Bulletin
http://ivory.trentu.ca/www/cl/ahb/

An index of volumes 1 (1987) - 11.2-3 (1997) of the Ancient History Bulletin is available along with articles from volumes 8-11. Scholars searching for colleagues will find the links to directories of ancient historians quite useful.

Ancient History 21: Greece and Rome
http://ccat.sas.upenn.edu/rrice/anch021.html

This page has links to Rob S. Rice's class notes (outline form), past quizzes, all course materials, and links to other sites of interest to students enrolled in the general studies course, Ancient History 21.

Ancient Law (Henry Sumner Maine)
http://www.socsci.mcmaster.ca/~econ/ugcm/3ll3/maine/anclaw/index.html

This is an online version of an 1861 work by Henry Sumner Maine on ancient law. It is of interest as period literature and can be used to demonstrate how views of ancient law have changed since the 19th century.

Ancient Medicine/Medicina Antiqua
http://web1.ea.pvt.k12.pa.us/medant/

A peer reviewed site for scholars wishing to collaborate on developing resources for the study of ancient medicine. Current hypertexts include Galen's Commentary on Hippocrates and Galen, On the Natural Faculties as well as bibliographies on Greek and Roman medicine and links to other classics bibliographies.

Ancient Near East Map Series
http://www-oi.uchicago.edu/OI/INFO/MAP/Near_East_Map.html

The Oriental Institute is sponsoring what promises to be the definitive map collection for the Ancient Near East on the Web. Two separate series of maps will be linked together, one organized by modern country borders and including longitude and latitude lines, modern cities, principal archaeological sites and other information. The second series of maps will follow ancient settlement patterns and will be on the same scale as the modern map series which will facilitate comparisons between the two. Both maps are depicted on a background of terrain relief.

Ancient Tablets, Ancient Graves: Accessing Women's Lives in Mesopotamia
http://home.earthlink.net/~womenwhist/lesson2.html

Although written for a non-technical audience this essay provides both interesting questions and readings to illuminate the lives of women in Mesopotamia.

Andover-Harvard Theological Library
http://divweb.harvard.edu/library/

The Andover-Harvard Theological Library collection can be searched via the Hollis library catalog. In addition to links to that catalog the library homepage offers collections of Internet resources in religious studies ranging from "Scriptural and Historical Studies" to "Lesbian, Gay, Bisexual, and Transgender Resources." Useful bibliographies are also available on the homepage covering a wide range of topics of interest to divinity and religious studies students.

ANE: Discussion List for the Study of the Ancient Near East
http://www-oi.uchicago.edu/OI/ANE/OI_ANE.html

The homepage for the premier discussion list for topics relating to the Ancient Near East. ANE covers all topics relevant to Ancient Near Eastern Studies and was founded to promote scholarly discussion of these topics. Please read the policies for the list before joining or posting messages to the list. This website offers access to information concerning the list and archives of prior discussions. ANE is an example of excellent use of technology by the Oriental Institute to provide scholarly resources in Ancient Near Eastern studies.

Ancient World Web: The Ultimate Index
http://www.julen.net/aw/

The Ancient World Web seeks to be a complete listing of all Internet resources related to the ancient world. The site is organized by geographic location, subject and a "Meta Index" that lists all the sites indexed in the Ancient World Web. Links are provided to search engines and indices for those needing further resources and a Frequently Asked Questions (FAQ) provides additional information on the site.

Anglican Association of Biblical Scholars
http://members.aol.com/AngABS/

The Anglican Association of Biblical Scholars site offers access to information concerning the organization, the current and past issues of its newsletter and the Answer Line which is an email service which answers biblical questions from an Anglican perspective.

Anglican Electronic Book of Common Prayer
http://listserv.american.edu:70/1/anglican/bcp

This is an electronic edition of the 1979 American version of the Book of Common Prayer. The text was hand entered, although the Psalter was generated from an SGML-tagged version created by Robin and Michael Cover.

Anglican Mailing List (Archive)
http://listserv.american.edu:70/11/anglican/logs

Archives of the Anglican mailing list. Some of the files are quite large and represents logs of all the postings to the list ANGLICAN (anglican@listserv.american.edu).

Anglicans Online!
http://infomatch.com/~haibeck/anglican.html

Denominational site with links to home pages of Anglican churches with an Internet presence. Useful for scholars studying the use of the Internet by organized churches.

Annual Egyptological Bibliography
http://www.leidenuniv.nl/nino/aeb.html

The Annual Egyptological Bibliography is a bibliography with summaries begun by the Dutch Egyptologist Jozef M.A. Janssen in 1947. Due to the increased number of publications on Egypt and changes in editors, the print publication of this important resource has been somewhat erratic since 1983. The International Association of Egyptologists and the Netherlands Institute for the Near East have joined together to sponsor this publication and have placed the most recent issue, 1993, on the Internet for browsing. This is an important step in bringing bibliographic information to scholars in a timely fashion and deserves emulation by other scholarly organizations.

Antiquity
http://intarch.ac.uk/antiquity/

Antiquity is a quarterly journal for specialists in archaeological research. While continuing publication as a print journal, Antiquity has made the full contents of its most recent issues available online. (Vol. 270, No. 267 (March, 1996) to Vol. 272, No. 275 (March, 1998) as of the spring of 1998) Less recent volumes are available with summaries (Vol. 69 No. 266 (December 1995) to Vol. 68 No. 258 (March 1994)) and even older materials may be accessed via an index to volumes 1-70 (1927-1996). One of the leading publication in archaeological research, Antiquity lacks the timidity that has prevented other publishers of specialized academic and specialist journals from making them available over the WWW. Antiquity states its purpose to be: "to make good knowledge public." Perhaps that is not a goal shared by some of the publishers of academic journals in other disciplines.

Apostolic Fathers
gopher://ccat.sas.upenn.edu:3333/11/Religious/ChurchWriters/ApostolicFathers

This collection includes English translations of 1 Clement, 2 Clement, Barnabas, Didache, Diognetus, Hermas, the letters of Ignatius, the Martyrdom of Polycarp and Polycarp. All translations are by J. B. Lightfoot.

Aqaba Project Reports
http://www-oi.uchicago.edu/pub/OI/PROJ/AQA/Aqaba.html

Excavation reports from the Islamic Project at Aqaba, Jordan, Donald Whitcomb, director.

Arabic Fonts
ftp://rama.poly.edu/pub/reader/win3/BAGDAD2.ZIP

ftp://ftp.cs.sunysb.edu/pub/EN/_incoming/AbdelHadi_Bakres/BAGDAD2.ZIP

ftp://ftp.u.washington.edu/public/reader/win3/BAGDAD2.ZIP

These sites offer TrueType Arabic fonts for use with most word processing software.

Arabic at Dartmouth
http://grafton.dartmouth.edu:8001/lrc/lang/arabic.html

Information concerning local holdings and links to other Arabic language resources.

Arabic HTML
http://www.informatik.uni-stuttgart.de/ifi/bs/lagally/almira6.html

Yes, Arabic in an HTML environment. This demonstration illustrates one approach to displaying Arabic over the WWW. TeX and ArabTeX are used to present the Arabic shown.

Arabic Morphological Parser
http://www.xrce.xerox.com/research/mltt/arabic/

This program is a stunning display of the power of the Web and the Java programming language to deliver scholarly information. This program is donwloaded over the Web and displays true Arabic characters and allows submission of words in Arabic script for parsing. Detailed information on the software is available at this site.

Arabic Program
http://philae.sas.upenn.edu/Arabic/arabic.html

Brief description of the Arabic studies program at the University of Pennsylvania.

Arabic Software Map
http://www.cs.tu-berlin.de/~ishaq/arabic/asm/asm.html

Arabic software for a variety of platforms and operating systems can be found listed at this site. Major sections include Unix, DOS, Windows, OS/2, Macintosh, as well as general information for all platforms on other sources of information and code sets.

ArabTeX Version 3.03
ftp://ftp.informatik.uni-stuttgart.de/pub/arabtex

ArabTeX is a TeX macro package with associated Naskh fonts designed to generate the Arabic writing from texts coded in an ASCII transliteration as well as in some other popular encodings for Arabic and Hebrew. It is compatible with Plain TeX, LaTeX, NFSS, and the EDMAC package. Mirror sites: Cambridge, UK (ftp://ftp.tex.ac.uk/tex-archive/languages/arabtex) Huntsville, TX, USA (ftp://ftp.shsu.edu/tex-archive/languages/arabtex) Heidelberg, Germany (ftp://ftp.dante.de/tex-archive/languages/arabtex)

ARACHNION: A Journal of Ancient Literature and History on the Web
http://www.cisi.unito.it/arachne/arachne.html

Arachnion is an electronic journal concerned with ancient literature and history. Issues from volume 1 and the first issue of volume 2 are available at this website. Unfortunately, it appears that Arachnion has not published any new material since early in 1996.

Archaeobotanical Bibliography
http://www.sas.upenn.edu/~nmiller0/

The homepage of Naomi Miller contains an exceptional archaeobotanical bibliography that covers Central Asia, Iran, Iraq, the Levant, Syria, Turkey and beyond.

Archaeological Data Archive Project
http://csa.brynmawr.edu/adap.html

The Archaeological Data Archive Project is an important effort to create a repository for archaeological information in digital form. This website offers helpful information on the issues surrounding the creation and preservation of digital archaeological information. Materials are currently being accepted for archiving and several interesting examples of archived materials are available from the ftp site maintained by the Archive. One example of deposited materials is a CAD model of older propylon on the Athenian Acropolis with associated databases that includes more than 200 drawing layers segmenting the remains according to date, material, and other criteria. While the project does not perform conversions from analog to digital formats, it will render assistance to scholars seeking to prepare materials for digital archiving.

Arachaeological Dialogues
http://archweb.LeidenUniv.nl/ad/home_ad.html

The website offers basic information on this English language journal that focuses on a broad approach to theoretical issues. The editorial policies for the journal, subscription information and the contents of its most recent issue can be found here.

Archaeological Excavations 1998
http://www.israel-mfa.gov.il/archdigs.html

The Information Division of the Israel Foreign Ministry maintains this website listing of archaeological sites in Israel, organized by month and site name. Contact information for each site is listed and other helpful information for volunteers is available.

Archaeological Institute of America
http://www.archaeology.org

Homepage contains membership information for the Archaeological Institute of America and links to its journal Archaeology.

Archaeology
http://www.he.net/~archaeol/index.html

Archaeology is the official publication of the Archaeological Institute of America. Back issues are available for reading online from January of 1996 to present.

Archaeology Email Lists
http://darwin.clas.virginia.edu/~dew7e/anthronet/subscribe/archlists.html

A listing of email lists of interest to those in the field of archaeology. Contains links to descriptions of the email lists and has email subscription forms for use with forms capable Web browsers. Useful both for the substance of its presentation and the technique of allowing the use of Web forms for email list subscriptions.

Archaeology of King Solomon's Harbor, Tel Dor, Israel
http://www.qal.berkeley.edu/arf/newsletter/1.1/tel_dor.html

This newsletter covers the ongoing excavations at King Solomon's Harbor, Tel Dor, Israel.

Archaeological and Environmental Investigation of Yemeni Terraced Agriculture
http://www-oi.uchicago.edu/OI/PROJ/YEM/Yemen.html

1993-94 Annual Report by M. Gibson and T. J. Wilkinson of the Oriental Institute, University of Chicago concerning their investigations into the emergence of the Himyarite Kingdom.

Archaeological Excavations at Sha`ar Hagolan - A Neolithic Art Center in the Jordan Valley,Israel.
http://www2.huji.ac.il/~applbaum/golan/main.htm

Sha`ar Hagolan is a Neolithic village from which over 150 art objects have been collected. Systematic excavation has not previously been possible due to agricultural use of the site. Due to economic conditions the use of the site for agricultural production has temporarily ceased and this web site urges that advantage should be taken of this lull in activity. A history of the site along with images of artifacts to demonstrate the importance of this site and further information are available.

Archaeological Fieldwork Server
http://durendal.cit.cornell.edu/TestPit.html

The Fieldwork server offers a collection of archaeological fieldwork opportunities from sources ranging from submissions, postings to mailing lists or newsgroups. It does not contain announcements for professional academic or staff archaeologist positions. The postings are arranged by geographic areas, and this server has links to other archaeological resources on the WWW.

Archaeological Institute of America
ftp://oi.uchicago.edu/pub/aia

Contains newsletters for the Archaeological Institute of America and its current calendar.

Archaeological Resource Guide to Europe (ARCE)
http://www.bham.ac.uk/ARGE/

ARGE is a collection of over 1,100 links from over 38 countries that provide information on archaeological resources in or concerning Europe. The links can be browsed by country, subject, period or from a database search. Links are verified and evaluated prior to being added to the new links section of the site.

Archaeological Survey in the Eastern Desert of Egypt
http://rome.classics.lsa.umich.edu/projects/coptos/desert.html

Preliminary report of the University of Michigan/University of Asiut Project on their archaeological survey of the eastern desert of Egypt by Henry T. Wright and Sharon Herbert. Summaries of data are presented with images relevant to the area under discussion.

Archaeology Bibliography Database
http://super3.arcl.ed.ac.uk/dbs.html

Sponsored by the Department of Archaeology, University of Edinburgh, the database server requires a user name and password for use of the database.

Archaeology on the Net
http://www.serve.com/archaeology/

This site offers an index to over 1200 sites on the Internet classified into some 33 categories of archaeological interest. Categories of links include Academic Departments, Bibliographies and Documentation, Course and Teaching Material, Discussion Groups, Field Projects and Reports, Fieldwork Opportunities, Journals, Maps and Atlases, Museums, Newsgroups, Organizations and Institutes. Topical areas include Anthropology, Archaeobotany and Zooarchaeology, Archaeological Computing, Archaeological Conservation, Archaeometry, Cultural Heritage Protection, Dendrochronology, Ethnoarchaeology, GIS and Remote Sensing, Linguistics, Lithics, Rock Art and Underwater Archaeology. Sites are also listed by geographic area. This site is a useful collection of links that allow for rapid location of resources in particular areas of interest.

Archives of ARCH-L@listserv.tamu.edu
http://listserv.tamu.edu/archives/arch-l.html

This is a searchable archive for the archaeology list Arch-L. The archive extends back to the foundation of the discussion list in May of 1992.

ArchNet: WWW VL Archaeology: Updated
http://www.lib.uconn.edu/ArchNet/

Noted as a comprehensive archaeology site in the first edition of this work, ArchNet continues to be one of the best archaeology sites on the Internet. Its homepage can now be found in Catalan, Dutch, French, German, Italian, and Spanish language versions and its resource collection is ever growing. In any language lay as well as professional archaeologists should bookmark this site for permanent reference.

Argo ASBL, Centre D'etudes Comparees Des Civilisations Anciennes
http://www.ulb.ac.be/recherche/uni/uni_b021.html

An investigation of the different techniques used by separate disciplines to investigate ancient civilizations.

Argos
http://argos.evansville.edu/

Argos is a search engine that limits its contents to a chosen set of Internet sites. These sites are the leaders in the areas of ancient and medieval studies, which results in Argos returning more relevant and useful results to search requests. At present the Argos database includes Abzu: Guide to Resources for the Study of the Ancient Near East (Oriental Institute), Byzantium: Byzantine Studies on the Internet (Fordham University), The Cambridge Classics External Gateway to Humanities Resources (Cambridge University), Diotima: Materials for the Study of Women and Gender in the Ancient World (Associated Colleges of the South/Miami University), Exploring Ancient World Cultures (University of Evansville), Kirke: Katalog der Internet-Ressourcen für die Klassische Philologie aus Erlangen (Universität Erlangen-Nürnberg), The Labyrinth: A World Wide Web Server for Medieval Studies (Georgetown University), NetSERF: The Internet Connection for Medieval Resources (The Catholic University of America), The Perseus Project: An Evolving Digital Library on Ancient Greece (Tufts University), Rassegna degli Strumenti Informatici per lo Studio dell'Antichità Classica (University of Bologna), and Romarch: Roman Art and Archeology (University of Cincinnati).

Arion: A Journal of Humanities and the Classics
http://web.bu.edu/ARION/

The Arion website offers information concerning the journal and a table of contents for the Third Series. Submission guidelines for contributors and a useful collection of links for classicists are also found at the site.

Aristotle's Works
gopher://gopher.vt.edu:10010/11/39

This directory of Aristotle's works includes his "Metaphysics" (trans. W. D. Ross), "De interpretatione" (trans. E. M. Edghill), "On the Soul" (trans. J. A. Smith), "Physics" (trans. R. P. Hardie and R. K. Gaye), "Poetics" (trans. S. H. Butcher), and "Rhetoric" (trans. W. Rhys Roberts).

Art Images for College Teaching
http://www.mcad.edu/AICT/index.html

No real epigraphic images but a very good collection of art images for use in undergraduate courses

ARTFL Project
http://estragon.uchicago.edu/Bibles/

The ARTFL Project, University of Chicago, has made this unique interface to the Bible available on the Internet. The Bible can be searched in any one of four editions: King James Version, French translation by Louis Segond, German Revidierte Elberfelder Bibel, or Jerome's Latin Vulgate. When the search is completed the relevant portion of that edition is displayed, and the interface provides a link to the relevant chapter in the other three editions.

Art History 201: Survey of Ancient and Medieval Art
http://www.wisc.edu/arth/ah201/index.html

A useful syllabus, lecture notes, and course materials for a survey course on Ancient and Medieval art.

ArtServe
http://rubens.anu.edu.au

Michael Greenhalgh, Professor of Art History, Australian National University, is responsible for this important site on art history. In addition to his book, The Greek and Roman Cities of Western Turkey, published on the Internet instead of hard copy, this site offers access to approximately 11,500 images related to art and architecture. For classical architecture of the Mediterranean Basin (approximately 2,500 images) there is a search interface which allows searching by country, site and type of work. (There are other fields that can be chosen but Professor Greenhalgh suggests that little to be gained from the use of those fields.) This site also offers images of prehistoric ritual monuments within the British Isles, a classical architecture supplement with additional 3,281 images of classical, medieval and renaissance architecture and sculpture, and a database of images of artwork. Professor Greenhalgh concludes this page with the technologies used for the creation of these data files and their limitations.

Ascent of Mount Carmel by St. John of the Cross
http://www.cs.pitt.edu/~planting/books/john_of_the_cross/ascent/ascent.htm

This is an English translation of the "Ascent of Mount Carmel" by E. Allison Peers. Available in text, PDF and RTF formats.

Asclepion
http://www.indiana.edu/~ancmed/intro.HTM

A webpage devoted to the study of ancient medicine that acts as a companion to a course taught by Professor Nancy Demand of Indiana University Bloomington. The site hosts essays by Professor Demand as well as gathering links to other sources of information on the Internet.

Ashkelon Excavations: The Leon Levy Expedition
http://fas-www.harvard.edu/~peabody/ashkelon_dig.html

Offers brief information concerning the ongoing excavations at Ashkelon by the Leon Levy Expedition. There is one large image linked to this page which shows several of the artifacts recovered to date. Unfortunately, no additional information is listed for any of the items shown.

Ashmolean Museum Home Page
http://www.ashmol.ox.ac.uk

While far from complete, the Ashmolean Museum home page holds great promise for the future. The Cast Gallery has several images with links to dictionary entries and other materials. The depth of the Ashmolean collection and the care that is evidenced in the current presentations make this a site worth careful attention as it develops.

The Palace of Ashurnasirpal II
http://ccat.sas.upenn.edu/arth/asrnsrpl.html

A 3-D animated fly-through of the Palace of Ashurnasirpal, which is a short part of a larger version created by Francine Jaskiewicz. While the files are large (Quicktime > 4MB, MPEG > 2MB) they are worth the time necessary to download these files. Holly Pittman provides the narration.

Asian Classics Input Project (ACIP)
http://acip.princeton.edu/

The ACIP website offers extensive information concerning the ongoing efforts to create a textual database of classical collections of Sanskrit literature in Tibetan translation and Tibetan commentaries on these texts. As part of its ongoing efforts, the ACIP has prepared listings of Sanskrit and Tibetan literature cataloged by the Library of Congress and computer programs that can be used in the study of these texts.

Asian Studies WWW Virtual Library
http://coombs.anu.edu.au/WWWVL-AsianStudies.html

This is the Asian Studies section of the World Wide Web Virtual Library. Supported by the Australian National University and edited by T. Matthew Ciolek, this site offers links to hundreds of information facilities around the world. The home page of this site offers searchable databases of sites, as well as a listing of sites by country for researchers interested in particular geographic areas.

The Association for History and Computing
http://www.let.rug.nl/ahc/welcome.html

The AHC seeks to promote the use of computers in all types of historical studies. A search feature allows multiple term searches of the complete AHC History and Computing bibliography.

Assemblage: The Sheffield Graduate Journal of Archaeology
http://www.shef.ac.uk/uni/union/susoc/assem/index.html

Assemblage is an electronic journal published by the Research School of Archaeology and Archaeological Sciences at the University of Sheffield. The most recent issue online (Issue Three: January 1998) contains the following: Graham Robbins (Sheffield University) on 'Crop Landscapes and Domestic Space' in the later prehistoric and Roman landscape of South Yorkshire and regular features including: Graham McElearney, in 'Graham's Guide to Software for Archaeologists'. Assemblage includes coverage of recent developments in archaeology, the use of technology by archaeologists and other issues of interest to the archaeology community.

Associates for Biblical Research
http://christiananswers.net/abr/abrhome.html

The Associates for Biblical Research sponsor archaeological excavations and publications based on the premise that archaeology can demonstrate the historical accuracy of biblical narratives. Their website offers information on their continuing excavations and publications program devoted to that proposition.

Association Internationale des Egyptologues International Association of Egyptologists Internationaler Ägyptologen-Verband
http://www.ashmol.ox.ac.uk/IAEPage.html

The homepage of the International Association of Egyptologists contains a wide variety of information on the organization. Membership information, a listing of addresses of Egyptologists, conference and meeting information as well as information on scholarships and grants are easily accessible at this site. This site is made available courtesy of the Ashmolean Museum, Oxford.

Assyria On-Line
http://www.cs.toronto.edu/~jatou

This collection of resources is relevant to both ancient and modern Assyrians. It includes both academic and popular resources available over the Internet.

The Assyro-Babylonian Mythology FAQ
http://pubpages.unh.edu/~cbsiren/assyrbabyl-faq.html

While not for the specialist, this document, written by Christopher B. Siren, provides a summary of Assyro-Babylonian mythology in the FAQ style familiar to many long time users of the Internet. It does end with a respectable bibliography for the interested lay person.

Asynchronous School of Buddhist Dialectics
http://faraday.clas.virginia.edu/~wam7c

Texts of the Tibetan Buddhist tradition, including Presentation of the Selfless in the Middle Way Consequence School (Prasangika), Three Principle Aspects of the Path by Dzong-ka-ba and The Object of Negation in the Middle Way Consequence School (Prasangika), drawn from Jam-yang-shay-ba's Great Exposition of Tenets Project. Fonts following the Classical Sanskrit and Classical Sanskrit Extended conventions of the International Association of Sanskrit Studies are under development at this site for use on the WWW.

The Athanasian Creed (c 500 AD)
ftp://pharos.bu.edu/CN/texts/AthanasianCreed.txt

The Athanasian Creed is the underlying basis for the Nicene Creed. English with no translator listed.

Athanasius, On the Incarnation
http://listserv.american.edu:70/1/catholic/church/fathers/others/ath-inc.txt

English translation of St. Athanasius's work On the Incarnation. No translator listed.

Atlantic School of Theology
http://cfn.cs.dal.ca/cfn/Education/AST.html

Basic information on the founding of the Atlantic School of Theology and contact information for the school.

ATLA WWW Guide to Theological and Religious Reference Works
http://library.dickinson.edu/webguide/awgfram1.htm

The American Theological Libraries Association sponsors this online bibliography to theological and religious reference works. The site is organized like the many excellent finding aids offered by theology libraries and cites printed reference materials only. The titles of the materials cited appear to be hyperlinks but do not actually access the cited works.

Atlas historique de l'Antiquité tardive -Régions
http://www.geocities.com/Athens/Acropolis/6200/regions.html

A historical atlas of late antiquity this collection of maps offers a readily usable and accessible map collection for this period.

Atlas of the Greek and Roman World
http://www.unc.edu/depts/cl_atlas/

A product of the Classical Atlas Project this site offers a wide variety of maps focusing on the classical world. The maps are accompanied by bibliographies that will be useful to those teaching classical history as well as their students. Of particular note is the use of one key for all the maps, which allows the user to move from one map to another without learning the key appropriate to each map.

Atrium
http://web.idirect.com/~atrium/

Atrium is a guide that features "The Ancient World on Television" rather than the latest political scandal. Atrium also offers: "This Day in Ancient History," "Bibliotheca" (a listing of resources on the WWW), and, "The Rostra" Nuntii Latini (for those unfamiliar with Nuntii Latini, it is a five minute news broadcast entirely in Latin.).

Augustine on the Internet
http://ccat.sas.upenn.edu/jod/augustine.html

This site is the home of Professor James J. O'Donnell's Internet seminar on Augustine. In addition to extended comments by Professor O'Donnell on the Confessions and the City of God , the following papers presented for the seminar are also available: E. Vance, "Text as Tomb"; F. Asiedu, "The Example of a Woman"; S. Katz, "Memory and Mind: Intro. to Aug.'s Epistemology"; W. Ferguson, "Beyond the Problem of Evil"; S. Elkatip, "Reason and Faith for Aquinas and Scotus"; L. Warner, "Sacrificing the Son"; S. Riker, "Concupiscence in Augustine and Aquinas." Additional materials include a reading list, syllabus and several essays by Professor O'Donnell, which include "Propositiones Quodlibetales," "The Authority of Augustine" and "Augustine's Idea of God." The full texts of the Confessions, the Enchiridion, and De dialectica are also available.

Ausonius' Mosella
http://kufacts.cc.ukans.edu/ftp/pub/history/Europe/Medieval/latintexts/mosella.txt

Latin text provided by Oliver Philips.

Australian Centre for Egyptology
http://www.ancient.mq.edu.au/ahist/ace/hello.html

A good source of information on Egyptology websites and organizations located in Australia.

Autobiography of Weni (6th Dynasty c. 2345-2181 BCE).
http://www.ccer.ggl.ruu.nl/texts/ael/weni.ael/index.htm

An early bibliography from the Old Kingdom (Egypt) translated by Geoffrey Graham.

Babylonian and Egyptian mathematics
http://www-groups.dcs.st-and.ac.uk/~history/HistTopics/Babylonian_and_Egyptian.html

A fairly complete picture of both Babylonian and Egyptian mathematics with links to illustrative materials that were hand written in antiquity. Treats both the underlying techniques used as well as actual practices of calculation, such as the construction of reciprocal tables

Babylonian Mathematics (With a section on the Plimpton 322 tablet).
http://aleph0.clarku.edu/~djoyce/mathhist/babylonia.html

A subsection of the History of Mathematics homepage maintained by David E. Joyce of the Department of Mathematics and Computer Science, Clark University. This page contains a link to more detailed material on tablet 322 of the G. A. Plimpton Collection at Columbia University. That link provides an image of the tablet, bibliography, a transcription of and a commentary on possible interpretations of the mathematics set forth on the tablet.

Babylonian Square Roots
http://www.seanet.com/~ksbrown/kmath190.htm

A short but complete technical explanation of how to extract the square roots of numbers using Babylonian mathematical techniques.

Bahai Faith
http://www.biologie.uni-freiburg.de/~amueller/religion/bahaifaith.html

This is the Bahai section of the WWW Virtual Library. A good collection of Internet resources for scholars of the Bahai faith or those interested in development of modern religious movements.

Baker Book House
http://www.bakerbooks.com/

This is the website for the Baker Book House publishing company. The site has a comprehensive list of books published, academic titles, books for church leaders and other information of interest to authors or customers of Baker Book House. One feature that should be emulated by other presses is the presence of online excerpts from books to allow users to browse a book much like in a traditional bookstore before purchasing the work.

Banias Archeological Project
http://www.pepperdine.edu/seaver/Banias/Home.htm

A consortium of American universities and the Nature Reserves Authority and the Antiquities Authority of the State of Israel are excavating Banais (Caesarea Philippi). A short history of the site and some images of the site and artifacts are available at this web site. A web page is under development to display coins found at the excavation.

Edgar James Banks: Bismya or The Lost City of Adab
New York : G. P. Putnam's Sons, 1912
http://eos.lib.uchicago.edu/cgi-bin/LIB_preserve_title.sh?CALL_NUMBER=DS70.B2

A scanned copy of this work by the Electronic Open Stacks project at the University of Chicago Library. The work can be viewed by chapters or a reader can "jump" to a particular page in the work. These image-based texts avoid the expense of creating full text searchable versions and yet provide usable access to materials too fragile for regular use.

Basic Lessons in Hieratic
http://home.prcn.org/~sfryer/Hieratic/index.html

This web site offers a basic introduction to the reading of hieratic, a cursive form of hieroglyphics. Lessons include: "Alphabetic" Signs, Common Determinatives, Common Bi- and Tri-Consonantal Signs, Ligatures and Numbers. In addition to the lessons, the hieratic text of The Story of the Shipwrecked Sailor (Papyrus Leningrad 1115) is reproduced as images with a linked hieroglyphic transcription.

Before the Coming of the Pickaxes
http://research.haifa.ac.il/~archlgy/colloq2.html

Abstracts for a colloquium sponsored by the Department of Archaeology and the Zinman Institute of Archaeology, Before the Coming of the Pickaxes: Aspects of the Archaeological Surveys in Israel, May 1, 1997. The abstracts include "Underwater Surveys In Israel", Ehud Galili and Ya'aqov Sharvit; "Spatial Analysis In Biblical Archaeology", Dr. Yossi Garfinkel; "Fifteen Years After: What We Have Learned From The Negev Survey", Prof. Steven A. Rosen, and others. Some of the abstracts are followed by bibliographies.

"Beginning From Jerusalem . . .": Re-examining Canon and Consensus
http://daniel.drew.edu/~ddoughty/miller.html

This essay by Merrill P. Miller of Pembroke State University examines the role of the Jerusalem church in the origins of Christianity. Miller challenges the notion that "messianic confrontations, claims, or titles" were involved in the death of Jesus or the identity of his followers.

Beinecke Library: Yale University Papyrus Collection
http://webtext.library.yale.edu/

A catalog and inventory of the Yale Papyrus Collection at the Beinecke Rare Book and Manuscript Library, Yale University. An introduction to the catalog describes the cataloging procedure and terms used for this important collection. The catalog is searchable from the Internet and covers P.CtYBR inv. 1-3299.

Beinlich Wordlist
http://www.trin.cam.ac.uk/pub/data/beinlich.html
or check
http://www.newton.cam.ac.uk/egypt/test/beinlich.html

The Beinlich Wordlist is a handlist of Ancient Egyptian words with the Egyptian word in transliteration, a German translation, and a brief reference to the Wörterbuch or other more recent publications. It is a valuable contribution to the field of Egyptology, and the authors, Horst Beinlich and Friedhelm Hoffman, deserve praise and recognition for allowing free electronic distribution of this resource. Using the "Manuel de codage" transliteration scheme, it is possible to represent diacriticals in a uniform way. Nigel Strudwick is responsible for the development of this WWW database that provides access to this important new resource in Egyptology.

The Order of Saint Benedict (Rule of St. Benedict in English)
http://www.osb.org/osb/rb/index.html

The Rule of St. Benedict is available in English, Latin, French, Hungarian, Italian, and Spanish language editions either at this site or by links to other sites. An extensive bibliography of works pertaining to the Rule of Benedict will be of interest to scholars of religious orders and their history. A telnet link is available to take the reader to the PALS library database that includes three Benedictine libraries in Minnesota.

Bibelwissenschaft
http://www.asn-linz.ac.at/schule/religion/frame.htm

The best European site for biblical studies and related areas, with extensive links to source materials and other resources on the Internet. Of particular interest are the link collections found under Bible & Theology Gateways and Computereinsatz in der Exegese.

Bible, Arabic
http://www.accent.net/alne3mat/

An online version of the Bible translated into Arabic.

Bible, Chinese Union Version
http://www.ifcss.org/ftp-pub/org/bcec/cbible/

In addition to a Chinese version of the Bible, this site offers a variety of tools for students and scholars. Various encodings of the Chinese text, tools for creating concordances of Chinese and English versions (Bible TOOL 1.3 for DOS), and links to other resources for Chinese Bible study are listed.

Bible, Czech
http://www.fee.vutbr.cz/~michal/kr/

An online version of the Czech Bible of Kralice originally published in six volumes (1579-1593). This work is available only in the Czech language and requires use of the proper document encoding.

Bible, Finnish
http://www.funet.fi/pub/doc/religion/christian/Bible/html/finnish/1992/Raamattu.html

This is a Finnish translation of the Bible.

Bible, French (Louis Segond)
http://saturn.colorado.edu:8080/Christian/LSG/lsg.html

This is an online version of the Louis Segond version of the Bible in French (1910).

Bible, Hungarian
gopher://gopher.mek.iif.hu:7070/11/porta/szint/human/vallas/biblia

This is a Hungarian translation of the Bible.

Bible, Indonesian
http://www.parokinet.org/docs/bible.html

This is an Indonesian translation of the Bible.

Bible, Italian
http://www.crs4.it/~riccardo/Letteratura/Bibbia/Bibbia.html

This is an Italian translation of the Bible.

Bible, King James with Apocrypha)
gopher://ccat.sas.upenn.edu:3333/11/Religious/Biblical/KJVBible

Text of the King James Bible with a search option.

Bible, King James
http://saturn.colorado.edu:8080/Christian/KJV/kjv.html

Text of the King James Bible tagged for HTML display.

Bible, Korean
http://kcm.co.kr/bible/bible.html

Appropriate Korean font and character encoding required for this site.

Bible, Korean
http://bible.wisenet.co.kr/

Appropriate Korean font and character encoding required for this site. This site also functions as a gateway to other Korean Bible resources.

Bible, Luther
http://nobi.ethz.ch/bibel/buecher.html

This is an online version of Martin Luther's translation of the Bible into German.

Bible, Norwegian
http://www.menfak.no/bibel/

Revised edition of the Norwegian Bible from 1930. Searchable by verse or passage with links to other translations and dictionaries.

Bible, Polish
http://david.silesia.pik-net.pl/biblia/

This is a Polish translation of the Bible.

Bible, Russian
http://www.serve.com/irr-tv/Russian/Bible/index.html

The Russian Bible site uses KOI8 Cyrillic fonts that are available at this site.

Bible, Spanish
http://www.mit.edu:8001/afs/athena.mit.edu/activity/c/csa/www/documents/Spanish/Bible.html

The origin of the Spanish text used for this web site is unknown.

Bible Analysis and Related Software
http://www.chorus.cycor.ca/hahne\bible.html

This site offers an excellent hypertext discussion of Bible analysis software for Biblical scholars. The availability and usefulness of several font packages for Hebrew and Greek are also discussed. Harry Hahne, the author of this resource, is also responsible for the more technical treatment of Biblical analysis software found under "Interpretive Implications of Using Bible-Search Software for New Testament Grammatical Analysis."

Bible Browser Advanced
http://goon.stg.brown.edu/bible_browser/pbform.shtml

The advanced version of the Bible Browser program from Richard Goerwitz. It is possible to search biblical texts by keyword, substring or word pattern. Unlike most other bible searching programs, it is possible to perform logical operations on groups of passages, retrieve passages from different versions and other options.

Bible Browser Basic
http://goon.stg.brown.edu/bible_browser/pbeasy.shtml

The Bible Browser program by Richard Goerwitz allows online searching of the bible or referencing a passage by book, chapter and verse number. Versions of the bible available for the basic version of this program are Revised Standard Version, King James Version, and Jerome's (Latin) Vulgate. The interface for the basic version is straightforward and should cause no difficulties for even neophyte computer users.

Bible Gateway
http://www.gospelcom.net/bible

The Bible Gateway allows searches of various translations of the Bible, by passage or search words with Boolean operators. The full text of the NIV, RSV, KJV, Darby and the YLT are available for searching. It also offers searchable translations of the Bible into other languages, including French (LSG), German (Elberfelder), Latin (Vulgate), Spanish (RVA), Swedish (SV1917) and Tagalog (only the books of John and James are available for Tagalog).

Bible Search Engine
http://www.thechristian.org/bible/bible.htm

A very useful Bible search site that allows searching of various translations of the Bible, including Darby, the King James Version, the New King James Version, the Authorized Standard Version, the Revised Standard Version, Young, Weymouth as well as Spanish, French and German editions. Some of the texts include references to study aids such as Strong's numbers or Strong's Old and New Testament definitions. Greek New Testament versions such as the Byzantine/Majority, Westcott-Hort edition, and the Textus Receptus and the Hebrew Bible are also available for searching. Students are cautioned against relying upon electronic texts of unknown proofing or providence when conducting biblical research. All results should be checked against a known scholarly edition or electronic text.

Biblia Sacra Vulgatae Editiones
http://www.umkc.edu/networking/chris/www/languages/latin/etexts/vulgate.html

Latin text of the Vulgate arranged as separate books of the Bible.

Biblia Sacra Vulgate Editionis
http://davinci.marc.gatech.edu/catholic/scriptures/vulgata-clementina.html

This is another edition of the text of the Vulgate online.

Biblical Archaeologist
http://www.asor.org/NEA/NEAHP.html

Biblical Archaeologist has changed its name to Near Eastern Archaeology. (To avoid confusion it has been listed under both names herein.) This site offers the table of contents from recent issues for viewing. The full text of some back issues of this journal are being placed online as part of the SELA project.

Biblical Archaeology Society
http://www.bib-arch.org

Best known for its journal Biblical Archaeology Review the Biblical Archaeology Society through its site offers access to an interesting variety of resources. Included on its homepage are links to information on its other publications such as Bible Review, Archaeology Odyssey and contact information for those wishing to join archaeological excavations. A listing of links to other sites of interest to biblical scholars is also available.

Biblical Institute of Fribourg University
http://www.unifr.ch/bif/

Provides timely information on the current activities of the Biblical Institute, which includes the new edition of the Biblica Hebraica. Information on volumes of Orbis Biblicus et Orientalis and Novum Testamentum et Orbis Antiquus, backlist and new/forthcoming, as well as the activities of the Swiss Society for Ancient Near Eastern Studies are available at this site.

Biblical Related and Sacred Texts
http://bramm.ucsm.ac.uk/bible.htm

An extensive collection of links to online bibles and related links based in the UK. As of May 1998, it listed some thirty-one online sites with one or more editions of the Bible in a variety of languages.

Biblical Studies on the Web
http://www.bsw.org/

Biblical Studies on the Web is an electronic journal focused on the study of Jewish and Christian biblical theology. The journal is interested in scholarly university papers from graduate students for publication at this site. In addition to the journal itself, links are maintained to Bible resources, libraries, software and other materials of interest to biblical scholars. Note that the site charges a subscription fee for access to articles or book reviews.

Biblical Studies Reference Sources
http://alcon.acu.edu/www/hsu/bible.htm

Written for the Hardin-Simmons University Libraries user community this listing of reference works for biblical studies deserves a wider audience. Non-professional scholars will find the listing useful in guiding their selection of reference materials from the large number of items currently available.

Biblical Theology Bulletin
http://www.shu.edu/programs/jcs/bulletin.html

The website for the Biblical Theology Bulletin lists the table of contents for the years 1995-1997 and provides subscription information for the journal.

A Bibliography of Hellenistic Poetry
http://wwwlet.leidenuniv.nl/www.let.data/gltc/hellenistic.bibl/hellenistic.bibl.html

A bibliography consisting of over 3200 records, the Bibliography of Hellenistic Poetry is a good resource for scholars interested in Hellenistic poetry. Topics include Aratus, Callimachus, Theocritus, Apollonius Rhodius (main subject of bibliography, 1360 records from 1496-1997), Nicander, Hellenistic Epigram, Quintus Smyrnaeus, Nonnus, and, Hellenistic Poetry 1992-1997.

Bibliographie zu Jesus Sirach, Version 3
http://www.ktf.uni-passau.de/mitarbeiter/boehmisch/BenSira.bibliographie.html

This is a very impressive bibliography on Jesus ben Sirach by Franz Böhmisch. Some 1,117 entries in length, it would make a worthy object for updating and annotation by an enterprising graduate student.

A Bibliographic Guide to Vergil's Aeneid
http://classics.rutgers.edu/vergil.html

Shirley Werner prepared this extensive bibliography on Vergil's Aeneid. While Werner disclaims any intent to list every possible resource on the Aeneid, her bibliography will be useful in all areas of Aeneid studies. The bibliography covers the following topics: ancient scholarship; anthologies; bibliography; biography; commentaries; cultural context; editions; electronic encyclopedia; ideology; individual books and passages; major studies; patronage; predecessors and literary traditions; reception and influence; religion, philosophy, cosmology; Rome and Italy; style, themes, techniques; theory and approaches; translation; and, transmission and text.

Bir Umm Fawakhir Survey Reports
http://www-oi.uchicago.edu/OI/PROJ/FAW/Fawakhir.html

Excavation reports from the Bir Umm Fawakhir survey, 1991-92 and 1992-93 seasons. This site was not systematically surveyed nor excavated prior to the beginning of this effort in 1992 under the direction of Carol Meyer. Bir Umm Fawakhir is a 6th-7th century A.D. Byzantine site in the Eastern desert of Egypt near Wadi Hammamat.

Blais, The Online Catalog of The librairies of The Claremont Colleges
http://blais.claremont.edu/

Blais is the online catalog for all the libraries of the Claremont Colleges. Of particular note is the library for the School of Theology at Claremont.

Blood and Purity in Leviticus and Revelation
http://www.stolaf.edu/people/kchanson/blood.html

Reprint of an article by K. C. Hanson which first appeared in Listening: Journal of Religion and Culture 28 (1993): 215-30. Hanson compares the purity assumptions that underlie the treatment of blood in both Leviticus and the Book of Revelations.

Blueletter Bible
http://www.khouse.org/blueletter/

The Blueletter Bible site offers the usual searching tools found with online bibles but also interlinear Hebrew and Greek for each text with optional Strong's reference numbers. A variety of older commentaries, concordances, lexicons, and dictionaries are also linked to the bible text.

Body and Sexuality in the Art of the Ancient World
http://www.umich.edu/~twilfong/bodysyll.html

A syllabus from a course at University of Michigan taught by Terry G. Wilfong, Visiting Assistant Curator, Kelsey Museum of Archaeology. Instructive reading references are mentioned in the body of the syllabus.

Boethius
http://ccat.sas.upenn.edu/jod/boethius.html

This is the WWW homepage for the course on Boethius that was taught by James J. O'Donnell in the Fall of 1994. This course offering was unique since participants not physically present at University of Pennsylvania could register for the course for full graduate credit. Links lead to "De Consolatione Philosophiae" by Boethius, Latin text, translation, and commentary by O'Donnell;

the Latin text of Boethius' "de musica" courtesy of T. Mathiesen (Thesarus Musicarum Litinarium project, Indiana University); assigned readings for the course and a searchable log of all the posting made during the course.

Dietrich Bonhoeffer
http://204.245.208.1/bonhoef/index.htm

Links to Web resources on Bonhoeffer, including the International Bonhoeffer Society are available at this site. The site allows the posting of public messages in the Bonhoeffer Forum, seeking suggestions on resources to be offered by the site.

Bonn Archaeological Statistics Package Ver. 4.5
ftp://ftp.uni-koeln.de/pc/msdos/statistics/basp4dos.zip

The Bonn Archaeological Statistics package is statistical software for archaeology that runs on DOS platforms.

Book of Kells
http://www.tcd.ie/kells.html

Three images drawn from the Book of Kells, two from the Gospel of Matthew and one from the Gospel of John.

Book of Mormon
gopher://ccat.sas.upenn.edu:3333/11/Religious/Mormon

This gopher menu at UPENN offers the text of the Book of Mormon, separated into separate books, with a search interface to the Book of Mormon as a whole.

Brepols Publishers
http://www.brepols.com/d1_1e.htm

The homepage for Brepols Publishers is offered in English, Dutch and French versions. A searchable backlist of over 4,000 titles and information concerning periodical publications and other topics are available here. Perhaps best known for its Corpus Christianorum, Typologie des Sources du Moyen Age occidental, Cetedoc Library of Christian Latin Texts, available only at large and well funded research facilities.

British Archaeology
http://britac3.britac.ac.uk/cba/ba/ba.html

British Archaeology, the primary publication of the Council for British Archaeology, is available in full text on the Web some two months after print publication. Available issues begin with No. 1 (February 1995) and continue to present.

British Museum
http://www.british-museum.ac.uk/

The British Museum site offers useful information about the museum and its collections. Some the images will interest teachers but none have enough detail to be useful for professional work.

British Association for Near Eastern Archaeology (BANEA)
http://www.art.man.ac.uk/arthist/banea.html

BANEA was formed to "promote the study of the archaeology, history, and languages of the ancient Near East at all levels" and this site is in furtherance of that goal. In addition to information concerning the society, jobs, scholarships and conference announcements, this site offers a reading list suitable for primary (coloring books) and secondary instruction on the Ancient Near East.

Brown University Department of Egyptology
http://www.brown.edu/Departments/Egyptology/

Information on the Egyptology department at Brown University is the main focus of this homepage. It provides useful information to students thinking about undergraduate or graduate studies in Egyptology. A selected bibliography on Ancient Egypt is also available at this site.

Bryn Mawr Classical Review
gopher://gopher.lib.Virginia.EDU:70/11/alpha/bmcr

The Bryn Mawr Classical Review offers reviews of recent monographs in the area of classical studies. At this gopher site previous "issues" are available by year, and there is a search interface for searching all the reviews currently online.

Buddhism
http://www.biologie.uni-freiburg.de/~amueller/religion/buddha.html

This site is part of the WWW Virtual Library, which focuses on electronic resources relating to Buddhism. It contains links to resources such as Buddhist Studies at the Australian National University, the Electronic Buddhist Archives, IRIZ (a collection of Chinese electronic texts, tools and bibliographies on Zen Buddhism), the Journal of Buddhist Ethics, the Taoism Information Page, and Early Tibetan Mandalas.

Buddhist Image Bank
ftp://sunsite.unc.edu/pub/academic/religious_studies/Buddhism/Tantric_Studies/Iconography

An ftp archive with 72 images related to Iconography and Tantric Studies, available for downloading.

Buddhist Studies
http://coombs.anu.edu.au/WWWVL-Buddhism.html

T. Matthew Ciolek of Australian National University, editor of the Asian Studies site noted above, is also responsible for this comprehensive listing of Buddhist Studies resources on the Internet. It is the best starting place for finding Buddhist resources on the Internet.

Buddhist_sutra_archive__in_Chinese
gopher://dongpo.math.ncu.edu.tw/11/buda

Buddhist sutra archive in Big-5 (a method of representing Chinese characters electronically) code.

Bulletin of the Asia Institute
http://www.bulletinasiainstitute.org/

Along with ordering information for the journal Bulletin of the Asia Institute, the table of contents for prior issues can also be found at this site. A subject index which breaks the contents in to rather large areas such as "Iranian Studies" and "Near East" also provide a listing of prior published articles. Unfortunately the content of articles from the Bulletin of the Asia Institute is not available at this site.

Cambridge University Press
http://www.cup.org/

The Cambridge University Press website offers an on-line catalog of all its publications, information for authors and ordering information for both booksellers and individuals. This is a well-organized site that reflects the quality for which Cambridge University Press is known.

Canadian Society for Mesopotamian Studies (CSMS)
http://www.chass.utoronto.ca/nmc/rim/csmshome.html

The Canadian Society for Mesopotamian Studies seeks to interest the general public in the culture, history, and archaeology of Mesopotamia. The society is a co-sponsor of the Canadian Expedition to Syria, and offers a variety of lectures and evening courses on archaeology.

Canons of the Council of Orange (529 AD)
http://www.iclnet.org/pub/resources/text/history/council.orange.txt

This is an anonymous English translation of the Canons of the Council of Orange.

Canticles
gopher://ftp.std.com/11/obi/book/Canticles

Sarah Keefer has provided an important source of information for those interested in the liturgical use of individual canticles. The text file of each canticle contains both the text and additional source and reference material. Keefer also maintains LITMSS.DBF (available at this site), which is a database file containing more than three hundred records of manuscripts owned or written in Anglo-Saxon England prior to 1100 and containing material from the liturgy.

CANTUS: Database of Divine Office Gregorian Chant
gopher://vmsgopher.cua.edu:70/11gopher_root_music%3A%5B_cantus%5D

A searchable database of chants used for the Divine Office. Searchable fields include folio number, feast day, office, genre, liturgical position, text incipit, letters indicating sources in which the chant appears as surveyed by Hesbert, CAO reference number, mode, and differentia.

CANTUS PLANUS
http://www.uni-regensburg.de/FzE/Musikwissenschaft/index.html

Cantus Planus is a study group of the International Musicological Society and seeks to promote the exchange of data in electronic format. This site, at University of Regensburg, offers inventories of representative medieval manuscripts of chants for the Mass. The two inventories available are Lateinische Handschriften des liturgischen Chorals and the Inventare lateinischer Handschriften des liturgischen Chorals.

Michael C. Carlos Museum, Emory University
http://www.emory.edu/CARLOS/carlos.html

The Carlos Museum, like many other museums around the world, has begun placing images of its objects on the WWW. Of particular interest for scholars of the Classics and the Ancient Near East will be objects drawn from its collections of artifacts from Ancient Egypt, the Ancient Near East and Classical Greece and Rome. While the current selection of objects represents a very limited part of the overall collection, it is an important first step in removing physical distance as a barrier to the viewing of such artifacts.

Cassiodorus
http://ccat.sas.upenn.edu/jod/cassiodorus.html

"Cassiodorus" by James J. O'Donnell is the standard treatment of the life and work of Flavius Magnus Arurelius. First published in 1979 by the University of California Press, the entire work is now available at this site.

A Catalogue of the Edward William Lane Collection in the Griffith Institute, Ashmolean Museum, Oxford
http://www.ashmol.ox.ac.uk/gri/4lane.html

This is a detailed record of the Edward William Lane Collection in the Griffith Institute, Ashmolean Museum, Oxford. This collection contains such important mss. such as Lane MSS 6.3 Manuscript draft of the first portion of Lane's Arabic-English Lexicon.

Catholic Files
http://listserv.american.edu/catholic/

This site offers links to most of the major repositories of Catholic documents on the Web and links to Catholic religious order sites.

Catholic Church, Official Church Documents
http://www.mcgill.pvt.k12.al.us/jerryd/cm/docs.htm

This site offers links to documents held at a variety of locations for all the Ecumenical Councils, Encyclicals and Other Papal Documents and a wide variety of other official documents of the Catholic Church. It is a very good starting place for quickly determining if a Church document is available online.

Catholic Resources on the Net
http://www.cs.cmu.edu:8001/Web/People/spok/catholic.html

This site, located at Carnegie Mellon University, is the home of a number of resources related to Catholicism and provides links to others. The contents of this site include Books, Catholic Information Sites, Catholic Organizations, Church Councils, Early Church writings, History and Culture (Miscellaneous), Liturgy and Worship, Papal Writings, Saints, Scripture, The Vatican, and Related Resources.

Center for Advanced Research on Language Acquisition (CARLA)
http://carla.acad.umn.edu/

CARLA sponsors this website which includes a page devoted to LCTL (Less Commonly Taught Languages). Some of the languages listed at this site are Akkadian, Amharic, Ancient Greek, Aramaic, Armenian, Assyrian, Avestan, Classical Hebrew, Coptic, Egyptian, Ethiopic, Greek, Hebrew, Hittite, Middle Iranian, Judeo-Arabic, Latin, Old Persian, Pahlavi, Sanskrit, Sumerian, Syriac, Ugaritic, and Vedic. The site also offers links to information on the use of technology in language teaching and other topics in language acquisition.

Center for Computer Analysis of Texts (CCAT)
http://ccat.sas.upenn.edu/

This update of the CCAT gopher site offers a variety of guides, tools, texts and software. Among the etext resources are a morphologically analyzed Septuagint text, along with the parallel aligned Hebrew-Aramaic and Greek Jewish Scriptures, which is based upon the Michigan-Claremont BHS consonantal text and the TLG LXX. A morphologically analyzed Hebrew Bible can also be searched from this site. Augustine's Confessions and Lightfoot's translation of the Apostolic Fathers can be found under Church Writers. An English translation of the Quran by M. H. Shakir is also available.

Centre for Computer-aided Egyptological Research (CCER)
http://www.ccer.ggl.ruu.nl/ccer/ccer_newton.html

The Centre is on the forefront of the use of computers for egyptological research. Projects such as the Coffin Texts Word Index, the Multilingual Egyptological Thesaurus, and the Prosopographia Aegypti, all noted elsewhere in this work, are examples of their work. It also maintains an extensive list of links to Egyptological institutions and museums, a list of Egyptologists, and information on projects by CCER and others to promote the use of computers in Egyptology.

Centre for the Study of Ancient Documents (Oxford University)
http://www.csad.ox.ac.uk/CSAD/

Like other Oxford University initiatives, the influence of the Centre for the Study of Ancient Documents is spreading beyond the confines of Oxford University. While established to provide a focus on the study of ancient documents at Oxford, the Centre has taken a leadership role in experimenting with delivery of images of inscriptions held in their squeeze collection over the WWW. A newsletter from the Centre is also available on the WWW. Details concerning other Centre activities and contact information are available from the Centre homepage.

Centre for Textual Studies
http://info.ox.ac.uk/ctitext/index.html

One of twenty-three Computers in Teaching Initiative (CTI) Centres for Textual Studies, established to promote the use of computers in university teaching. This homepage offers access to the Centre's Resources Guide, which is an introduction to the software, techniques and literature of electronic textual analysis for academics seeking to use computers in teaching and research. Resources on the Internet, other sources of electronic texts, texts for religious studies and classics, fonts and scanning, as well as a bibliography, are found in this guide. The site also has links to the Oxford Text Archive and the Canterbury Tales Project.

Centre of Non-Western Studies: Leiden University
http://www.leidenuniv.nl/interfac/cnws/

Information on all aspects of the Centre of Non-Western Studies at Leiden University is available at this site. A newsletter from the Centre covers current research projects and detailed information on the Centre's activities.

CenturyOne Bookstore
http://www.centuryone.com/

The CenturyOne Bookstore offers a wide selection of traditional books as well as electronic publications of interest to biblical scholars. Sponsored by the CenturyOne Foundation, this site also offers links to sites of interest to those working in biblical studies.

Champollion Project
http://www.ccer.ggl.ruu.nl/champollion/default.htm

The Champollion Project is an effort to honor the founder of Egyptology, Jean François Champollion, by making collections of Egyptian objects held by European museums more accessible to both scholars and the public. Ten separate museums have agreed to participate in this project which will make available images of objects in their collections on a series of CD-ROMS. Each museum is contributing access to approximately 1,500 objects each for a total of approximately 15,000 objects to be imaged and released on ten CD-ROMs. The price of approximately 50 EUC per volume will allow virtually every interested person to own a copy of this unique resource. The interface for access will be available in Dutch, English, French, German, Italian, Portuguese, Spanish and Swedish. Portions of the Champollion database will be accessible from the Internet although principal access to the materials will be via the CD-ROMs. This is truly a remarkable project not only for its scope but the securing of the cooperation of diverse parties to produce a scholarly product that is priced within the range of most scholars. The organizational and technical lessons from this project should be applied in other areas of Ancient Near Eastern studies.

Catholic Biblical Association of America
http://www.cua.edu/www/org/cbib/welcome.htm

Homepage for the Catholic Biblical Association of America based at the Catholic University of America. Extensive information on the organization and its meetings as well as its various publications and grant opportunities.

Checklist of Editions of Greek and Latin Papyri, Ostraca and Tablets
http://odyssey.lib.duke.edu/papyrus/texts/clist.html

The preface to this site notes: "The primary purpose of the Checklist of Editions of Greek and Latin Papyri, Ostraca and Tablets is to provide for scholars and librarians a ready bibliography of all monographic volumes, both current and out-of-print, of Greek and Latin texts on papyrus, parchment, ostraca or wood tablets." The information in the bibliography is updated on a regular basis and for ease of use and access sets an example that deserves emulation.

Chicago Assyrian Dictionary Project
http://www-oi.uchicago.edu/OI/PROJ/CAD/CAD.html

Annual Reports on the Chicago Assyrian Dictionary Project.

Chicago Demotic Dictionary Project
http://www-oi.uchicago.edu/OI/PROJ/DEM/Demotic.html

Annual Reports on the Chicago Demotic Dictionary Project. There is also a link to the Oriental Institute's ftp server for obtaining documents describing the abbreviations used by the Chicago Demotic Dictionary at: ftp://oi.uchicago.edu/pub/oi/demotic/Text_Info.ascii.txt.

Chicago Hittite Dictionary Project
http://www-oi.uchicago.edu/OI/PROJ/HIT/Hittite.html

Annual reports from the Chicago Hittite Dictionary Project.

Chicago House Bulletin
http://www-oi.uchicago.edu/OI/PROJ/EPI/Epigraphic.html

Bulletins from the Chicago House, the headquarters in Egypt for the Oriental Institute.

The University of Chicago Library Catalog
http://www.lib.uchicago.edu/webpac-bin/wgbroker?new+-access+top

The University of Chicago Library offers access to its library catalog over the Internet at this site. Scholars at various locations can now access one of the better university libraries in the United States for research on any topic concerning the Ancient Near East without leaving their offices.

Chogha Mish Project
http://www-oi.uchicago.edu/OI/PROJ/CHO/Chogha_Mish.html

A brief note on the excavations at Chogha Mish, Iran and present plans for publication.

Chorus: A Resource for Academic and Educational Computing in the Arts/Humanities
http://www.chorus.cycor.ca/chorus.html

Chorus is a resource for academic and educational computing in the arts/humanities. The reviews of popular software for use by humanists take some of the uncertainty out of software purchases.

Christian Classics Ethereal Library
http://ccel.wheaton.edu/

The Christian Classics Ethereal Library relies upon public domain translations and editions to make a large number of works available over the Internet. Most of the works are available in a variety of formats, ranging from ASCII text to compressed Postscript, and some appear in different translations. The authors to be found here include St. Alphonsus (1696-1787), St. Augustine (345-430), John Bunyan (1628-1688), John Calvin (1509-1564), Jonathan Edwards (1703-1758), Brother Lawrence (c. 1605-1691), John Milton (1608-1674), and John Wesley (1703-1791).

The Christian Coptic Orthodox Church of Egypt
http://cs-www.bu.edu/faculty/best/pub/cn/Home.html

A very good collection of information and links for anyone working on topics related to the Christian Coptic Orthodox Church of Egypt. It includes information directed at casual users as well as links of interest to professional coptologists.

Christian Theology Page
http://apu.edu:80/~bstone/theology.html

A useful collection of links to sites with material of interest on Christian theology.

Christian WWW Resource List
http://saturn.colorado.edu:8080/Christian/list.html

Simon Damberger has compiled a fairly comprehensive set of links to selected Christian resources found on the Internet. The links are arranged by topics and are not limited to scholarly materials, although links to many of the sites listed in this work may also be found at this site.

Excavations at Tell Chuera, Syria
http://mlucom6.urz.uni-halle.de/orientarch/chuera.html

A guide to current excavation efforts at Tell Chuera, Syria, including a selective bibliography of publications concerning the site and a satellite image of the area. Very good image maps and plans of excavated areas as well as a brief history of the site placing it in historical context. The excavation and this website are projects of the Martin-Luther-Universität Halle-Wittenberg, Institut für Orientalische Archäologie und Kunst.

The Cicero Homepage
http://www.utexas.edu/depts/classics/documents/Cic.html

An excellent collection of the texts of Cicero (in Latin) along with a proposed chronology for the placement of those works in his lifetime. An extensive bibliography of works on Cicero and his texts can also be found at this site.

Chaironeia: Plutarch's Home on the Web
http://www.utexas.edu/depts/classics/chaironeia/

A very complete listing of links to Web resources on Plutarch, including links to translations of his "Lives" in English as well as links to the Perseus Project for selected lives in Greek.

Chinese Character Genealogy: Web-Based Etymological Dictionary for Learning Chinese Characters
http://zhongwen.com/

This is an interesting online tutorial for learning Chinese characters. The dictionary offers access to over 4,000 characters and guides are given to pronunciation. An FAQ (Frequently Asked Questions) documents answers a variety of common inquiries concerning the development and use of Chinese characters.

Chloris
http://www.chass.utoronto.ca:8080/fine_arts/chloris/index.html

Organized by site of excavation on the mainland of Greece and Crete, Chloris maintains a bibliography of Bronze Age archaeology references to these sites. The bibliography can be searched for publications concerning particular sites.

Church Fathers (Edinborough edition)
http://www.sni.net/advent/fathers/
http://ccel.wheaton.edu/fathers2/

English translations of the Church Fathers based upon the 38-volume Edinborough edition.

Claretian Missionaries
http://http1.brunel.ac.uk:8080/depts/chaplncy/cmfs.htm

This is the homepage of the Claretian Missionaries. General information on the order and some links to other sites with collections of links to religious material.

Classical Mediterranean E-Mail List Archives
http://www.umich.edu/~classics/archives.html

A searchable archive of prior postings from several discussion lists focusing on the ancient world.

Classics and Mediterranean Archaeology
http://rome.classics.lsa.umich.edu/welcome.html

Sebastian Heath of the Department of Classical Studies, University of Michigan, maintains this collection. In addition to its completeness, the other notable feature of this site is a search feature at the top of the home page that allows searches by the title of resources. A very helpful tool for cases where only the title of a resource has been mentioned without its specific Internet location.

Classics at Chicago
http://humanities.uchicago.edu/humanities/classics/Resources/Net.html

This site has a very extensive collection of links to classics resources on the Internet. The links are divided into the following categories: Overviews, Summaries, and Useful Collections; Texts, Images, Vistas; Libraries and Related Resources; Electronic Journals and Mailing Lists; Learned Societies, Professional Associations, and Related Groups; and, Other Classics and Archaeology Programs. The site is well maintained and any difficulty in reaching particular resources is noted for that link.

Classics at Oxford
http://units.ox.ac.uk/departments/classics/

This is the home page of the Faculty of Literae Humaniores at Oxford University. Created by Don Fowler, Stuart Lee, and Andrew Wickham, this resource for the classics offers a wide variety of links to resources, both within and without the UK.

Classics Ireland
http://www.ucd.ie/~classics/ClassicsIreland.html

Classics Ireland is the journal of the Classical Association of Ireland and is available both in print and in electronic format. Beginning with volume 1 (1994), all issues of the journal are available on the WWW. This journal and other electronic journals noted herein demonstrate that scholarship is not a function of the medium of publication.

Classics Resources at Wisconsin
http://polyglot.lss.wisc.edu/classics/resource.htm

A listing of the resources sponsored by the Classics Department at the University of Wisconsin and links to other resources on the Web. Home to the Bibliotheca Latina Latin listing of Web resources, the Aeneid (Books One and Four, as well as Ovid's Metamorphoses. The link collections to other sites on the Web are very extensive and should be consulted along with Linda Wright's Classics homepage for recent additions to Web resources.

Classics On-line Course Database
http://www.colleges.org/ctts/clscourses.html

This is an excellent example of the use of technology to provide information that was not easily accessible prior the advent of the WWW. The database consists of courses offered in the classics and includes the subject, instructor, institution, semester and year the course was offered. It is possible to search the database by any of these fields and new courses can be added by use of a form on the website. An excellent way to find other scholars teaching similar courses or to investigate particular classics programs.

Classical Philology
http://www.journals.uchicago.edu/CP/

The Classical Philology website offers information on the journal Classical Philology and access to the tables of contents from volume 91 (1996) to volume 92 number 2 (1997).

The Classical Quarterly
http://www.oup.co.uk/jnls/list/clquaj/

This site offers access to the table of contents for the Classical Quarterly for all of 1996 and part of 1997. Information for authors and prospective subscribers is also available.

The Classical Review
http://www.oup.co.uk/jnls/list/clrevj/

This site offers access to the table of contents for the Classical Review for all of 1996 and 1997. Information for authors and prospective subscribers is also available.

Classical Studies Home Page for the University of North Carolina at Greensboro
http://www.uncg.edu/~shelmerd

In addition to information concerning courses, faculty and other departmental matters, this home page offers links to other classics departments, both domestic and non-U.S.

Cobb Institute of Archaeology: Lahav DigMaster Digital Archaeology Archives
http://www.cobb.msstate.edu

Joe Seger has pioneered the use of WWW technology to bring vast amounts of information from archaeology digs to scholars. Currently the Lahav database offers: 564 figurines in the database, 548 thumbnail pictures of the figurines, 548 full size front photos, 1273 full size alternate photos, 1821 full-scale color photos of the figurines, 330 drawings of figurines, 58 section or profile drawings, 67 QuicktimeVR Object files, 6 VRML Models of objects, and 15 Area Reports and 1 Field Summary in the database. There have been few, if any, archaeological excavation reports that have published in this degree of detail and certainly none that have done so in such a cost effective manner. The DigMaster publication model is one that should be explored and followed by archaeologists who are concerned more with advancing scholarship than hoarding artifacts for eventual publication or to attract graduate students.

Coffin Texts Word Index (CCER)
http://www.ccer.ggl.ruu.nl/ct/ct.html

The Coffin Texts Word Index consists of 108,000 records which index all words from the hieroglyphic text of Adriaan De Buck, The Egyptian Coffin Texts, Vol. I-VII, Chicago, 1935-61. Searches may be for a single word, two words, by viewing the quick-index, or by browsing the original De Buck edition by page or spell.

Colby College Archaeological Projects in Israel
http://www.colby.edu/rel/Israel.html

Thomas Longstaff maintains this homepage which focuses on the excavations of Colby College at Sepphoris, Israel. Reports for the 1993 and 1994 season are available. An experimental publication on the WWW of "The Location and Identification of Ancient Shikhin (Asochis)" by James F. Strange, Dennis E. Groh, and Thomas R. W. Longstaff also appears at this site.

A Collection of Ancient Documents
http://www.stolaf.edu/people/kchanson/ancdocs.html

This set of links constructed by K. C. Hanson allows quick access to a variety of images of ancient documents located at various sites on the WWW. These documents include: Aramaic, Tel Dan Inscription (9th-7th cent. BC), Petition to Authorize Elephantine Temple Reconstruction Aramaic (407 BC); Hebrew, The Gezer Calendar/Almanac (c. 925 BC), The BytYhwh Inscription (c. 9th-7th centuries BC), The Yavneh-Yam (Mesad-Hashavyahu) Ostracon (c. 639-609 BC), 1QpHab: The Habakkuk Pesher (c. 100 BC); Moabite, The Mesha Stele (aka: "Moabite Stone")(c. 930 BC); Greek, The Gallio Inscription (a.k.a. Delphi Inscription) (AD 52), The Proclamation of Nero's Succession as Roman Emperor (AD 54), The Jerusalem Temple Warning Inscription (1st century AD), The Theodotus Inscription (1st century AD), Census Edict of Gaius Vibius Maximus, Prefect of Egypt (AD 104), Gospel of John (P52) (c. AD 125), A Widow, Orphans, and the Evil Eye (c. AD 280-281), The Pilate Inscription (AD 26-37), Pliny/Trajan Correspondence (c. AD 100), The Hammurapi Stele (c. 1790 BC), and, the Ishtar Gate Inscription (c. 600 BC). As scholars make images (with or without translations) of biblical or related materials available on the Internet a short note should be sent to Hanson to aid in the maintenance of this very useful listing.

Combined Ceasarea Expeditions
http://www.inform.umd.edu/Caesarea/

The University of Maryland and the University of Haifa are the sponsors of this excavation at Caesarea Maritima. This web site is an excellent example of the type of information that can be made available for an excavation on the World Wide Web. Under the Research hyperlink there are further links to field reports, research articles, an extensive bibliography for the site, and research initiatives. The "Combined" in the title to the expeditions refers to the investigation of both the land remains of the site as well as a harbor located at this ancient city.

Comparative Religion
http://weber.u.washington.edu/~madin/

This site offers a well organized and extensive listing of links to resources for a variety of religious traditions. Despite its title, the site is more of a collection of links to separate traditions and not focused on comparative religion as an academic category. This is an excellent starting place for students and non-specialists interested in comparing religious traditions.

A Comprehensive Guide Map to the Giza Plateau for Tourists, Travel Agents, Scholars and Students
http://interoz.com/egypt/Antiq.htm

This is one of the most comprehensive guides to Egypt that is available on the WWW. The site features a history of Egypt, ancient monuments that includes pharonic, Islam and early Christianity, rulers of Ancient Egypt, a guide to Egyptian religion, and a glossary of terms. Unfortunately the entries are uneven; some drawing upon sources such as E. Wallis Budge and serious students will need to check many of the facts recited on this site. On the whole a very notable effort with flaws that could be readily corrected by using more current information concerning Egyptian history.

Computer-Assisted Theology on the Internet
http://info.ox.ac.uk/ctitext/theology/

Formerly called "Routes to Religion," this site contains a generous listing of links to resources in the area of religious studies. In addition to this WWW site, Michael Fraser is also the administrator of several email discussion lists that post notices of new resources for religious studies and the author of a list of email discussion groups for theologians. The information found here is always accurate, timely and of interest to scholars, a feat not always duplicated at other sites.

Computed Tomography and Archaeology
http://www2.huji.ac.il/~applbaum/ct/ctindex.htm

This site offers important information on the use of computed tomography in the study of archaeological artifacts. This technique has been used to study cuneiform texts on tablets that remain sealed within clay envelopes. A useful history of this technique in archaeology is also available at this site.

Computers and Ancient Languages
http://anes235-1.ff.cuni.cz/caal/caal.htm

The homepage for the Computers and Ancient Languages discussion list. The CAAL discussion list focuses primarily on the use of computers in the analysis and publication of Ancient Near Eastern languages. This WWW site is a collection of the postings to that list.

Computer Assisted Collation of New Testament Manuscripts
http://www.entmp.org/entmp/papers/coll.html

An important article by Tim Finney, Baptist Theological College of Western Australia, that examines methods of using computers to collate New Testament manuscripts. Beginning with the question of which manuscripts are significant enough to merit collation, Finney also details a method for preparing texts for use of Peter Robinson's excellent Collate program to produce a collated text. Finney has made the source code for his programs mentioned in this article available for use by other scholars.

Computer Technologies and the Classics
http://www.colleges.org/ctts/nycc97.html

A very useful summary of the Computer Technologies and the Classics Conference held by the New York Classical Club, February 8, 1997, by Barbara F. McManus. Topics included "Modeling the Past with Computers," by Harrison Eiteljorg, II and "Information Technologies and the Renewal of Classical Studies," by Roger Bagnall.

The Concise Matthew Henry Commentary on the Bible
http://www.cs.pitt.edu/~planting/books/henry/mhc/mhc.html

This online version of Matthew Henry's Commentary is part of the Christian Classics Ethereal Library project. The files are available in HTML, RTF and plain ASCII.

G. Contenau: Umma sous la Dynastie d'Ur Paris : Librairie Paul Geuthner, 1916
http://eos.lib.uchicago.edu/cgi-bin/LIB_preserve_title.sh?CALL_NUMBER=PJ4075.C76

A scanned copy of this work by the Electronic Open Stacks project at the University of Chicago Library. The work can be viewed by chapters or a reader can "jump" to a particular page in the work. These image-based texts avoid the expense of creating full text searchable versions and yet provide usable access to materials too fragile for regular use.

Conversation Analysis and the Book of Jonah: A Conversation
http://www.ualberta.ca/ARTS/JHS/Articles/article2.htm

Published in the online Journal of Hebrew Scriptures, this conversation (article) offers contributions by Cynthia L. Miller, Kenneth M. Craig, Jr. and Raymond F. Person, Jr. on the use of conversation analysis and the Book of Jonah.

COPAC
http://copac.ac.uk/copac/

COPAC is an online public access catalogue (OPAC) that provides a uniform interface to the catalogues of major university research libraries in the UK and Ireland. The database currently has 4.7 million records, with approximately 7.7 million holding statements. Access can be gained through this web interface, telnet or Z39.50 clients. Libraries currently included in the database are: Cambridge University Library, Edinburgh University Library, Glasgow University Library, Imperial College Library, Leeds University Library, Nottingham University Library, Oxford University Library, Trinity College Dublin Library, University of London Library, and University College London Library. Libraries that will be added in the near future are: Birmingham University Library, Durham University Library, Kings College Library (London), Liverpool University Library, London School of Economics Library, Manchester University Library, Newcastle University Library, School of Advanced Study (London), School of Oriental and African Studies (London), Sheffield University Library, Southampton University Library, Warwick University Library, and The Wellcome Institute.

COPAC is an indication of the rapid progress in the development of OPAC technology as well as a commitment to providing user-friendly interfaces to library catalogues. Online help is available along with guides to using COPAC that can be downloaded for viewing or printing. COPAC is a major bibliographic resource that will be of assistance to scholars without regard to geographic location.

The Coptic Language
http://www.stshenouda.com/coptlang.htm

Hany Takla is responsible for one of the more useful language sites to be found on the WWW. The Coptic language pages offer access to basic information on Coptic as well as lessons for learning Coptic. Information on software for learning Coptic, histories on the use of Coptic for religious texts, locations of Coptic manuscripts and other resources can be found here. A very valuable resource for any scholar working in Coptic studies.

Coptologia Journal
http://www.interlog.com/~hishak/copt.htm

The Coptologia webpage provides access to the tables of contents for volumes 1-15 and other information concerning the journal. Unfortunately there is no provision for access to older volumes of this publication over the Internet.

Cornell AsiaLink
http://cucjk.eap.cornell.edu/asialink.homepage.html

Offers information and links to software for CJK/Multiligual computing for both Macs and DOS machines. Also the site for Cornell courses Asian Studies 250: Introduction to Asian Religions and Asian Studies 358: Chinese Buddhism. Due to copyright restrictions some materials listed under these classes may not be accessible beyond the Cornell community. AAR program offerings for the 1995 Annual meeting and courses on the Lotus Sutra and Zen prepared in conjunction with AAR panels are also available.

The Cornell Halai East Lokris Project
http://128.253.68.14/chelp.htm

Online information concerning the excavation project at Halai, Greece. J. E. Coleman is directing this joint excavation effort by the Cornell Halai and East Lokris Project. There is an abundance of textual information concerning the information gained from the site for various historical periods, numerous images of the excavation site itself and a clickable map of the Acropolis of Halai.

Council of Remiremont
http://ccat.sas.upenn.edu/jod/remiremont.html

A twelfth century story about nuns who discuss what type of men they prefer. The original text was written in Latin and Paul Pascal prepared this text for the Bryn Mawr Commentary series. James O'Donnell prepared this hypertext edition as an experiment for the WWW. All the notes in the commentary are linked to the appropriate passage in the text. A brief bibliography is also available. This is a good demonstration of the use of hypertext linking for presentation of an original text with commentary.

Council of Societies for the Study of Religion
http://www.cssr.org/

The homepage for the CSSR offers information on the CSSR and its member societies as well as an index to Religious Studies Review. Of particular interest to prospective graduate students will be the listing of approximately 1,600 departments and programs in religious studies in North America.

Counting in Babylon
http://www.phys.virginia.edu/classes/109N/lectures/babylon.html

A brief treatment of counting and number systems in ancient Sumer and Babylonia, including the writing system used to represent numbers.

CSA Newsletter
http://csaws.brynmawr.edu:443/web1/newslet.html

The CSA Newsletter is published by the Center for the Study of Architecture and covers a number of important topics to scholars working with computers in the humanities. Two recent articles were: "The Lerna Database Experiment Experiment complete, data now available on the Web" (Susan C. Jones and Harrison Eiteljorg, II) and "A CAD Guide to Good Practice." All articles since volume 7, number 4, have been posted to the WWW with a selection of earlier articles in volume 7.

Cultural Map of Hellas
http://www.culture.gr/2/21/maps/hellas.html

Maps are used to connect users with information for museums, archaeological sites or monuments in particular regions. Overall organization into the following main districts: Athens, Peloponnese, Ionian Islands, Thessaly, Macedonia, Epirus, Crete, Aegean Islands, and Thrace. Museums, archaeological sites or monuments can be found by selecting a district on a map, selecting a district from the table that underneath the map or the search engine can locate a particular site of interest.

Cushitic Lexicon Project Reports
http://www-oi.uchicago.edu/OI/PROJ/CUS/Cushlex.html

The Cushitic Lexicon Project is gathering information to provide comparative lexical information contained in sets of cognate words from members of the Cushitic and Omotic language families. Gene Gragg's Cushitic-Omotic Etymological Database has been implemented in a standard FoxPro database format. Links are provided to a number of data files and other information located on the Oriental Institute FTP server.

Cyber Mummy
http://www.ncsa.uiuc.edu/Cyberia/VideoTestbed/Projects/Mummy/

Cyber Mummy is a K-12 presentation using modern technology to unlock the secrets of a mummy.

Cybermuslim Information Collective
http://www.uoknor.edu/cybermuslim

This site covers Muslim interest generally, with links to a wide variety of resources. Of particular interest is the link to the HyperQur'aan Project, which offers a variety of translations of the Qur'aan, and a version that displays the Arabic text by use of inline images. (One of the last hurdles to be cleared before the Internet can become a fully useful scholarly tool is the transmission and display of non-ASCII character sets.)

St. Cyprian
http://listserv.american.edu:70/1/catholic/church/fathers/cyprian/cyprian.html

A short biographical essay precedes the presentation of links to the selected texts of St. Cyprian listed below. Unfortunately, the source of the texts and translations does not appear with these materials. The following texts are available: To Demetrian, To Donatus, The Dress of Virgins, That Idols Are Not Gods, Jealousy and Envy, The Lapsed, The Lord's Prayer, Exhortation to Martyrdom, To Fortunatus, Mortality, The Good of Patience, The Unity of the Catholic Church, and Works and Almsgiving.

Czech Institute of Egyptology, Charles University
http://www.ff.cuni.cz/~krejci/Welcome.html

This site offers basic information concerning the Institute and its projects with some links to other Egyptology resources.

Dante's Epistle to Cangrande
http://ccat.sas.upenn.edu/jod/cangrande.latin.html
http://ccat.sas.upenn.edu/jod/cangrande.english.html

James Marchand of the University of Illinois is responsible for supplying the Latin text and English translation of this work by Dante.

Dante's Epistle to Cangrande: The Current Debate
http://ccat.sas.upenn.edu/jod/barlow.int.html

Professor Robert Hollander of Princeton University lectures on the authenticity of the Epistle to Cangrande originally delivered in March of 1993.

Dark Night of the Soul by St. John of the Cross
http://www.cs.pitt.edu/~planting/books/john_of_the_cross/dark_night/dark_night.html

An electronic edition of Dark Night of the Soul, translated by E. Allison Peers from the critical edition of P. Silverio De Santa Teresa, C.D. This particular edition was prepared from the 3rd edition text published by Image Books in 1959. Unfortunately, almost 400 footnotes or parts of footnotes describing variations among manuscripts have been omitted from this edition.

Davidson, Michael, Early Hebrew Printing Homepage
http://www.uottawa.ca/~weinberg/hebraica.html

Michael Davidson's web page is a collection of links to sites with information on early Hebrew printing and in particular those with illustrations from early works. A very useful collection that leads not only to images of early works but also to text and archival projects dealing with early Hebrew manuscripts and books.

Dead Sea Scrolls: Religious Studies 225
http://ccat.sas.upenn.edu/rs/rak/kraft.html

This link leads to archives from Robert Kraft's seminar on the Dead Sea Scrolls at the University of Pennsylvania, spring 1995. For ten years Kraft edited Offline, a column in Religious Studies News, which introduced many religion scholars to the use of computers and ultimately the Internet.

The Dead Sea Scrolls Project Reports
http://www-oi.uchicago.edu/OI/PROJ/SCR/Scrolls.html

Annual reports from the Dead Sea Scrolls Project at the Oriental Institute can be found at this location.

Vinton A. Dearing
http://englishwww.humnet.ucla.edu/Individuals/dearing/

Vinton Dearing is widely known for his use of computers in examining the precepts and advancing the practice of textual criticism. Dearing's webpage offers corrections to his work "Principles and Practice of Textual Criticism" and improved versions of programs he used to analyze the Catholic Epistles. Dearing's techniques in textual criticism have been applied to New Testament as well as secular textual traditions.

Death in Ancient Egypt
http://www-oi.uchicago.edu/OI/DEPT/RA/ABZU/DEATH.HTML

Sponsored by the Oriental Institute of the University of Chicago, this web page offers excellent background information on death in Ancient Egypt. Explanations of tomb scenes, supplies for the after-life, shabtis, parts of the personality, with an extensive list for further reading and links to relevant Internet resources make this an excellent resource for the lay reader.

The Deh Luran Archaeological Project
http://www.umma.lsa.umich.edu/Oldworld/Deh_Luran/Deh_Luran.html

This is a very complete presentation on the excavations at Deh Luran. Small images are linked to larger, higher resolution versions of the same subject. A complete bibliography of source materials used for this exhibit enhances the usefulness of this site.

De Imperatoribus Romanis: An Online Encyclopedia of Roman Emperors
http://www.salve.edu/~dimaiom/deimprom.html

Short bibliographical essays of all the Roman emperors with bibliographies, illustrations and footnotes. Not every emperor is yet listed but enough to make the site useful for basic research or casual browsing.

Deir el-Medina Database
http://www.leidenuniv.nl/nino/dmd/dmd.html

Two extensive bibliographies of publications concerning Deir el-Medina have been combined to form the Deir el-Medina database. The first, compiled by L.M.J. Zonhoven, covers the time period 1867-1980, and the second, compiled by B. Haring, covers the time period 1980-1990. The bibliographies are divided into twenty-six separate categories with cross-references for items that should be listed in more than one category. The Deir el-Medina site has provided extensive information on Egytian life during the construction and decoration of tombs during the New Kingdom and this database serves as an important access point to scholarly analysis of that information.

De Laicis (The Treatise on Civil Government) by St. Robert Bellarmine
http://www.jbi.hioslo.no/dominican/doctors/delaicis.htm

This is an anonymous English translation of De Laicis by St. Robert Bellarmine SJ (1542-1621).

De Re Militari Information Server
http.cc.ukans.edu/history/deremil/deremain.html

This is the homepage of the Association for the study of Classical and Medieval Military Matters. Following the link Workstation and then the link Library, one finds a delightful assortment of classical texts via links to a number of sites. Most of the classical material ranges from the expected Aeschylus and Caesar to Plato and Plutarch, but one also finds the Code of Hammurabi (trans. by L. W. King, from the eleventh edition of the Encylopedia Britannica). The breadth of this site is not adequately represented by its name, which implies far more focus on military resources than is in fact the case.

The Demotic Dictionary Project, Directory of Institutions and Scholars
http://www-oi.uchicago.edu/OI/PROJ/DEM/Demotic_Directory.html

A directory of institutions and scholars involved in Demotic Studies. In addition to the directory there are online forms for adding institutions and scholars to the listing. This is a useful resource for scholars attempting to locate colleagues or students seeking institutions offering work in demotic studies.

Demotic Dictionary Project, Sample Documents
http://www-oi.uchicago.edu/OI/PROJ/DEM/DDP_Sample_Docs.html

Samples of the source materials for the Chicago Demotic Dictionary Project. Includes a scanned image of P OI 10551 (a land transfer document) along with translation, transliteration and other information relating to this document. The dictionary authors should note this demonstration of the utility of an electronic version of the Demotic Dictionary.

Demotic Texts
http://www-oi.uchicago.edu/OI/DEPT/RA/ABZU/DEMOTIC_WWW.HTML

This is the definitive collection of links to materials on the Internet related to Demotic texts. The links are organized by type of text, on-line collections and archives, bibliographies, directories, articles and discussion lists. The logical starting place to evaluate what Demotic materials are available or to plan a contribution to the growing number of text and other resources presently available.

Department of Archaeology - University of Edinburgh
http://super3.arcl.ed.ac.uk/arch/homepage.html

More than simply a departmental webpage, this site offers current information on new WWW resources around the world, acts as a mirror for the Bonn Archaeological Software collection, and operates a bibliography database on archaeology.

Department of Archaeology, University of Haifa
http://research.haifa.ac.il/~archlgy/engframe.html

Mainly a departmental page for the Department of Archaeology at the University of Haifa but still under construction with the expectation that more resources will be added as the site develops. The site can be accessed through either English or Hebrew Web pages.

Department of Classics Rutgers University
http://classics.rutgers.edu/

The Classics department at Rutgers University is home to a number of innovative projects in the classics using the Web as a means of delivering traditional scholarly information and content. While noted elsewhere, commentaries on individual odes of Pindar and a short bibliography of Thucydides by Lowell Edmunds as well as a bibliographic guide to Vergil's Aeneid by Shirley Werner can be found here. These are only examples of the resources that are being produced by the classics department in its adaptation of modern technology to a traditional classics program.

Deus absconditus in Ezekiel's Prophecy
http://shemesh.scholar.emory.edu/scripts/SBL/ezekiel/tuell.html

A paper presented at the Society of Biblical Literature Seminar Theological Perspectives in the Book of Ezekiel by Dr. Steven S. Tuell, Randolph-Macon College.

Development of the NT Canon
http://shell5.ba.best.com/~gdavis/ntcanon/index.shtml

Based upon the works of Bruce Metzger and Wilhelm Schneemelcher this site contains a listing of works on: Early Christian Authorities, Apocryphal New Testament Writings, Cross Reference

Table: Writings and Authorities, Early Lists of the Books of the New Testament, The Bibles of Constantine, Map of Early Christianity, Closing the Canon in the West and Closing the Canon in the East. Links to English translations of cited ancient works are provided whenevere possible. A useful quick reference source as well as a model for a scholarly resource in the original languages.

Dharma Electronic File Archive
http://sunsite.unc.edu/dharma/defa.html

An electronic file archive maintained by DharmaNet International. Most notable is the collection of Buddhist journals available online, including Gassho, Sakyadhita: International Association of Buddhist Women, Bhavana Society Newsletter, Forest Sangha Newsletter, Insight, Inquiring Mind, and Blind Donkey. This site also offers links to other Internet resources of interest to Buddhist scholars.

The Dialogue of the Seraphic Virgin by St. Catherine of Siena
http://www.cs.pitt.edu/~planting/books/catherine/dialog/dialog.html

Translation by Algar Thorold, with English modernized by Harry Planting.

Didache
gopher://ccat.sas.upenn.edu:3333/00/Religious/ChurchWriters/ApostolicFathers/Didache

English translation of the Didache by J. B. Lightfoot.

Didaskalia - Ancient Theater Today
http://www.warwick.ac.uk/didaskalia/didaskalia.html

Both a journal and website, Didaskalia focuses on the performance of Greek and Roman drama, dance and music. Current and back issues of the journal are available at the website which includes resources such as an "Introduction to Ancient Theater" and "Theater of Dionysus Reconstructions."

The DigSite
http://www.scriptorium.org/TheDigSite

Breaking from the tradition of documenting excavations in reports published years, if not decades, after concluding a dig, this web site is documenting an archaeological dig currently underway in Wadi Natrun, Egypt. The excavation and Web site are sponsored by The Scriptorium: Center for Christian Antiquities. A Coptic monastery dating from 385 CE is the subject of this excavation. It does presently lack the detail associated with traditional excavation reports, but that shortfall is not attributable to the method chosen to disseminate information concerning the dig.

Diotima: Materials for the Study of Women & Gender in the Ancient World
http://www.uky.edu/ArtsSciences/Classics/gender.html

A collaborative effort between Ross Scaife (University of Kentucky) and Suzanne Bonefas (Miami University, Ohio) to share approaches and materials for those teaching courses about women and gender in the ancient world. This site has expanded rapidly since the first edition of this work and offers such resources as: Course Materials (Over 70 reading lists, bibliographies, study guides, including a searchable course database), Bibliography (listed by topics and also searchable), Art Collections (Web accessible images and museum collection); Anthology of Translated Texts (very extensive, includes texts approved by the Diotima translation editor (Diane Arnson Svarlien of Georgetown College) and links to other relevant texts on the WWW); Essays (links to essays, lectures and journal articles); Additional Scholarship on Politics and Theory (Feminism, Gay theory, cultural studies); and, Bibles, Related Texts, Other Sites (focused on texts relating to women and gender but includes general biblical resources where relevant). A model for combining scholarship and the technology of the WWW on in an area of academic study.

Directory of Historians of Ancient Law
http://www.abdn.ac.uk/~law113/rl/dir.htm

A directory of historians interested primarily in Roman law and the history of civilian (as opposed to common law) legal systems.

Directory of North American Egyptologists - 1995/1996
http://www-oi.uchicago.edu/OI/DEPT/RA/ABZU/EGDIR_INTRO.HTML

Another important resource for scholars working in the Ancient Near East, courtesy of Charles Jones and his colleagues at the Oriental Institute at the University of Chicago.

Discovering Hebrew
http://www.ort.org/ort/hebrew/start.htm

This is the first three lessons of a projected sixty covering Modern Hebrew. To display Hebrew, small GIF images are used for Hebrew letters. Lessons are available in analytic or interactive format.

Disjecta Membra in Araneo - Scattered Remains on the Web
http://www-oi.uchicago.edu/OI/DEPT/RA/ABZU/ARCETALK.HTML

Alexandra O'Brien outlines in this presentation the progress of the use of computers in the humanities and the beginnings of such use in Egyptology. She makes it clear that the new technology will assist scholars in their traditional tasks and solve some problems, such as joining fragments held in separate locations or mounted, that cannot be approached by traditional techniques. A very persuasive presentation that merits reading by scholars seeking to make a case for the use of computers in Egyptology (or other humanities fields as well).

Displaying Non-Roman Characters with a Graphical Web Browser
http://shemesh.scholar.emory.edu/scripts/TELA/TELA-foreign-chars.html

This document discusses various options for displaying non-Roman characters on a Web page. Written by James R. Adair, it is updated periodically, whenever new options arise.

Diyala Miscellaneous Objects Publication Project
http://www-oi.uchicago.edu/OI/PROJ/DIY/Diyala1.html

The Diyala Miscellaneous Objects Publication Project (Oriental Institute, University of Chicago) is an effort to publish a database of all the miscellaneous objects found as part of the Diyala excavations. Those excavations took place in four separate locations: Tell Asmar/ancient Eshnunna, Khafajah/ancient Tutub, Ishchali/ancient Neribtum(?), and Tell Agrab, and resulted in the Diyala regional archaeological sequence. Questions have arisen concerning that sequence that can be explored due to the careful record keeping of the original excavators and the use of modern computer databases.

Djoser Pyramid Comples at Saqqara
http://ccat.sas.upenn.edu/arth/zoser/zoser.html

This is an excellent presentation of information on the Step Pyramid Complex of Djoser. A clickable map of the Precinct of Djoser and its Step Pyramid as well as separate illustrations allow exploration of this important archaeological site. This site made possible by Holly Pittman and Jay Treat of University of Pennslyvania.

Documents of the Roman Catholic Church (American University)
http://listserv.american.edu:70/1/catholic/church/church.html

An excellent collection of documents relating to the Catholic Church arranged by categories. The main menu lists the following choices: Documents of the Council of Trent; Documents of the Second Vatican Council; Encyclicals and Other Papal Documents, Vatican Statements; U.S. Bishop Statements, and Writings of the Church Fathers/Doctors/Saints.

Documentation of Theological and Interdisciplinary Literature
http://starwww.uibk.ac.at/theologie/theologie-en.html

These databases from the School of Theology at University of Innsbruck illustrate the use of the Internet to provide access to traditional scholarly literature. The databases are Biblical Literature (Biblical Literature and Biblical Archaeology), Canon Law, Girard-Documentation, and Systematic and Fundamental Theology. Over 60,000 monographs, articles from collected works and articles from relevant journals are presently contained in these databases. The search interface is quite easy to use, and this will prove to be an important resource for scholars in these areas of study.

Dominican (Order of Preachers)
www-oslo.op.org/op/menu.htm

A generous listing of resources pertaining to the Catholic Church in general and the Dominican Order in particular. Available materials range from a history of the order to Dominican art and email addresses for Dominicans on the Internet. Also notes mirror sites in other geographic regions for some resources.

Dove Booksellers
http://www.dovebook.com/

Dove Booksellers supplies scholars working in Biblical and Ancient Near Eastern studies with both new and used books as well as computer software. Lists of new used book lists are regularly posted to this website. A mailing list for announcements of new or used book lists is maintained by Dove and can be subscribed to at this site.

Duke Data Bank of Documentary Papyri
http://www.perseus.tufts.edu/cgi-bin/txtfind?cit=DDP/0001

A service of the Perseus Project this interface allows searching for strings in the Duke Data Bank of Documentary Papyri (DDBDP). A very good example of collaboration between two sites on the WWW to offer a service that combines the unique talents found at differing locals.

Duke Papyrus Archive
http://odyssey.lib.duke.edu:80/papyrus

The Special Collections Library at Duke University has undertaken to provide electronic access to the largely unpublished Duke papyrus collection of papyri from ancient Egypt. There is a search interface that allows the searching of over 1,000 online catalogue records for the Duke papyrus collection and 200 images of and texts about Duke papyri arranged by selected topics. The usefulness of this site is enhanced by the provision of both basic and advanced information on papyri in general and their languages, along with the information noted above.

Dynamic Equivalence: A Method of Translation or a System of Hermeneutics?
http://www.mastersem.edu/journal/j1th2.htm

An essay by Robert L. Thomas, Professor of New Testament at the Master's Seminary addressing the use of dynamic equivalence in the practice of bible translation.

Early Church On-Line Encyclopedia Initiative (ECOLE)
http://www.evansville.edu/~ecoleweb

The Early Church On-Line Encyclopedia Initiative (ECOLE) was begun by Anthony F. Beavers (General Editor) to create an online encyclopedia of church history up to the Reformation. The major division of the site are: Documents (translations contributed to the project and links to other translations); Glossary (short essays on various topics); Articles (article length treatments of major figures and topics); Images (a very extensive set of links to images categorized by the subject of the image); and, Chronology (timeline with a geographical cross-index.).

Easton's Bible Dictionary
http://www.cs.pitt.edu/~planting/books/easton/ebd/ebd.html

A hypertext version of the Illustrated Bible Dictionary by M. G. Easton, Third Edition, published by Thomas Nelson, 1897. The illustrations are not reproduced in this edition.

Edinburgh Ras Shamra Project
http://www.ed.ac.uk/~ugarit/home.htm

This project offers both images of tablets from Ugarit and information on the Ugaritic language. Transliterations and translations accompany the texts at this site. Sponsored by the Hebrew and Old Testament Department, New College, at the University of Edinburgh, this effort combines traditional scholarship with the new tools offered by the Internet in a manner worthy of emulation.

Egeria and The Fourth Century Liturgy of Jerusalem
http://users.ox.ac.uk/~mikef/durham/egeria.html

A hypertext linking of the Latin text of Egeria's Journal of the Jerusalem Liturgical Year with a translation and commentary based upon that of Louis Duchesme in his Christian Worship (London, 1923). A select bibliography of works concerning this text is also available.

Egypt and the Ancient Near East: Web Resources for Young People and Teachers
http://www-oi.uchicago.edu/OI/DEPT/RA/ABZU/YOUTH_RESOURCES.HTML

Alexandra A. O'Brien has collected this vast array of Internet resources for school children and their teachers on Egypt and the Ancient Near East. The majority of these resources could be found by other means but this listing by Ms. O'Brien and its topical organization provides better access to these materials for both teachers and students. Link cover topics such as pyramids (many with clickable tour maps), artifacts, maps, mummies, museum resources, recommended reading lists and even cross-curricula lesson plans.

The Egypt Exploration Society
http://britac3.britac.ac.uk/institutes/egypt/index.html

The EES site offers information on membership in the society and its publications. Unfortunately, its Journal of the Egypt Exploration Society, one of the leading journals in Egyptology, has not yet appeared at this site.

Egypt Interactive
http://www.channel1.com/users/mansoorm/index.html

A site devoted to providing information about Egypt. The most notable feature is an annotated list of resources on Egypt on the Internet, covering both ancient and modern Egypt. This list is current and contains resources of interest to the scholar as well as the interested lay person.

The Egypt Page (UPENN)
http://www.sas.upenn.edu/African_Studies/Country_Specific/Egypt.html

This site offers links to a number of important sites concerned with ancient Egypt, as well as the origin of resources such as the Djoser Pyramid Complex at Saqqara.

Egyptian History Class: Resources for History of Ancient Egypt
http://www.library.nwu.edu/class/history/B94

This WWW page of the Schaffner Library (Northwestern University) was created to assist students enrolled in the History of Ancient Egypt course being taught by Peter Piccione. A course description, syllabus, and background essays on irrigation, Egyptian language and the status of women in ancient Egypt can all be found at this site. Of particular interest is the posting many of the visual aids and images utilized in the classroom lectures complete with descriptions. Review for examinations and the dissemination of information is certainly enhanced by the availability of these images.

Egyptian Collection (Archaeological Museum of Bologna)
http://www.comune.bologna.it/bologna/Musei/Archeologico/egitto_e.htm

A few images of some of the more than 3,500 items in the museum collection are posted for viewing at this site. Of greater interest, for instructional purposes, is the reconstruction of the Horemheb tomb in Memphis for virtual presentation.

Egyptian Flood Cycle Flowchart
http://www.uni.uiuc.edu/departments/social_studies/history/hyper_flow/eg_flood_map.html

This is an interesting presentation that traces the flood cycle of the Nile from the time of the Old Kingdom to the final decline of Ancient Egypt. Background information and colorful flow charts make this a very useful presentation on this important cycle in Egyptian life.

Egyptian Law, Bibliography
http://www.law.pitt.edu/hibbitts/egypt.htm

A useful bibliography on Ancient Egyptian law and legal practices prepared by Professor Bernard J. Hibbitts in for courses taught at the University of Pittsburgh School of Law.

Egyptian Mathematics
http://aleph0.clarku.edu/~djoyce/mathhist/egypt.html

A short treatment of Egyptian mathematics with a bibliography mainly centered on the Rhind papyrus.

The Egyptian Museum
http://www.idsc.gov.eg/culture/egy_mus.htm

The website of the Egyptian Museum primarily offers images of a few of the important artifacts held by the museum in its permanent collection. These images could be useful for a general audience interested in the type of items created by the ancient Egyptians. Unfortunately, only a very few items are shown on the website and the images are available in resolutions that make them inappropriate for scholarly study.

Egyptian Tomb of Menna
http://www.doc.mmu.ac.uk/RESEARCH/Menna/

This site has extensive information concerning the tomb of Menna, including a virtual reconstruction of the tomb as it existed at its discovery in 1916. Excellent images and maps of the tomb.

Egyptological Bibliography
http://www.kv5.com/html/bibliography.html

This bibliography is part of the Theban Mapping Project but merits separate mention from the parent project. Over 30,000 references to studies of ancient Egyptian history, culture and archaeology will ultimately be indexed at this site. A helpful listing of abbreviations used in Egyptological bibliographies begins the collection of references that is organized under by museums with Egyptological collections, Etyptology as a Discipline, the Natural Environment, Science and Medicine, Theban sites and the Valley of the Queens. Professional as well as amateur (in the classical sense) Egyptologists will find this resource worth visiting on a regular basis.

Egyptological Fieldwork Directory
http://131.211.68.206/ccer/FIELDW.HTML

This site offers a searchable WWW directory of Egyptological fieldwork information. The present entries do not reflect all of the fieldwork presently being conducted but do illustrate the usefulness of the basic idea and this site. If you are conducting or associated with Egyptological fieldwork, a visit to this site and a contribution of information would increase the value of this resource to all of your colleagues.

Egyptologica Vlaanderen VZW On-Line
http://www.netvision.be/egyptologica/e_home.htm

An interesting collection of resources relating to Egyptology including a selective bibliography, an introduction to hieroglyphics, a picture gallery and a selected list of other scholarly sites on Egytology. The site is well on its way to reaching its announced goal of being an "...on-line library with scientifically sound information on the Ancient Egyptian civilization."

Egyptologist
http://www.iglobal.net/pub/wagers/ousia/Egyptologist.html

An extremely comprehensive and up to date site with numerous links to all areas of interest to the amateur or professional Egyptologist. Well organized and a pleasure to browse.

Egyptology & Hittitology Sites
http://www.dnai.com/~junko/egypt.htm

This site has a very impressive collection of Internet accessible materials on Egyptology and Hittitology. As of its update on February 12, 1998, this site offered an alphabetical index to 187 separate links for Egytology and 20 links for Hittitology.

Egyptology at UCLA
http://www.humnet.ucla.edu/humnet/egyptology/index.html

The homepage for the UCLA department of Egyptology offers departmental information and links to ongoing projects at Thebes, Askut and Tombos.

Egyptology Resources
http://www.newton.cam.ac.uk/egypt

Nigel Strudwick maintains this WWW page, which was originated with the assistance of the Newton Institute in the University of Cambridge, to provide a source of Egyptological information on the World Wide Web. Most notable for its clear focus on Egyptology and extensive links to resources, the regular updating of announcements of interest and John Baines' list of email addresses for Egyptologists.

Eisenbrauns
http://www.eisenbrauns.com/

This is the Web presence for Eisenbrauns, one of the premier publishing and book distribution concerns in the areas of Ancient Near Eastern studies, archaeology, Egyptology and biblical studies. Information concerning used books, the current catalog, typesetting services and the publishing department can all be accessed at this site. Like its print catalog and ordering service, this website emphasizes service to the academic community, an Eisenbrauns tradition.

Electronic Antiquity: Communicating the Classics
ftp://ftp.utas.edu.au/departments/classics/antiquity/

Electronic Antiquity, edited by Peter Toohey and Ian Worthington, qualifies as one of the earliest electronic journals in the area of classical studies. Beginning with the first issue in June of 1993 and continuing to the present date, all the issues are available for viewing or downloading.

Electronic Bodhidharma
http://www.iijnet.or.jp/iriz/irizhtml/irizhome.htm

Information page for the Electronic Bodhidharma, which has sponsored the use of computers in the creation of Chinese and Japanese electronic text archives. This is one of the largest collections of Buddhist primary text materials on the Web. Many text files are available for downloading or for minimal cost ($10) for the Zen KnowledgeBase CD-ROM. Articles are also available on issues that arise when creating electronic versions of Chinese or Japanese texts.

The Electronic Buddhist Text Initiative
http://www.acmuller.gol.com/ebti.htm

The Electronic Buddhist Text Initiative is composed of representatives of academic institutions and Buddhist clerical organizations who are interested in the use of technology for the preservation and dissemination of Buddhist texts. This website has sections on Art, Archeology and Multimedia; Document Preservation; Text Input Projects/Canonic and Text Databases; CJK Characters/Codes; Dictionary Projects; On-line and Network Data; Teaching and Research; and, General Regional Reports.

Electronic Journal of Vedic Studies
http://www.shore.net/~india/ejvs

Homepage of the Electronic Journal of Vedic Studies, with information on submissions, current and back issues of the journal and links to other resources of interest. All articles are protected by copyright but with automatic permission for the author to publish elsewhere, a policy designed to promote rapid dissemination of information. A refereed journal led by Michael Witzel (Harvard University) as Editor-in-Chief and Enrica Garzilli (Harvard University) as Managing Editor. All inquiries should be sent to the editors, ejvs-list@husc.harvard.edu.

Electronic New Testament Manuscripts Project
http://www.entmp.org

James K. Tauber is leading this volunteer effort to place transcriptions and images of New Testament manuscripts on the Internet. The importance of this effort and the computer tools being developed as part of the project cannot be overstated. Scholars who work with manuscripts in other areas of study should emulate this model of cooperation and access.

Electronic Resources for Classicists: The Second Generation
http://www.tlg.uci.edu/~tlg/index/resources.html

Maria C. Pantelia maintains this web site which in the field of classical studies is without equal either in terms of coverage or organization. A partial listing of the table of contents for this site reveals listings for: databases, web projects and information servers, home pages of projects, electronic publications, bibliographic indexes, bibliographies, collections of images, course materials and e-text archives. This site is a demonstration that it is possible to impose order on the anarchy of the World Wide Web and provide a service to scholars and students in an entire field.

The Electronic Text Corpus of Sumerian Literature
http://www-etcsl.orient.ox.ac.uk

This is a very important project that merits the support of everyone working with any Ancient Near Eastern texts. This project is using SGML based encoding methods, which divorce content from presentation, to prepare an electronic text corpus of Sumerian literature. Unlike some projects, samples of the encoded texts and the methods behind those texts are being made readily available at this site. The use of SGML for creation of textual databases will allow researchers to more effectively search the encoded texts and will result in an electronic archive that will outlast the hardware and software used to create it.

Encyclopedia of the Orient
http://i-cias.com/e.o/index.htm

The Encyclopedia of the Orient is a very complete guide to Islam and its history since its inception to the present day. Geographic locations and cities, people, historical events and concepts are organized in alphabetical order for easy browsing or searching.

Enlil
http://anes235-1.ff.cuni.cz/home.htm

Enlil is the WWW server for the Institute of Ancient Near Eastern Studies in Prague. A variety of resources of interest to scholars in this area reside on this site or are represented by hypertext links. The archives of the Computers and Ancient Languages (CAAL) reside at this site, as does the Semitistic Circle in Prague. The usefulness of this home page is enhanced by the ability to search the HTML documents of this site by keyword.

Epigraphic Survey Reports
http://www-oi.uchicago.edu/OI/PROJ/EPI/Epigraphic.html

The web pages for the Epigraphic Survey by the Oriental Institute offer a general history of the survey, a bibliography of its publications and access to reports from the project. The project reports are known as the Chicago House Bulletins and contain information on current plans and activities.

Library of Ethiopian Texts
http://anes235-1.ff.cuni.cz/projects/semetic/ethiopian/intro.html

Michal Jerabek has made a number of texts originally written in Ge'ez available over the Internet. The texts are transcribed in accordance with the Unicode Desta Based Table v0.2. These texts include: The Book of Enoch; The Rest of the Words of Baruch; The Acension of Isaiah; The Testament of Adam, and The Wisdom of Solomon. Other scholars working in this field are invited to contribute texts for non-commercial distribution at this site. Details are available from the homepage of this project.

European Centre for Upper Mesopotamian Studies (ECUMS)
http://users.skynet.be/lebeau/index.htm

ECUMS is one of the partners in the excavations at Tell Beydar (Syria) and promotes interdisciplinary Upper Mesopotamian studies. This site offer access to further details concerning the Centre's ongoing activities and provides further contact information.

Evaluation of an Ancient Egyptian Mummy Using Spiral CT and 3-D Reconstructions: Interactive Display Using the World Wide Web
http://www.rad.rpslmc.edu/rsnamumie/rsnamumie.html

Based on a exhibit originally seen at the annual meeting of the Radiological Society of North American, November 30-December 5, 1997, this presentation provides both an introduction to computed tomography and its use in the evaluation of ancient Egyptian mummies. The viewer is allowed to tour the discoveries made by the use of this technique along with following links to other resources on radiology, archaeology and Egyptology. This project combines the use of both modern scientific and communication techniques to provide a broad audience with the results of this study. (Note this page contains numerous images and is best viewed over a high-speed connection.)

Evangelical Lutheran Church in America (ELCA)
http://www.elca.org

Denomination resource with extensive links to resources such as WWW pages for member churches and guides to preparing WWW pages.

Everson Gunn Teoranta
http://www.indigo.ie/egt/

A remarkable resource featuring information on Unicode proposals (ISO/IEC 10646), fonts for a variety of languages, European Localization Requirements (CEN/TC304), a listing of discussion lists for various languages, and other resources.

Excavations at Khorsabad
http://www-oi.uchicago.edu/OI/PROJ/KHO/Khorsabad_Ex.html

A history of the Oriental Institute's excavations at present day Khorsabad, Iraq, formerly the capital city of King Sargon II (721-705 BCE). Links to a reconstructed view and plan of the palace and city near the palace and a bibliography of the excavation.

Exploring Ancient World Cultures
http://eawc.evansville.edu/index.htm

A general introduction to ancient world cultures over the WWW designed for college freshmen. Eight cultures are included: the Near East, India, China, Egypt, Greece, Rome, the Islamic World, and Medieval Europe. While this site does not attempt to be a complete index to all resources on these areas on the WWW, it is organized in a way that will be easy to recommend to students beginning their study of ancient world cultures.

Exploring the Internet
http://silicon.montaigne.u-bordeaux.fr:8001/HTML/ONLINE/IE10/Nigel.html

Nigel Strudwick, whose contributions to Egyptology both on and off the Internet have been noted at several places in this work, authored this paper which he presented to the Informatique et Egyptologie meeting in Geneva. Written in 1994 it does not address the latest technological advances but does fairly state the advantages to be found in using electronic technology in Egyptology.

Facets of Religion: Virtual Library of Religions
http://www.biologie.uni-freiburg.de/~amueller/religion

Part of the WWW Virtual Library with main links to resources on Bahai, Buddhism, Christianity, Hinduism, Islam, Judaism, Sikhism, and Zoroastrianism. The main page also allows for keyword searches of all the lists.

Fachinformationen für das Sondersammelgebiet Ägyptologie
http://www.ub.uni-heidelberg.de/helios/fachinfo/fachref/aegypt/welcome.htm

This site offers an excellent collection of Egyptology resources found around the Web. Maintained by Dr. Eckhard Eichler, the links are divided into helpful subject areas and there is also a telnet link for consulting the library collection at the University of Heidelberg.

Faiyum Diary — Forgotten Expedition to a Lost World
http://www.nh.ultranet.com/~granger/FaiyumCover.html

An adaptation of a 250-page diary keep by Walter Granger during a 1907 expedition to the Faiyum of Egypt. The main focus of the journey was on paleontology and this journal will be of interest to scholars studying explorations of Egypt and its past.

Fallacies Intentional and Canonical: Metalogical Confusion about the Authority of Canonical Texts
ftp://ftp.lehigh.edu/pub/listserv/ioudaios-l/Articles/bhcanon

An attempt by Baruch Halpern to define the terms for debating the canonicity of texts rather than settling questions of canonicity. Productive debate requires a common set of definitions to avoid confusion on the subject of the debate, not to mention its proposed resolution. This paper, which originally appeared on Ioudaios-l, is a step in the right direction.

The Family Letters of Paniskos
http://www.lib.umich.edu/pap/snapshots/paniskos/paniskos

Images of letters written in the late third or early fourth century between Paniskos with Ploutogenia, his wife, and Aion, his brother, as well as of Ploutogenia with her mother Heliodora.

Bir Umm Fawakhir: Insights into Ancient Egyptian Mining
http://www.tms.org/pubs/journals/JOM/9703/Meyer-9703.html

This article is a study of Ancient Egyptian gold mining techniques based on evidence derived from excavations at Bir Umm Fawakhir. It appeared in print form in JOM, a publication of the Minerals, Metals & Materials Society, Volume 49, No. 3 (1997), pp. 64-68.

Fear of Offending: A Note on Educators, the Internet, and the Bible Browser
http://www.dlib.org/dlib/april97/04goerwitz.html

Richard Goerwitz's Bible Browser is a neural interface that allows exploration of the Bible over the Internet in ways not possible with print versions. This article by Goerwitz sets forth his rationale for the development of the Bible Browser and his plans for future development of this important software resource.

Finding God in Cyberspace: A Guide to Religious Studies Resources on the Internet
http://users.ox.ac.uk/~mikef/durham/gresham.html

As a starting point for finding scholarly religious resources on the Internet, this site includes links to electronic indices of print resources, job openings, theological library catalogs, publishers, electronic journals, and much more.

Focusing the Early Christian Writings and Their Social World
http://www.hivolda.no/asf/kkf/rel-stud.html

A very comprehensive collection of links to sites with materials relating to early Christian writing and the social world of early Christianity. While providing source materials to Web users is very important, sites that carefully organize resources into customary categories serve a useful purpose as well. This is particularly the case when the links are well maintained and new materials are added when they become available. This site deserves a bookmark from all students or scholars of early Christianity.

Fonts from Scholars Press
ftp://shemesh.scholar.emory.edu/pub/fonts

This directory contains several public domain fonts for Macintosh and Windows computers. Currently offered are Hebrew (SPTiberian), Greek (SPIonic), Syriac Estrangela (SPEdessa), Coptic (SPAchmim), and transliteration (SPAtlantis) fonts. These fonts are used on the pages of the electronic journal *TC: A Journal of Biblical Textual Criticism*, among other places.

Food in the Ancient World: Subsistence and Symbol
http://www-personal.umich.edu/~salcock/Foodc.html

Professor Sue Alcock has posted her syllabus for this course on classical civilization along with a listing of food related sites on the Internet. Even more useful to scholars in this area of study will be the selected bibliography located at this site.

The Fourth Book of the Christian Topography of Cosmas Indicopleustes
http://ccat.sas.upenn.edu/~awiesner/cosmas.html

A useful site with the text of the Fourth Book of the Christian Topography of Cosmas Indicopleustes in linked Greek (Winstedt) and English (McCrindles) text. Cosmas Indicopleustes argues against the spherical view of the world on the basis of postulates drawn from the bible.

Franciscan Archaeological Insitute
http://198.62.75.1/www1/ofm/fai/FAImain.html

The homepage for the Franciscan Archaeological Institute this site offers links leading to further information on the Institute's activities at Mt. Nebo, the Madaba Mosaic Map, the Machaerus Fortress, excavations at Umm el-Rasas, and information for volunteers wishing to join in their efforts.

Franciscan Web
http://listserv.american.edu/catholic/franciscan

Information and some online resources related to the Franciscan religious order.

Front Door of the Ancient Egyptian Language Listserve
http://www.rostau.demon.co.uk/AEgyptian-L/index.html

This is the homepage for the AEgyptian-l discussion list on all periods of ancient Egyptian language. Archives of the list are held at this site along with links to texts with hieroglyphics and translations such as: The Autobiography of Weni (6th Dynasty c. 2345-2181 BCE); Westcar Papyrus (Tale of Khufu and the magician); and The Teachings of Ptahhotep, to mention only a few of the texts available. All Egyptologists should contribute text and translations to increase the availability of modern translations for students of Egyptology.

The Funerary Chapel of Ka(i)pura, Saqqara, Egypt
http://www.learningsites.com/Kapure/Kapure_home.htm

A sample of images from a presentation developed for a traveling exhibit on Egypt by the University of Pennsylvania Museum of Archaeology and Anthropology. A 3D model of the chapel has been created by LEARNING SITES that permits a flyover and flythrough the chapel.

FUNET Archives
http://www.funet.fi/pub/doc/religion/christian

A source for biblical texts in several different editions-KJV, Darby, Weymouth, Webster, Young- as well as a number of other languages, including Chinese, Danish, English, Finnish, French,

German, Greek, Hebrew, Latin, Swahili, Swedish, Tagalog, and Turkish. Also has software and texts for most popular computer platforms and other textual materials. This is a mirror site for texts posted by the NJB (Not Just Bibles project).

Free Catholics Web
http://listserv.american.edu/catholic

Links to Web pages for the Franciscan, Dominican, Jesuit, Claretian and Order of St. Benedict religious orders. Includes a numbers of resources of general interest.

Gabriel
http://portico.bl.uk/gabriel/en/services.html

Gabriel is a very impressive collection of links to European National Libraries. The links are divided into Online Public Access Catalogues, National Bibliographies, National Union Catalogues, Indexes to Periodical Contents, Gopher and WWW services. Instructions are offered in a variety of languages but most commonly English, Deutsch, and Français. Young scholars would be well served to learn the more prominent library systems represented on this website.

Galen, On the Natural Faculties
gopher://gopher.vt.edu:10010/02/86/1

This site offers A. J. Brock's English translation of Galen's On the Natural Faculties.

German Palestinian Society
http://www.uni-wuppertal.de/inst/kiho/dpv/english/index.html

The homepage of the German Palestinian Society is available in English, French and German. Among its more notable features is a search engine covering the Zeitschrift des Deutschen Palästina-Vereins (ZDPV - Journal of the German Palestinian Society) from 1976 to 1997. The search interface allows searching for titles, authors, authors and titles of reviewed books, maps, figures, biblical or non-biblical citations as well as permitting limitation of searches by range of publication date or volume. Contributor guidelines for the ZDPV - Journal of the German Palestinian Society and the Abhandlungen des Deutschen Palästina-Vereins (ADPV - Papers of the German Palestinian Society) are available in MSWord 6.0 format. Prior volumes in the ADPV - Paper of the German Palestinian Society are listed at the website.

Giza Plateau Computer Model
http://www-oi.uchicago.edu/OI/DEPT/COMP/GIZ/MODEL/Giza_Model2.html

Dr. Mark Lehner is directly an effort at the Oriental Institute (University of Chicago) to construct a computer model of the Giza Plateau. The 3D model is based upon actual data drawn from published maps, survey, and excavation reports. To date models have been completed of the Khafre Mortuary Temple, Khafre Valley Temple, the Sphinx Temple; Menkaure Mortuary

Temple, Menkaure Valley Temple; the interior chambers of the Khafre and Menkaure pyramids, and the interior chambers and temples of the Queens' pyramids for both the Khafre and Menkaure pyramids. While the model is not open to the public there are some wireframe and shaded images of some of the structures for viewing at this site.

Giza Plateau Mapping Project Reports
http://www-oi.uchicago.edu/OI/PROJ/GIZ/Giza.html

Annual Reports from the Giza Plateau Mapping Project, 1991-92 and 1993-94, under the direction of Mark Lehner, Assistant Professor of Egyptian archaeology. Lehner has pioneered the use of computer graphics and remote sensing technology to construct a model of the ancient Giza Plateau and the Sphinx. The primary focus of this project is on the construction during the Old Kingdom of the Sphinx, the Great Pyramids and associated Old Kingdom structures in this area.

Glassmaking Discovered
http://www.pennynet.org/glmuseum/edglmak.htm

The Corning Museum of Glass offers a short history glassmaking with an anonymous translation of instructions for making glass from a cuneiform tablet.

Global Resources for Buddhist Studies
http://www.cac.psu.edu/jbe/resource.html

An excellent collection of links to resources for Buddhist Studies sponsored by the Journal of Buddhist Ethics, a refereed electronic. Sites are separated into WWW, gopher, ftp and newsgroups.

Glossary of terms relating to Judaism
http://philo.ucdavis.edu/Courses/RST23/gloss.html

A public domain glossary originally begun by Robert Kraft for use in his course Judaism, Christianity and Islam.

Gnomon Online
http://www.gnomon.ku-eichstaett.de/

The Heidelberg Epigraphische Datenbank offers access to a number of Latin inscriptions drawn from the volumes of L'Année Épigraphique. The underlying database software allows simple or relatively complex searching for particular words or phrases.

The Gospel of Thomas
http://www.epix.net/~miser17/Thomas.html

This is the primary site on the Web for scholars interested in the Gospel of Thomas. A translation of the Gospel of Thomas (Stephen Patterson and Marvin Meyer), a bibliography of the Gospel of Thomas (over 300 entries), reprints of articles from traditional journals on the Gospel of Thomas, translations of the Gospel of Thomas into a variety of languages and links to other sites on the Web can all be found here. There is also a section on the Q source question with a number of resources and links.

Graham, Geoffrey
http://pantheon.yale.edu/~sokar/index.html

Geoffrey Graham, currently an Egyptology graduate student at Yale, has made significant contributions to the use of the Internet in the study of Egyptology. As a regular participant on the AEgyptian-l language discussion list, founder of the EEF list for advanced discussions of all areas of Egyptology, and creator of several WWW accessible resources in Egyptology, Graham has set a high standard for all scholars pursuing careers in the Ancient Near East. Rather than only discuss ideas and exchange materials with small closed groups of specialists, Graham has encouraged broad interest in this area of study. Links on his site lead to the The Nefertum Chapel of Sety I at Abydos, Scenes A, B, C, D, E1, E2, F, with hieroglyphic text and translations.

Grammatical Aids for Learning Medieval Latin
http://kufacts.cc.ukans.edu/ftp/pub/history/Europe/Medieval/aids/latgramm.aid

Lynn Nelson created this grammatical reference list for use with Medieval Latin. It lists translations for different uses of several noun cases and the endings of regular nouns, adjectives, active verbs, and present participles. Due to the layout of the text, an ordinary word processor can be used to search for particular endings.

Great Hymn to the Aten from the Tomb of Aye at Amarna
http://www.rostau.demon.co.uk/Aye/index.html

Transcribed and scanned by Geofrey Graham. This text represents an important source of information on the religious reforms of Akenaten (Amenhotep IV) and the worship of the Aten and is also available in English translation. Earlier translations and interpretations of texts from this time period were partially responsible for Sigmund Freud's *Moses and Monotheism* and similar works that have now been discredited.

Greco-Roman Studies and the Social-Scientific Study of the Bible: A Classified Bibliography (1970-1994).
http://www.stolaf.edu/people/kchanson/classbib.html

K.C. Hanson has provided scholars with access to several extensive bibliographies of interest to scholars working in biblical or Ancient Near Eastern Studies. The individual bibliographies give some idea of the breath of information to be found at this site: (1) The Old Testament: The Social Sciences & Social Description; (2) Parallels and Connections Between the Hellenic, Semitic, and Anatolian Cultures (1658-1997); (3) Ritual & Ceremony in the Ancient Near East (1970-1996); (4) Ritual & Ceremony in the Greco-Roman World (1970-1996); and, Publications of Walter Burkert (1961-1997). Professor Hanson should be commended for making this important resource available to scholars outside his home institution.

Ein Gedi Archaeological Excavation
http://www.hartford.edu/greenberg/eingedi.html

The Hebrew University of Jerusalem and University of Hartford's Maurice Greenberg Center for Judaic Studies are the co-sponsors of this excavation which has yielded the first archaeological evidence connected to the Essenes. A summary of the site, excavation activity, photos from the excavations and course offerings for academic credit are the main offerings of this web site.

Greek Fonts
http://www.compulink.gr/Users/heraclit/howto.html

If you are weary of transliterated Greek on the WWW, this page may hold the solution to that problem. Free fonts are offered for MS-DOS (SVGA), Windows, Macintosh, Unix and Linux, along with information for using these fonts to view Greek on the Internet. This solution is not as versatile as entity references in true SGML, but it is available for present use while scholars work towards SGML encoded texts for display over the Internet. See also "Displaying Non-Latin Characters with a Graphical Web Browser," above.

Greek Language
http://matt.clas.canterbury.ac.nz

An excellent source for Hypercard stacks for students learning Greek or those teaching Greek. There are two stacks to accompany use of the JACT Cambridge textbook, Reading Greek, which offer drills and tests on most of the exercises and the vocabulary. An authoring system is included to allow the creation of new stacks or modifications to the existing ones. Stacks are also available on the Reading Greek vocabulary, Greek Verb Help and a hypertext commentary with reference grammar on the Plato sections of the JACT textbook, The Intellectual Revolution. (Please note that these files reside on a personal computer which will be down each day from 1:00 to 5:00 GMT for maintenance and ordinary usage.)

Greek Law, Bibliography
http://www.law.pitt.edu/hibbitts/greek.htm

A useful bibliography on Classical Greek law and legal practices prepared by Professor Bernard J. Hibbitts in for courses taught at the University of Pittsburgh School of Law.

Greek Mathematics
http://aleph0.clarku.edu/~djoyce/mathhist/greece.html

A subsection of the History of Mathematics homepage maintained by David E. Joyce of the Department of Mathematics and Computer Science, Clark University.

Greek New Testament
http://www.znet.com/~broman/gnt.html

This is a listing of editions of the Greek New Testament currently available in machine-readable format. Notes on the various manuscripts of the Greek New Testament, papers on textual criticism, and, fonts for proper display or printing of the text are also available at this site.

Greek New Testament
ftp://ftp.funet.fi/pub/doc/bible/texts/greek/

A Greek New Testament and the UBS version of the Greek New Testament are available at this site. Both are compressed using the Unix utilities tar and gzip.

Gregorian Chant
http://www.music.princeton.edu:80/chant_html

Peter Jeffery of the Music Department at Princeton University has collected links to the important resources on Gregorian Chants for this WWW homepage. Among other resources, there are links to a tutorial on Gregorian chants, the Thesaurus Musicarum Latinarum at Indiana University, which includes texts of medieval treatises on music theory, and a host of related religious resources of interest to scholars of Gregorian chants.

Gregory of Nyssa
http://www.ucc.uconn.edu/~das93006/nyssa.html

David A. Salomon, a Ph.D. candidate at the University of Connecticut maintains this site on Gregory of Nyssa. English translations by Br. Casimir McCambly, OCSO, an extensive bibliography and links to other related material on the Internet are available at this site.

Griffith Institute
http://www.ashmol.ox.ac.uk/Griffith.html

The Griffith Institute, a leader in Egyptology and Ancient Near Eastern studies at Oxford, was among the first such institutions to appear on the WWW. This homepage offers general information about the Institute and more specific information concerning the various resources, such as its archives of papers from scholars available at the Griffith Institute. Present and forthcoming titles from the Institute as well as recent accessions in Egyptology to the library are also present on the homepage. The catalogue for the library can be reached at http://www.lib.ox.ac.uk/olis (choose option 3, Ashmolean Library).

Guide to Early Church Documents
http://www.iclnet.org/pub/resources/christian-history.html

A hypertext document with pointers to Internet-accessible files relating to the early church, including canonical documents, creeds, the writings of the Apostolic Fathers and other historical texts relevant to church history. All of the links checked for this work pointed to English translations of the original documents, some attributed to translators and others not so attributed.

Guide to Latin Texts on the Internet
http://www.georgetown.edu/labyrinth/subjects/latin/latin.html

Part of the Labyrinth project at Georgetown University, this guide has pointers to Latin text databases on the Internet such as the MALIN archive at University of Kansas, articles on Latin texts and culture, reference tools, teaching resources and other resources. There is also a pointer to the Armarium Labyrinthi: Labyrinth Latin Bookcase, which has pointers to both Latin texts and translations available over the Internet.

Hadith Database
http://www.usc.edu/dept/MSA/reference/searchhadith.html

This website offers a searchable hadith database that supports some Boolean operators in queries. The collection holds the following texts: Sahih Bukhari (complete collection), Sahih Muslim (partial collection), Sunan Abu-Dawud (partial collection), and Malik's Muwatta (complete collection).

The Hadrianic Baths at Leptis Magna
http://archpropplan.auckland.ac.nz/People/Bill/hadrians_bath/hadrians_bath.html

A reconstruction of the Hadrianic Baths at Leptis Magna by computer model. The reconstruction is presented by use of computer generated images. In addition to placing this remarkable work on the Internet, Bill Rattenberry has made it all the more useful by the inclusion of extensive notes on the reconstruction process, the effect of the computer on the reconstruction process and a short bibliography of material on the baths themselves.

Hanson, K. C.
http://www.stolaf.edu/people/kchanson/

The homepage for K. C. Hanson, now of St. Olaf College, has an extensive series of materials some originating from Hanson or classified for easier access. These materials include photo galleries of Syria & Palestine, Greece & Rome, Mesopotamia, extensive classified bibliographies, classified WWW sites on the ancient world (240 sites), religion on the web (90 sites) and links to images of ancient documents on the web. Several of these items are of such significant that they have been treated separately in this work.

Harrassowitz
http://www.harrassowitz.de/

A web site offering access to library services offered by Harrassowitz.

Harvard Divinity School
http://www.harvard.edu/divinity_school/public_html

Course information for the divinity school and a link to the Andover-Harvard Theological Library.

Harvard Semitic Museum
http://fas-www.harvard.edu/~peabody/museum_semitic.html

This site offers primarily background and contact information for the Harvard Semitic Museum, with some images drawn from current exhibits. Hopefully this will be expanded along the lines of the Cobb Institute of Archaeology: Lahav DigMaster Digital Archaeology Archives to provide useful access to the extensive collections held by the museum.

The Hashemite Kingdom of Jordan: Sami Shalabi
http://www.mit.edu:8001/activities/jordanians/jordan

This site offers information on the country of Jordan, with an interesting series of links to additional information on its history. More images are being added, but at present there are links to images drawn from Petra, Jarash, Wadi Rum and Aqaba. (Look under the main menu topic "Tourism.")

Hatshepsut's Obelisk at Karnak
http://www.rostau.demon.co.uk/Hatshepsut/index.html

The hieroglyphic text of Hatshepsut's Obelisk at Karnak typeset by Al Berens. The text is separated into sections, one for each face on the obelisk, each with approximately 5-6 lines of hieroglyphics. A very good resource for practicing inscription reading.

Hatti
http://www.geocities.com/CollegePark/Union/3659/frame.html

Homepage for a group of French Hittology graduate studies which contains links to Haluka, a newsletter by the group as well as links to other useful information on the Hittites. Extracts from the newsletter are available in French but work is proceeding to make the abstracts available in English as well.

Hazor Excavations
http://unixware.mscc.huji.ac.il/~hatsor/hazor.html

Information for volunteers, a basic bibliography, excavation reports, a history of Hazor can all be found at this web site. A picture gallery is available and has some items that would be of interest to those using web sites for access to images of artifacts not readily available in most school libraries.

Hebrew: A Living Language
http://www.macom.co.il/hebrew/index.html

This is a guide to Hebrew as a spoken language. It is possible to view and hear, with the proper software and hardware, both traditional and contemporary phrases.

Hebrew Bible Bibliography
http://www.library.vanderbilt.edu/divinity/bibs/hebrewbi.html

The Divinity Library, Vanderbilt University short bibliography of the Hebrew Bible.

Hebrew Syntax Encoding Initiative
http://www.chass.utoronto.ca/~decaen/hsei/intro.html

The Hebrew Syntax Encoding Initiative is an effort to create a theory neutral encoding for Hebrew syntax. There are several working papers and a proof of concept text (Jonah) available at this site. Recommended for scholars strong in Hebrew syntax and modern linguistic theory.

The Reuben and Edith Hecht Museum - Haifa University
http://research.haifa.ac.il/hecht/index.html

This museum is build about a private collection donated by Reuben Hecht to Haifa University. There are approximately fourteen items drawn from this collection, which covers the time period between the Chalcolithic period and ends with the Talmudic Era, that are available for viewing as images.

Hellenistic Greek Linguistics Pages
http://www.entmp.org/HGrk/grammar/

James K. Tauber of the University of Western Australia is responsible for this WWW homepage on Hellenistic Greek linguistics. Details of the Reference Grammar Project and the archives of the Greek-Grammar mailing list as well as other links of interest can be found here. The Reference Grammar Project is an effort by the Greek Grammar Seminar of the Westar Institute to produce a successor the Blass-Debrunner-Funk grammar, A Greek Grammar of the New Testament and Other Early Christian Literature, University of Chicago, 1961.

Hermas
gopher://ccat.sas.upenn.edu:3333/00/Religious/ChurchWriters/ApostolicFathers/Hermas

The text of The Shepherd of Hermas, translated by J. B. Lightfoot. The notation at the head of the text notes that it has been adapted and modified by Athena Data Products, but there is no apparent specification of what adaptations and modifications were made.

The Heliand
http://kufacts.cc.ukans.edu/ftp/pub/history/Europe/Medieval/latintexts/heliand.txt

Latin text of Heliand, provided courtesy of James Marchand, University of Illinois at Urbana Champaign.

Heidelberg University Library
http://www.ub.uni-heidelberg.de/sonder/Welcome.html

A web interface with this important university library.

Hieroglyphica: Sign List - Liste des Signes - Zeichenliste
http://131.211.68.206/hiero/hiero.html

Hieroglyphs drawn from the book Hieroglyphica, by Nicolas Grimal, Jochen Hallof, and Dirk van der Plaswhich, and it lists all 4,700 signs available in the Extended Library, a hieroglyphic computer font for Glyph for Windows and MacScribe. Categories presently represented follow the categories found in Gardiner's Egyptian Grammar, such as "Man and his occupations," which has 707 small GIF images. A fast workstation link or a great deal of patience is required for viewing this helpful array of images. Ordering information for this important work and Proceedings of the IAE Computer Working Group are also available.

Hill Monastic Manuscript Library
http://www.csbsju.edu/hmml

Located at St. John's University, the Hill Monastic Manuscript Library is the home to microfilm copies of more than 25 million pages from nearly 90,000 volumes in libraries and archives of classical and medieval handwritten manuscripts. A few images of manuscripts are present at this site, but more important is the information concerning the efforts of the library to make its collection and indices available in electronic format. This site represents a fitting continuation of the tradition that preserved the manuscripts now represented in the microfilm collection of the Hill Monastic Manuscript Library.

Hindu-Christian Studies Bulletin
http://www.acusd.edu/theo/hcs-l/bulletin.html

Published by the Society for Hindu-Christian Studies, the Hindu-Christian Studies Bulletin includes articles, book reviews, reports on meetings that would be of interest to members of the society. This web site offers further information concerning the journal, including the tables of contents from new or recent issues but no substantive information from the journal.

Historical Christian Documents
http://www.realtime.net/~wdoud/fathers.html

A small collection of historical Christian documents, including Athanasius, Clement and Ignatius. The documents are available in anonymous English translations.

Historical-Critical Method in its Application to Statements Concerning Events in the Holy Scriptures
http://daniel.drew.edu/~ddoughty/hartlich.html

A very interesting re-appraisal of the historical-critical method as applied to Holy Scriptures. This article originally appeared as "Historisch-kritische Methode in ihrer Anwendung auf Geschehnisaussagen der Hl. Schrift," in ZThK 75 (1978), 467-484 and was translated for the Journal of Higher Criticism by Darrell J. Doughty.

The History of Herodotus
http://classics.mit.edu/Herodotus/history.html

The History of Herodotus as translated by George Rawlinson.

The History of Plumbing - Jerusalem
http://www.theplumber.com/jerus.html

This article outlines the history of plumbing in the city of Jerusalem. This article appeared in Plumbing & Mechanical Magazine, July 1989 and illustrates the importance of water in the history of the Near East.

HISTOS: The New Electronic Journal of Ancient Historiography
http://www.dur.ac.uk/Classics/histos/

A peer-reviewed journal of 'ancient historiography' that appears both on the WWW and in hard copy editions. Articles and notes, a guide for authors, reader's responses, and more information on HISTOS can be reached at this site. The articles and notes published in HISTOS demonstrate that peer-review is alive and operating well in the new electronic medium.

Hittite Home Page
http://www.asor.org/HITTITE/HittiteHP.html

This developing site is a resource for scholars interested in the study of the Hittites. Resources at this site include the Catalog of Hittite Texts, Hittite Literature in Translation, images of Hittite sites, as well as links to other sites.

Hittite Law Bibliography
http://www.law.pitt.edu/hibbitts/hitt.htm

A useful bibliography on Hittite law prepared by Bernard J. Hibbitts, University of Pittsburgh School of Law.

Hittite/Hurrian Mythology
http://pubpages.unh.edu/~cbsiren/hittite-ref.html

This site offers a summary of Hittite and Hurrian mythology from a variety of scholarly sources. While the presentation is apparently oriented towards the non-specialist, references are given for those wishing to pursue the information given in more detail.

The Holy See
http://www.vatican.va/

The Vatican website offers access to its materials in a variety of modern languages. Selections from the homepage include links to further information on the Holy Father, the Roman Curia, the Vatican Museum, Jubilee 2000 and News Services.

Homosexuality in History - A [Partially] Annotated Bibliography
http://www.qrd.org/qrd/culture/history.of.homosexuality

Paul Halsall has created this partially annotated bibliography of homosexuality in history.

Horn Archaeological Museum
http://www.andrews.edu/ARCHAEOLOGY/HORNMUS/A-INTRO.htm

The Horn Archaeological Museum at Andrews University is primarily concerned with conserving and exhibiting objects from ancient Biblical cultures. Information concerning the museum and its programs as well as archaeological activities at Andrews can be accessed from this site. Unfortunately, the site offers little access to items actually held in the museum's collections.

The House of Ptolemy
http://pw1.netcom.com/~aphilipp/index.html

An extremely complete web site focusing on Ptolemaic Egypt (331 to 30 BCE) that includes sites treating the subsequent Roman and Byzantine rule in Egypt. There are over 250 links to Ptolemaic resources, some 50 links to sites treating the Roman period and approximately 30 links concerning the Byzantine period. Resources are organized by topics and time periods and include sub-topics on various subjects. A very good starting place for anyone interested in any of these periods in Egyptian history.

Houses of Worship
http://www.housesofworship.net/

Sponsored by Ekklesia, Inc., a partnership of the American Bible Society, the Pittsburg Leadership Foundation, and OnTV Pittsburg, LP, Houses of Worship is an effort to provide a web presence for all Christian congregations in North America. Web pages are offered without charge and a good deal of effort has gone into making the Web more user friendly for non-technical users. At present over 13, 000 congregations can be found here making it a logical starting place for locating North American congregations. Houses of Worship is also working on the development of markup that will make web pages more useful, such as their <HOW_PRAYER> or <HOW_SCRIPTURE> elements that allow indexing of prayers or scriptural references in HTML pages. Recommended both for its content and efforts to expand use of the Web to the general population.

How Honorable! How Shameful! A Cultural Analysis of Matthew's Makarisms and Reproaches
http://www.stolaf.edu/people/kchanson/mak.html

An examination of Matt 5:3-12 and 23:13-36 in light of an honor/shame value system. K. C. Hanson argues for interpretations that take into account the social value system of the context of the text.

How To Research a Paper in Classics/Ancient History
http://web.idirect.com/~atrium/research.html

While part of the Atrium website listed separately, this guide by David Meadows to using both Web and traditional resources for researching a paper in the classics merits separate mention. Meadows' guide covers much of the same ground as traditional research paper guides but also demonstrates how to use both traditional sources and Web based resources to their best advantage. Advice is also given on proper citation practices and the need for careful proofreading. A guide that emphasizes all the traditional values of research and scholarship while recognizing that the tools used by scholars are changing rapidly.

Huet, Gérard
http://pauillac.inria.fr/~huet/SKT/indo.html

Gérard Huet is the author of an electronic Sanskrit to French dictionary that is currently in progress. He has made this resource available in postscript but hopes to make a browseable version available at some point in the future. Links are also available to his ongoing work on Tantric lore and a French translation of Henrich Zimmer's Kunstform und Yoga im indischen Kultbild.

Hugoye: Journal of Syriac Studies
http://www.acad.cua.edu/syrcom/Hugoye/index.html
European Mirror:
http://www.cl.cam.ac.uk/users/gk105/syrcom/Hugoye/index.html

A peer reviewed online journal dedicated to the study of the Syriac tradition. The first issue of this journal has appeared with articles such as: "The Baptismal Anointings According to the Anonymous Expositio Officiorum", "Ms Vat. Syr. 268 and the Revisional Development of the Harklean Margin", and "A Bibliographical Clavis to the Works of Jacob of Edessa". Hugoye is Hosted by the Catholic University of America, known for its *Review of Metaphysics* which should dispell any lingering doubts about scholarship on the Internet.

Humanities Computing at Oxford
http://www.ox.ac.uk/depts/humanities

This is a collection of all the links to the humanities computing efforts at Oxford University. Contains links to such efforts as the Centre for Humanities Computing, the Humbul Gateway (international resources for the humanities), projects undertaken by various departments at Oxford, and a variety of other important resources.

Hunterian Museum University of Glasgow
http://www.gla.ac.uk/Museum/HuntMus/egypt/mus.html

An interesting collection of images of Egyptian artifacts held by the Hunterian Museum at the University of Glasgow. Of particular note is that the images are all downloadable for off-Web viewing.

John C. and Susan L. Huntington Archive of Buddhist and Related Art
http://kaladarshan.arts.ohio-state.edu/

This is a very image-intensive site that can best be appreciated over a fast Web connection. The Huntington Archive, from which images are drawn for web delivery, contains almost 300,000 original color slides and black and white and color photographs of Asian art and architecture. The archive also contains the largest collection of images of the art and architecture of Nepal. An extensive guide is available detailing how art and architecture should be documented with photographic methods. It should be noted that the site uses the Dublin Core Metadata standard (a standard for data about resources that facilitates finding and classification of resources) and represents one of the best examples of use of the Web to provide access to important scholarly materials held in archives.

Hypertext Halacha
http://www.torah.org/learning/halacha/

The Hypertext Halacha brings a translation of the Shulchan Aruch and Mishna Berurah to the Web.

IDAP - International Directory Aegean Prehistorians
http://classics.lsa.umich.edu/IDAP.html

The latest version of the International Directory of Aegean Prehistorians is available for downloading from this site. There is a Word for Macintosh and Rich Text Format version of this document. This is very useful resource in this area, characteristic of the growing acceptance of computer technology in the field of classical studies.

Index to Sumerian Secondary Literature (ISSL)
http://ccat.sas.upenn.edu:80/psd/www/ISSL-form.html

This is the Web interface to the Index to Sumerian Secondary Literature. A very impressive search program that allows researchers to search this index for graphemes using a variety of separators, words in transliteration, boolean operators and regular expressions. The software for searching the database was written by Steve Tinney.

Ignatius: Bishop of Antioch in Syria
gopher://ccat.sas.upenn.edu:3333/11/Religious/ChurchWriters/ApostolicFathers

The CCAT archives at the University of Pennsylvania offer the following texts translated by J.B. Lightfoot of Ignatius, Bishop of Antioch in Syria to: Polycarp, the Ephesians, the Magnesians, the Philadelphians, the Romans, the Smyrneans the Trallians and the Martyrdom of Polycarp.

Images of Ancient Iran
http://Tehran.Stanford.EDU:80/Images/Ancient/ancient.html

A series of nine small GIF images that lead to larger images of the same scene or object. While nine images is inadequate for any ancient civilization, it is a useful repository of what is presented.

Images of Egypt (UPENN)
http://www.sas.upenn.edu/African_Studies/Egypt_GIFS/menu_Egypt.html

This is a collection of images of both scenery and Egyptian artifacts. The scenery images include the tombs in Luxor, the temple at Karnak and other prominent sites. Most of the object images are of items associated with King Tutankhamen, such as his burial mask.

Images of Orality and Literacy in Greek Iconography of the Fifth, Fourth and Third Centuries BCE
http://ccat.sas.upenn.edu/~awiesner/oralit.html

An interesting collection of images depicting the view of Greeks on the invention and use of writing. Some of the images are accompanied by commentary and the collection is enhanced by the inclusion of a bibliography of sources for the images, some of which address the issue of the rise of literacy in Ancient Greece.

The Imitation of Christ by Thomas Kempis
http://www.cs.pitt.edu/~planting/books/kempis/imitation/imitation.html

Part of the Christian Classics Ethereal Library and available in HTML, RTF, PDF, text and Hypercard formats. English translation by Aloyius Croft and Harold Bolton.

In the Steps of Tutankhamun
http://www.geocities.com/Athens/7171/romersteps.html

This site presents a report of the survey and mapping of the tomb of Ramesses XI in the Valley of the Kings. In addition to many fine photographs, there are extracts from the expedition diary of John Romer, the leader of this project. This is one important step to document tombs located in the Valley of the Kings, which are threatened by natural as well as other hazards.

The India Resources Page
http://www.clas.ufl.edu/users/gthursby/ind/index.htm

A general listing of resources on the WWW relating to India. Of particular interest to scholars will be the collection of links to academic libraries, research grant sources, current news sources, and online journals.

Indologist
http://www.iglobal.net/pub/wagers/ousia/Indologist.html

A comprehensive listing of Internet resource for the field of Indology. Maintained by Will Wagers, who also maintains a similar site for Egyptologists.

Indology Home Page
http://www.ucl.ac.uk/~ucgadkw/indology.html

Dominik Wujastyk, founder of the Indology discussion list, is the author of this WWW home page. Links to electronic journals, multilingual software, Indological publishers and bookshops and library catalogs are some of the valuable resources available from this site. Of particular note is the collection of links to Indic e-texts which includes those offered by the site and links to Rome University "La Sapienza" Sanskrit Text Archive, the Vienna E-Text Archives and other important sources of electronic versions of Indic texts.

Informationsblatt der deutschsprachigen Ägyptologie online
http://www.ub.uni-heidelberg.de/helios/fachinfo/fachref/aegypt/info/index.htm

An impressive collection of links to German-language sites dealing with Egyptology. From museums and libraries to universities, this site is the logical beginning place for any inquiry concerning German-language Egyptology resources.

Inscriptions from the Land of Israel
http://www.iath.virginia.edu/mls4n/home.html

A project to collect all inscriptions found in the Land of Israel that can be dated between the Hellenistic period (ca. 330 BCE) and the Persian conquest (614 CE). Only the inscriptions from Beth She'arim are available at present but that will expand as more materials are brought online. This project is notable not only for the scholarly content being made available over the WWW but also for its use of Unicode and SGML for the storing of the data records from this project. The chapter on SGML covers this topic more fully but the project's choice to use SGML will mean this data will be available for future generations of researchers instead of only the present project.

Institute for Christian Leadership
http://www.iclnet.org

While focusing on the popular and devotional aspects of Christianity, this site does offer a helpful guide to a wide variety of information sources on the Net that would be of interest to scholars. Current links to FTP sites, Gophers, World Wide Web sites, Bulletin Board systems, USENET groups and other resources are found at this site. Directories of software for common personal computers and denominational resources can also be found here.

Institute for Islamic-Judaic Studies
http://www.du.edu/~sward/institut.html

This is the homepage for the Institute of Islamic-Judaic Studies at University of Denver. Listings include calls for papers for upcoming conferences sponsored by the Institute and information on its publications.

Institut für Orientalische Archäologie und Kunst at Martin-Luther-Universität Halle-Wittenberg
http://mlucom6.urz.uni-halle.de/orientarch/contents.html

This site offers basic information on the Institut für Orientalische Archäologie und Kunst such as its staff and examination rules. Links are offered to projects sponsored by the Institute and other WWW sites of interest.

Institut für Papyrologie, Universität Heidelberg
http://www.uni-heidelberg.de/institute/fak8/papy/

Information on the faculty of the Institut für Papyrologie, University of Heidelberg, current projects and a useful directory of email addresses. This site includes the logs of the PAPY-L discussion list, which is mentioned below.

Institute for the Study of Languages and Cultures of Asia and Africa (ILCAA)
ftp://ftp.aa.tufs.ac.jp/pub/tool/TeX/languages/kannada/

The ILCAA at Tokyo University of Foreign Studies maintains this FTP server with files for implementing use of the Kannada script with TeX software. A perl script to convert files written in transliteration into the Kannada script is also available.

Institute of Archaeology: Andrews University
http://www.andrews.edu/ARCHAEOLOGY/ARCHFIEL/Intro.htm

Site report information on the ongoing excavations at Tell Hesban, Tell el-`Umeiri, Tel Gezer, and Tell Jalul as well as North American Sites. The most notable resource at this site is the 1997 report of operations at Tell Hesban which are directed at making the excavation more meaningful to non-specialists (tourists). Support from the general public is an increasing concern in an era of budgetary restraint and this report demonstrates that scholarship and public presentation of findings need not conflict.

Institute of Archaeology: The Hebrew University of Jerusalem
http://www2.huji.ac.il/~applbaum/archaeom.html

This homepage offers extensive information on the Institute of Archaeology and its resources. Links are available to some of the projects presently underway by staff members of the Institute such as: Sha'ar Hagolan 1998, Tel Rehov 1998, Tel Hazor, Tel Dor, Ein Gedi, Archaeology and GIS Project, and Computed Tomography and Archaeology.

The Institute of Archæology University of California, Los Angeles
http://www.ioa.ucla.edu/

The webpage of the Institute of Archaeology at University of California, Los Angeles, offers extensive information on its various programs, including forms for research proposals.

The Institute of Egyptian Art and Archaeology
http://www.memst.edu/egypt/main.html

The user can select from this homepage the option of taking a tour of Egyptian artifacts residing at the University of Memphis or learning more about the Institute of Egyptian Art and Archaeology. The artifacts on display include a statuette of Nedjemu (Old Kingdom, Dynasty V), a block statue of Nedjem (New Kingdom, Dynasty XIX, reign of Ramesses II), and the mummy of Iret-iruw (Ptolemaic Period). All of these images are accompanied by information that places them in abbreviated historical context.

Institute of Indology and Tamil Studies (IITS) University of Cologne, Germany
http://www.uni-koeln.de/phil-fak/indologie/index.e.html

Based at the University of Cologne, Germany, IITS offers a wide range of excellent resources for scholars working in Indology or Tamil studies. Available in English and German versions, these webpages offer access to the IITS-Font, a True Type font used to transliterate Sanskrit, Prakrit, Pali, Hindi, Marathi, Bengali, Dravidian languages, and tribal languages (like Toda or Alu Kurumba). A digital database offers an easy interface to: the Cologne Digital Sanskrit Lexicon, Cappellers Sanskrit-English Dictionary, the Tamil Text Thesaurus (TTT), the Online Tamil Lexicon (OTL), EMDEN Tamil-German Dictionary, the IITS Library Catalogues, the Tamilnadu Geographical Names Server, and Tamilnadu Tribes and other Minorities. Other resources include an Index of Translations of Ancient Tamil Sangam-Poetry, and the Lexicon of Iranian Languages. IITS also offers a listing of other academic materials on the WWW but should be noted primarily as a source (and example) of extremely useful material on Indology and Tamil studies.

The Institute of Microfilmed Hebrew Manuscripts
http://www2.huji.ac.il/~jnul/imhm/imhm.htm

Ben Gurion, then Prime Minister of Israel founded the Institute of Microfilmed Hebrew Manuscripts, in 1950. The Institute now possesses copies of more than 90% of known Hebrew manuscripts on over 60,000 reels of microfilm. This site offers a history of the Institute, bibliographic information for works listing microfilms of manuscripts held by the Institute, a helpful guide to the card entries for the collection distributed on microfiche (very helpful), and, reproduction permission forms for the various libraries and collections that hold the originals of the manuscripts. The search for Hebrew manuscripts continues but has been hampered by a lack of funding to publicize the search and to reach small collections, those in private hands and to find manuscripts used in the binding of other works. Scholars and librarians should notify the Institute if they discover Hebrew manuscripts in bindings of other works or small or private collections that are not currently contained in this collection.

International Association for Coptic Studies
http://RmCisadu.let.uniroma1.it/~iacs/

The International Association for Coptic Studies site is a very useful collection of information for both scholars and students of Coptic Studies. The site has lists of Coptologists, links to recommended Coptic Studies sites and IACS Newsletters online. Of interest to both scholars and students will be the listing of courses on Coptic language, literature, art, archaeology, or theology. Future additions to the site include the contents of recently published journals and biographies of Coptologists.

International Council on Monuments and Sites (ICOMOS)
http://nickerson.icomos.org/canada

Home page of ICOMOS Canada, an organization devoted to the preservation of the worlds built cultural heritage. ICOMOS also publishes an online Bulletin, which documents the work of the organization. Articles on the preservation of St. George's Church in Halifax and on the conservation problems of the walled city of Nicosia, Cyprus, are included, as is the full text of the Oaxaca Declaration, a statement concerning cultural pluralism and indigenous populations drafted at a meeting of the International Seminar on Education, Work, and Cultural Pluralism convened by UNESCO.

International Directory of Aegean Prehistorians
http://classics.lsa.umich.edu/IDAP.html

The homepage for the International Directory of Aegean Prehistorians offers an electronic version of the 1995 directory in two separate formats for downloading. A database containing all the information contained in the downloadable versions of the directory can be searched at this site. The preface to the 1995 edition of the directory can be read at this location.

International Dunhuang Project (IDP)
http://www.bl.uk/collections/oriental/dunhuang.html

The IDP is the focal point for efforts to study and preserve manuscripts and printed documents from Dunhuang and other Central Asian sites. Based at the British Library the project is creating a database of all known Dunhuang manuscripts from various collections and investigating the problems of cataloging and delivering images of these manuscripts. The database should be available by the summer of 1998. A newsletter for the IDP can also be read online at the website.

International Journal of Hindu Studies
http://web.clas.ufl.edu/users/gthursby/ijhs/

The International Journal of Hindu Studies is a new journal focusing on Hindu studies. A peer reviewed journal that appears in print, IJHS has made the tables of contents and abstracts of articles available on the Internet. Information concerning submissions to the journal and other administrative information is available at this web site.

International Journal of Nautical Archaeology
http://www.hbuk.co.uk/ap/journals/na/

The International Journal of Nautical Archaeology is a traditional print journal that offers information for prospective authors and subscribers on its website. The journal covers all areas of nautical archaeological research. The table of contents for the most recent issue with abstracts can be accessed from this page.

International Journal of Tantric Studies
http://www.shore.net/~ijtslist

A journal devoted to Tantric Studies in Sanskrit, with particular attention to the Trika schools of Kashmir. The journal holds copyright on published articles but with automatic permission for the author to publish elsewhere at a later time. This journal provides an interesting resolution to the supposed conflict between rapid dissemination of information and copyright issues and one that deserves both study and emulation. This is the companion WWW site to the electronic journal listed under mailing lists and has both current and back issues of the journal, information on how to submit papers and other information of interest to those involved in Tantric studies.

International Organization for Targumic Study
http://www.uwyo.edu/a&s/relstds/ts/iots.htm

A listing of papers presented at its organizational meeting in the summer of 1995 and contact information for the IOTS can be found at this site. A link to the homepage of the Newsletter for Targumic & Cognate Studies (see listing below) provides the more interesting information at this site.

The International Papyrological Photographic Archive
http://www.usask.ca/classics/paparch.html

The International Papyrological Photographic Archive, at the University of Saskatchewan, has turned to the Web to make a comprehensive listing of its holdings available to the larger community of scholars. The Archive is composed of photographic copies of papyri from the Cairo Museum in Egypt, the Bodleian Library and Birmingham University in England, and the University of Aberdeen in Scotland. One problem being addressed by the archive is the difficulties caused by papyri having several common names that may not correspond to its name as held by the archive.

Internet Archaeology
http://intarch.ac.uk/

Access to the first four issue of Internet Archaeology is free but requires registration for full access. Internet Archaeology publishes the results of archaeological research such as photographs, data, drawings and interpretations. It will also publish data sets and programs for use with data sets.

Internet Classics Archive
http://classics.mit.edu/index.html

Based at MIT, the Internet Classics Archive has since 1994 made classical works available in English translation. The collection of 440 works of Greek and Roman authors can be browsed or searched, with links leading to additional materials on an author or work.

The Internet Public Library
http://readroom.ipl.org/bin/ipl/ipl.books-idx.pl?type=deweystem&q1=220

The Internet Public Library is an effort to collect links to texts on the Internet and to organize those links according to the Dewey Decimal classification system. Following the link listed above will take the user to the listing of texts for the subject area of religion under the Dewey Decimal system.

Internet Sites about Ancient Egyptian Women
http://php.indiana.edu/~ajgillen/Ewomen.html

A potentially useful collection of links to Internet sites focusing on women in Ancient Egypt. Unfortunately it has not been updated since early 1997 and does not represent the breath of material currently available on the Internet concerning this topic.

Interpreting Ancient Manuscripts
http://www.stg.brown.edu/projects/mss/overview.html

The Interpreting Ancient Manuscripts site is an adaptation of an original Hypercard stack developed at Brown University focusing on ancient manuscripts on which current versions of the New Testament are based. More than fifty images of original manuscripts are reproduced in this introduction to the process of textual criticism. Introductory information on materials, writing formats and other issues germane to textual criticism are covered in this online overview of ancient manuscripts and their interpretation. This site takes an important first step in bringing textual criticism and its evidence (manuscripts) onto the Internet.

Interpretive Implications of Using Bible-Search Software for New Testament Grammatical Analysis
http://www.chorus.cycor.ca/hahne/ntgram.html

An important paper that should be required reading for everyone interested in the encoding or computer-assisted analysis of Biblical texts. Harry Hahne demonstrates the effect of grammatical tags, errors in tagging and program limitations on the results of the use of Bible search software. All of these factors can lead to serious errors in the results of computer assisted searches and the conclusions based thereon. This paper does not caution against the use of computers for Biblical analysis, but argues that such use must be with an awareness of the limitations of the tagged text and the program in question.

The Intertexture of Divine Presence and Absence in the Book of Ezekiel
http://shemesh.scholar.emory.edu/scripts/SBL/ezekiel/allen.html

A paper presented by Dr. Leslie C. Allen, Fuller Theological Seminary at the Society of Biblical Literature Seminar Theological Perspectives in the Book of Ezekiel. This seminar has taken an important first step to make the papers from the seminar available to a larger audience of scholars over the World Wide Web.

Introduction to Ancient Egypt
http://www-oi.uchicago.edu/OI/COURSES/EGYPT101/egyptpub.html

This web site is the home for an adult education course on the history and culture of Ancient Egypt being offered over the Internet by the Education Program of the Oriental Institute Museum. A restricted web site will offer students access to: "detailed syllabus, bibliographies, lists of weekly reading assignments, chronologies, a detailed king-list of ancient Egypt, informative essays—as the instructor's bi-weekly lectures, on-line readings from our exclusive Web Library, translations of ancient inscriptions, a multitude of original and breath-taking color graphics, including photographs, maps, charts, and line illustrations." A closed discussion list will also be available for students to communicate with each other and the instructor. It is hoped that a positive experience with this innovative offering will lead the Oriental Institute to offer graduate classes in Ancient Near Eastern languages and similar topics that can be delivered over the Internet.

Introduction to Judaism
http://pubweb.ucdavis.edu/Documents/RST23/infordir.html

Information for the Introduction to Judaism course taught by Bruce Rosenstock of the University of California, Davis. Includes a glossary of terms related to Judaism, bibliographies and links to other sources of information on the Internet.

An Introduction to Latin Epic
http://www.sjc.ox.ac.uk/users/gorney/

A very useful site for an introduction to Latin Epic with information on many of the works and authors encountered in the study of Latin Epic. Short bibliographies are included where appropriate, making this an excellent resource for beginning research on any of the authors or works listed at this site.

Ioudaios
http://listserv.lehigh.edu/lists/ioudaios-l/Articles.html or
ftp://ftp.lehigh.edu/pub/listserv/ioudaios-l

Articles previously appearing on the IOUDAIOS list indexed by author for retrieval. If you cannot retrieve the articles via the WWW, use the second address to access the files by FTP.

Ioudaios Review
http://www.lehigh.edu/lists/ioudaios-review or
ftp://ftp.lehigh.edu/pub/listserv/ioudaios-review

The WWW homepage of the IOUDAIOS Review, a companion to the discussion group IOUDAIOS-L, which focuses on reviews of materials of interest to scholars of early Judaism and related fields. Ioudaios reviews are indexed by author, reviewer, and title, and there is a bibliographic index. It should be noted that efforts such as this one provide more timely information than print bound reviews that appear many months, if not years, after the reviewed materials are published. If you cannot retrieve the reviews via the WWW, use the second address to access the files by FTP.

Ioudaios-L Basic Bibliography
http://ccat.sas.upenn.edu/ioudaios/biblio/basic.html

An excellent resource for those interested in or teaching courses concerned with Judaism in the Greco-Roman period. To assist in the selection of materials from this bibliography the entries have been coded to indicate those appropriate for students with no background in the subject up to graduate students who are pursuing studies in this area.

Ioudaios-L Discussion List
http://ccat.sas.upenn.edu/ioudaios/

Ioudais-L is an email discussion list focusing on the discussion of Judaism in the Greco-Roman world. This website serves as an information center for the discussion list, containing archives of recent messages sorted by thread, date, subject, author, along with useful bibliographies and biographies of list members. For those new to email discussion lists or who have simply forgotten a necessary command there is a guide to commands for the discussion list.

Iranshahr
http://weber.u.washington.edu/~iranshar

A WWW site by the Middle East Center at the University of Washington. Provides general information on Iran and links to sites covering both the Middle East and Iran in particular.

IRIZ: Zen Buddhism
http://www.iijnet.or.jp/iriz/irizhtml/irizhome.htm

This is the homepage of the International Research Institute for Zen Buddhism at Hanazono University, Kyoto, Japan. As part of the Zen KnowledgeBase project directed by Urs App, this site offers information on over seventy Zen text files in JIS and Big-5 as well as a variety of tools for the creation and analysis of electronic texts. Fonts, articles on the creation of electronic texts (drawn from the journal Electronic Bodhidharma), programs for JIS/Big5 and Big5/JIS code conversion on both Mac and DOS, concordance tools and annotated bibliographies, including Urs App's Annotated Bibliography of Reference Works for Chan Studies and Yanagida Seizan's Annotated Bibliography of Chan Texts (Zenseki kaidai), can also be found at this site.

Islamic Architecture
http://www.anglia.ac.uk/~trochford

Thomas Rochford, the head of Computer Services at Anglia Polytechnic University, Cambridge, is responsible for making this study of Islamic architecture in Isfahan available on the WWW. The city, one of ten designated by UNESCO as a universal heritage, contains Islamic architectural styles dating from the 11th century CE to the 19th. Images accessible from this site were made by Rochford and his wife and may be freely used for academic purposes with proper acknowledgment. The images are organized into categories, which include mosques and shrines, minarets, palaces and bridges, and other sites of interest. A short bibliography on Islamic architecture is also found at this site.

Israel Antiquities Authority
http://www.israntique.org.il/

This web site has current information on the activities of the Israel Antiquities Authority. Its listing of contact information for the various departments and sections of the Authority will be helpful to scholars contacting the Authority.

Israel: Information Servers
http://www.ac.il

This is a central access point to most of the Internet Servers (WWW/Gopher/FTP) that are located in Israel. Notable not only for its extensive listings of servers, it also provides support for the use of Hebrew in a WWW environment and a clickable map of some of the servers listed. An excellent starting place for resources known to be located in Israel but for which the exact address is unknown. Listings for servers are divided into several categories, academic vs. non-academic, by subject and by region, to assist in the location of a particular server.

Israel Information Service
http://www.israel.org or gopher://israel-info.gov.il

The Information Division of the Israeli Foreign Ministry sponsors this set of resources on Israel. Of particular interest is the information on archaeological sites located in Israel, the text and images of which were prepared by Richard T. Nowitz. This overview of sites includes such areas as the Judean Foothills, the Judean Desert and the Negev, The Mediterranean Coast, the Galilee and the Golan, and Jerusalem. While such presentations lack the number of images associated with serious study of an archaeological site, they are most useful for survey or overview courses.

Israel Museum, Jerusalem
http://www.imj.org.il/

The Israel Museum website offers information concerning its own collections and links to other information that will be of interest to the scholar or lay visitor. Of particular interest is its page that organizes archaeological information beginning with the Old Stone Age (Lower Paleolithic) and ending with the Late Islamic Period.

Isaeli Law, Bibliography
http://www.law.pitt.edu/hibbitts/isr.htm

A useful bibliography on law in Ancient Israel and legal practices prepared by Professor Bernard J. Hibbitts in for courses taught at the University of Pittsburgh School of Law.

Izmir Excavations and Research Project (IRERP)
http://www.geocities.com/Athens/Forum/8635/irerp.html

Information on excavations at Liman Tepe, Bakla Tepe, and Panaztepe, three sites in the Izmir Region of Turkey is available at this site. Background information is currently available but preliminary results from the excavations will also be placed on the WWW. Evidence of occupancy of one or more if these sites ranges from the Chalcolithic period to the 5th century CE.

Jamieson, Robert, A. R. Fausset and David Brown Commentary Critical and Explanatory on the Whole Bible (1871)
http://ccel.wheaton.edu/j/jfb/jfb/JFB00.htm

Part of the Christian Classics Ethereal Library based at Wheaton College this older commentary is now available over the Internet. While the age of a work is not a reliable guide to its usefulness, witness the continued study and citation of the Summa Theologica in both Latin and translation, most 18th and 19th century bible commentaries are of little present relevance in biblical studies. Advances in archaeology, Hebrew and Greek lexicography and linguistics as well as textual criticism have rendered such works unsuitable for both the lay and academic reader.

The Jebel Hamrat Fidan Project
http://weber.ucsd.edu/Depts/Anthro/classes/tlevy/Fidan/Fidan01.html

This project is a study in the social context of early metallurgy in the Jebel Hamrat Fidan in southern Jordan. The project will use "copper metallurgy as a lens for examining social change through time in the southern Levant...." An interesting project that bears watching as more information is made available from both excavations and surveys in this region.

Jerusalem 3000: Three Millennia of History
http://www.usm.maine.edu/~maps/exhibit1/

An eminently useable and interesting site on the history of the city of Jerusalem. Notes that set each in its historical context accompany maps and images of Jerusalem. The presentation is marred only by copyright restrictions that prohibited the inclusion of some images into this web version of the catalog.

A Jesuit's Jesuit Home Page
http://maple.lemoyne.edu/~bucko/jesuit.html

Raymond Bucko, S.J., at Le Moyne College, has assembled an interesting collection of links to a variety of resources relating to the Jesuit order in particular and the Catholic Church in general. Links are provided to resources concerning Jesuit texts, history, colleges and universities, personal Jesuit home pages, and other religious orders, to list only some of the subject areas covered by this page.

Jesuits and the Sciences, 1600-1995
http://www.luc.edu/libraries/science/jesuits/index.html

This presentation includes images of rare scientific works from the Cudahy Collection of Jesuitica at Loyola University of Chicago. It is significant both for its use of WWW technology in the delivery of this information and for making important resources concerning the Society of Jesus more widely available.

Jewish Bible Association
http://www.jewishbible.org/

The Jewish Bible Association website offers a variety of resources for those interested in the Jewish Bible. A twenty-four year index to the Jewish Bible Quarterly (JBQ), JBQ Weekly Bible Quizzes, and other information are readily accessible at this site.

Jewish Prayer Bibliography
http://newark.rutgers.edu:80/~zahavy/biblio.html

This site offers a bibliography on Jewish prayer from Tzvee Zahavy's work *Studies in Jewish Prayer*.

Jewish Studies Judaica eJournal
http://shamash.org/~ajhyman/jsjej.html

Home page for the Jewish Studies Judaica eJournal, which is sponsored by the Shamash Project of the New York State Educational Research Network and the Humanities On-Line Project of the University of Illinois at Chicago. Back issues of the journal are available for browsing as well as links to other resources for the academic study of Judaism. Both the journal and this site are excellent resources for anyone working in the field of Jewish Studies.

Jewish Theological Seminary of America
http://www.jtsa.edu

A well constructed site with numerous links to further information on the Jewish Theological Seminary of America and its departments. It also has links to other sites and institutions of interest to those engaged in Judaic studies. A site to visit on a regular basis as it originates more resources and provides links to new resources offered by others. Of particular note is access to the Jewish Theological Seminary of American library through a web interface.

Josephus, Flavius
http://wesley.nnc.edu/josephus/

The complete works of Flavius Josephus, translated by William Whiston, available for online viewing or downloading.

Journal of Semitics
http://www.unisa.ac.za/dept/press/onjourn.html

Titles and abstracts for articles appearing in volumes 6 (1994) and 7 (1995) of the Journal of Semitics, as well as several other journals from the University of South Africa.

Journal of the British School of Archaeology in Jerusalem and the British Institute at Amman for Archaeology and History
http://www.art.man.ac.uk/arthist/LEVANT.HTM

The index for volumes I-XXVIII and abstracts for articles published in 1966-1996 in the Journal of the British School of Archaeology in Jerusalem and the British Institute at Amman for Archaeology and History are available at this site.

Journal of Buddhist Ethics
http://www.cac.psu.edu/jbe/jbe.html

One of the new electronic journals that has all the scholarly attributes-blind peer review, editors and an editorial board-of a traditional print journal, without the delays, costs and vagaries of delivery associated with traditional journals. The Journal of Buddhist Ethics is devoted entirely to Buddhist ethics and is edited by Damien Keown, University of London (Goldsmiths College) and Charles S. Prebish, Pennsylvania State University.

Journal of Hebrew Scriptures
http://www.ualberta.ca/ARTS/JHS/jhs.html

The Journal of Hebrew Scriptures is an electronic, refereed academic journal focusing on the Hebrew Scriptures. Articles published to date include: Bernon Lee, "A Specific Application of the Proverb in Ecclesiastes 1:15."; Philip R Davies, "Loose Canons. Reflections on the Formation of the Hebrew Bible."; Michael V. Fox, "What Happens in Qohelet 4:13-16."; Caetano Minette de Tillesse (Fortaleza, Brazil), "The Conquest of Power: Analysis of David and Solomon's Accession Histories."; Cynthia L. Miller, Kenneth M. Craig Jr. and Raymond F. Person Jr., "Conversation Analysis and the Book of Jonah: A Conversation."; Helmut Utzchneider, "Text - Reader -Author. Towards a Theory of Exegesis: Some European Views." The articles are available in HTML, MS Word (Mac or PC) and PDF formats.

Journal of Near Eastern Studies
http://www.journals.uchicago.edu/JNES/home.html

The homepage for the Journal of Near Eastern Studies offers basic information concerning the journal, a listing of tables of contents and instructions for authors.

The Journal of Northwest Semitic Languages
http://www.sun.ac.za/local/academic/onos/jnsl/jnslhome.html

At this site you can review the rules for submission of articles, obtain subscription information and see the table of contents with indexed abstracts and book reviews beginning with volume 21, number 1. Unfortunately, at this point, there are no full text articles available and no plans mentioned to make any such texts available in the future.

Journal of Religious Ethics
gopher://gopher.lib.virginia.edu:70/11/alpha/jre

Basic information concerning the *Journal of Religious Ethics*, its editorial board and submission practices are available on this gopher server. A searchable cumulative index to the journal and a cumulative index as text are also present.

Journal of Roman Archaeology
http://www-personal.umich.edu/~pfoss/jra/JRA_Home.html

The table of contents for the *Journal of Roman Archaeology* can be browsed or searched for authors, articles or book reviews in all annual issues or supplements for JRA. Selected articles or reviews are available in full, along with editorial guidelines for submitting articles.

The Journal of Semitic Studies
http://www.oup.co.uk/jnls/list/semitj/

Web site for the *Journal of Semitic Studies* published by Oxford University Press. Internet access to the contents of the journal is possible only with a paid institutional subscription. An institutional subscription is required for viewing more than the table of contents. Basic information concerning journal policies is also available without charge.

Journal of South Asia Women Studies
http://www1.shore.net/~india/jsaws/

The Journal of South Asia Women Studies is a peer-reviewed electronic journal that publishes articles, abstracts and news on all subjects relating to women in South Asia. All of its contents are available on the WWW and authors retain the right to publish their work in other forums. The board of editors reflects the level of international participation in the editorial process made possible by the growth of the WWW.

Journal of the Association of Graduates in Near Eastern Studies
http://ishi.lib.berkeley.edu/~hsp/JAGNES/

Produced by the Association of Graduates in Near Eastern Studies, JAGNES is composed of papers submitted in a series of colloquia sponsored by this group. The journal does not appear available online, a rather odd circumstance for a graduate school publication when many professional journals are moving in the direction of electronic access, at least for non-current issues. A series of links to other resources reflects the broad nature of Near Eastern Studies and is organized by subject matter.

Judaica Archival Project
http://www.archival.org/

The Judaica Archival Project is an effort to create a virtual library for Judaic Studies. Since 1990 the project has preserved over 500,000 pages of materials in Rabbinic from the library at Jewish National and University Library. A free catalog lists all the works held by the collection and is updated frequently. Reproductions are available in microfiche, paper or digital format for any of the works listed in the catalog.

Judaism and Jewish Resources
http://shamash.org/trb/judaism.html

If not the most complete, certainly one of the most complete listings of both links to other sites and original source material related to Judaism and Jewish Studies. Since it does cover a wide range of interest, it is not as focused as the Jewish Theological Seminary of America WWW site, but it is well organized and is a pleasure to browse.

KanTeX
http://langmuir.eecs.berkeley.edu/~venkates/KanTex_1.00.html

Website for KanTeX font package for Kannada script.

Kapatija (1998)
http://www.duke.edu/web/jyounger/kapat98.html

A very comprehensive listing of Bronze Age and Classical Aegean world information sites on the WWW. A separate listing is kept of relevant discussion lists and prior listings are also available.

Karanis Project
http://classics.lsa.umich.edu/Kelsey/OutKaranis.html

A collection of images of artifacts from excavations sponsored by the University of Michigan in Karanis between 1926 and 1935. These images include views of the site, glass and other containers, wall paintings, sculpture and figurines, and coins. The presentation in designed to provide access to objects too fragile for general classroom examination.

Katholieke Universiteit Leuven, Department of Classical Studies
http://www.arts.kuleuven.ac.be/facdep/arts/onderz/dep/klass.htm

More than a simple listing of faculty, this site offers information concerning ongoing research projects as well as the more traditional contact information for its faculty.

Krannert Art Museum - Old World Antiquities
http://www.ncsa.uiuc.edu/General/UIUC/KrannertArtMuseum/Guide/OldWorld/OldWorld.html

Images of a few artifacts drawn from the collection of the Krannert Art Museum, University of Illinois at Urbana-Champaign, three from Greece and one from Egypt to demonstrate contrasting styles.

Keilschrifttexte des dritten Jahrtausends v.Chr. im Vorderasiatischen Museum, Berlin
http://fub46.zedat.fu-berlin.de:8080/~uruk/VAM

This project is seeking to make images of all published cuneiform tablets held at the Vorderasiatischen Museum, Berlin, available at this site.

Kemet
http://ourworld.compuserve.com/homepages/kemet/

Kemet is a German language journal on Egypt for non-specialists.

Kerkenes
http://www.metu.edu.tr/home/wwwkerk/non/index.html

The Kerkenes Project is an excavation located on a mountain in central Turkey. The site has been identified as the Hittite Mount Daha. This web page offers a very complete exposition of the techniques used at this site and the artifacts recovered during the excavation. Background information on the history of the site and more technical information for specialists is available. The project hopes to make raw geophysical data and photographs from the site available over the Internet.

Kings' Valley Project
http://www.cpsc.ucalgary.ca/~attia/kings/kings.html

This Web site describes the project to find the tombs of Pharaoh Akhu En Aten and his wife Nefert Iti by the use of sonic imaging. The site offers a brief review of the proposed technique and expected benefits from this relatively new technology for determining fruitful excavation sites.

KMT: A Modern Journal of Ancient Egypt
http://www.sirius.com/~reeder/kmt.html

An English language journal devoted to all aspects of ancient Egypt. This WWW site offers a listing of current articles and allows the viewing of a few sections, such as For the Record by David Moyer, which reports new publications, museum news and exhibits in the U.S. and abroad, and lectures and symposia both in the U.S. and abroad. Nile Currents may also be viewed, and it offers recent news and developments on excavation sites and projects. Unfortunately, the main articles are not available for viewing over the Internet.

Koch-Ludwig Giza Plateau Mapping Project
http://www.pbs.org/wgbh/nova/pyramid/excavation/fullreport.html

A full report on the 1997 excavation season by Mark Lehner on the Koch-Ludwig Giza Plateau Mapping Project. Contains a summary of prior seasons and highlights the findings from the current season, which include further work on bakeries discovered at the excavation site.

Kolam: A Mirror of Tamil Culture
http://www.uni-koeln.de/phil-fak/indologie/kolam/kolam.html

Kolam is an electronic journal focusing on all aspects of Tamil culture. The name is derived from a type of drawing that has been made by women on the ground in front of their homes and is an essential aspect of Tamil culture. The journal includes articles on classical literature, modern literature, indigenous sciences, and folklore and culture.

Korte, Gustav and Alfred Korte Gordion Ergebinisse der Ausgrabung im Jahre 1900 Berlin : Druck und Verlag von Georg Reimer, 1904 Jahrbuch des Kaiserlich Deutschen Archaologisch
http://eos.lib.uchicago.edu/cgi-bin/LIB_preserve_title.sh?CALL_NUMBER=CC27.D481_vol5

A scanned copy of this work by the Electronic Open Stacks project at the University of Chicago Library. The work can be viewed by chapters or a reader can jump to a particular page in the work. These image-based texts avoid the expense of creating full text searchable versions and yet provide usable access to materials too fragile for regular use.

Robert Kraft
http://ccat.sas.upenn.edu/rs/rak/kraft.html

For ten years Kraft was the editor of Offline, a column in Religious Studies News, which introduced many scholars to the use of computers and ultimately the Internet, in religious studies. Links to materials from the following classes led by Kraft can be found at this location: Religious Studies 014: Judaism, Christianity, Islam; Religious Studies 135: Christian Origins; Religious Studies 225: Dead Sea Scrolls; Religious Studies 435: Ancient Traditions Concerning Joshua/Jesus; Religious Studies 436: Life and Letters of Paul; Religious Studies 525: Varieties of Early Judaism; Religious Studies 535: Varieties of Early Christianity, and, Religious Studies 735: Seminar on Early Judaism and Early Christianity. These materials are only part of his continuing contributions to his chosen field of study with new tools and means of communication.

Ksowada's Egyptology Page
http://www.zeta.org.au/~ksowada/

Karin Sowada, Assistant Curator at the Nicholson Museum of Antiquities (University of Sydney), has constructed a very useful list of museums with Egyptology collections in Australia with very complete contact information. A useful guide for scholars planning a research trip to Australia or anyone interested in Egyptian artifacts in Australian museums.

KV5
http://www.pathfinder.com/@@jbUGhtDkZwAAQKlt/time/magazine/domestic/1995/950529/950529.cover.html

Time magazine coverage of the discoveries in KV5, the possible resting place of the sons of Ramesses II. Includes a multimedia clip of Egyptologist Kent Weeks giving brief tour of the tomb and several single images.

Labyrinth
http://www.georgetown.edu/labyrinth

Labyrinth is a major resource for all scholars working in medieval studies. Sponsored by Georgetown University, this site can be searched by keywords, a very helpful feature when you are uncertain of which menu choice will lead to the desired link. Among the main menu choices are the Labyrinth Library (links to texts in Latin, French, Italian, Old English, and Middle English), Subject Menus leading to resources such as General Medieval History and Manuscripts (Paleography, Codicology), Labyrinth On-Line Bibliographies, and Pedagogical Resources. The Daedalus's Guides to the Net and Web: Resources and Tools option on the main menu will be of interest to those seeking more information on effectively using the Internet and World Wide Web, including tools for searching the entire Web.

Lachish and Sennacherib
http://home.uleth.ca/geo/htmjoel/frames.htm

A recounting of the Assyrian conquest of the city of Lachish by Sennacherib in 701 B.C.E. Reliefs from Ninenah are used as sources for information on styles of dress, technologies for war and other social structures. Archaeological information is presented concerning the site and its history with good use of images to illustrate the context of the fall of Lachish.

Lahav DigMaster Digital Archaeology Archives

See entry under Cobb Institute of Archaeology

Language Interactive: A Trailguide to Creating Dynamic Web Pages
http://www.vcu.edu/idc/li/interact.html

Language teachers may assume that many of the technologies of the Web are not relevant or difficult to adapt to the teaching of languages. This site by Bob Godwin-Jones should dispel both of those assumptions. Focusing specifically on the teaching of languages, this site gives practical examples of the use of plug-ins, JavaScript, Java, CGI scripts and other web methods to fashion tools for language instruction. Many of the examples are useable programs in their own right and need only simple modifications to adapt them to a particular language or classroom situation. Highly recommended for all language instructors.

Latin dictionary of Saxonian Latin
http://www2.dk-online.dk/users/christ_h/latin/

A dictionary of Saxonian Latin by Professor Franz Blatt, and revised by Reimer Hemmingsen.

Latin Library at Ad Fontes Academy
http://patriot.net/~lillard/cp/latlib

This is a very wide ranging collection of Latin texts from a variety of public domain sources. While these are not critical editions, they do provide access to materials which would otherwise not be available online.

A Latin Wordlist for Learning Medieval Latin
http://kufacts.cc.ukans.edu/ftp/pub/history/Europe/Medieval/aids/latwords.aid

A suggested Latin wordlist for those learning Medieval Latin. In this same directory are files on Latin grammar and a Latin wordlist for the Vulgate.

Latin Papyri
http://odyssey.lib.duke.edu:80/papyrus/texts/latin.html

Latin Papyri found in the Duke Papyrus Archive. For a full description, please see the entry for the Duke Papyrus Archive

Latin Vulgate
http://tuna.uchicago.edu/forms_unrest/VULGATE.form.html

Jerome's Latin Vulgate Bible may be searched or browsed at this site. Part of the ARTFL Project, this search interface illustrates the possibilities of present technology, including limiting the search to certain books, selecting a phrase search, or having the output of the search returned as KWIC report (key word in context) or frequency by title. The search engine uses the powerful Unix regular expression search parameters, and it is possible to specify accented vowels.

Learning Greek with Accordance
http://info.ox.ac.uk/ctitext/publish/comtxt/ct14/kraabel.html

Professor Tom Kraabel describes his use of Accordance, a tool developed for the grammatical analysis of the Greek New Testament, in the teaching of a Biblical Greek class.

Learning Sites, Inc. Digitally Reconstructed Ancient Worlds for Interactive Education and Research
http://www.learningsites.com/

Learning Sites uses VRML (Virtual Reality Modeling Language) 2.0 to create models or virtual worlds for museum, educational or scholarly projects. Samples available for viewing include reconstruction of archaeological excavations and structures such as the Funerary Chapel of Ka(i)pura, Saqqara, Egypt. Links to text, image and sound databases can be integrated into the virtual presentation.

Leiden Ur III Project
ftp://enlil.museum.upenn.edu/pub/Ur3

A collection of numerous Sumerian texts from the Ur III period, from a variety of sources. The transliteration standards used in transcribing the texts can be found in ftp://enlil.museum.upenn.edu/pub/Ur3/convntns.txt. This site provides an excellent example of using the Internet to disseminate information from archaeological excavations.

Le Ramesseum Temple de Millions d' Années de Ramsès II à Thèbes-Ouest
http://ourworld.compuserve.com/homepages/Gerard_Flament/

This is a very complete and enjoyable presentation of findings from a temple complex build by Ramesses II. The site plan is available in French and English and offers not only information on what was discovered at the site but also sets findings in their appropriate religious context. Finally a virtual reconstruction of the temple complex without out buildings allows the viewer some idea of the scale and beauty of the original structure.

The Levant Cultural MultiMedia Servers
http://www.hiof.no/almashriq

An index and guide to multimedia cultural material on Lebanon and the Levant. It is not limited to material of historical interest but very current and useful for scholars working in this area.

Levis exsurgit zephirus
http://www.georgetown.edu/labyrinth/library/levis_exsurgit_zephirus.html

A Latin text drawn from Cambridge University Library, Gg 5.35 (s.xi, med., Canterbury), f. 441ra, with English translation, which is linked back to the Latin text by Martin Irvine. Bibliographic information on this work is included. Another demonstration from classical studies of the usefulness of hypertext links in the WWW environment.

Liberation Philology Software
http://members.aol.com/libphil/

This site offers free or very nominal cost language software for students working in a variety of languages. The languages offered include Ancient and NT Greek, Latin, Old English, Sanskrit, Old Norse and others. For languages not listed, contact Liberation Philology concerning creation of similar software.

Library Catalogs with Web Interfaces
http://www.lib.ncsu.edu/staff/morgan/alcuin/wwwed-catalogs.html

A listing of library catalogs that have WWW interfaces. Includes libraries that provide access to their own catalogs as well as catalogs of Internet resources.

Library of Congress Classics WWW Page
http://lcweb.loc.gov/global/classics/classics.html

Maintained by the Library of Congress, this site allows searching of the Library of Congress online catalog and has a useful collection of links to other resources for the classics as well as on electronic texts and publishing.

Life in Ancient Egypt
http://www.clpgh.org/cmnh/tours/egypt/walton.html

This site is a guide to the Walton Hall of Ancient Egypt at the Carnegie Museum of Natural History. The Carnegie Museum collection holds approximately 2500 Egyptian artifacts with some 600 items on display. Extensive contextual information is offered for the items shown on this Web site with an excellent teacher's guide to Ancient Egypt with references for further reading. The usefulness of this site for teaching would be enhanced if more images drawn from its collection were offered to accompany the reading materials.

Look It Up!
http://www.uky.edu/ArtsSciences/Classics/lexindex.html

An outstanding collection of searching tools for Internet resources on the classics and the ancient world. This collection deserves a bookmark by every scholar or teacher concerned with any aspect of classical Greece or Rome. The search interfaces on this site include Perseus (search by words, phrases, reverse lexicon, and position of text), Lewis & Short Latin Dictionary, A Handbook of Rhetorical Devices, A Glossary of Literary Terms, The Internet Classics Archive, ANCIEN-L archives (Archives for aegeanet, ancien-l, ane-l, byzans-l, classics-m, greekarch, lt-antiq, numism-l, romarch-l), and, Gnomon Online to name only a few of the resources found at this site.

Loose Canons. Reflections on the Formation of the Hebrew Bible
http://www.ualberta.ca/ARTS/JHS/jhs-article.html#A5

Philip R. Davies offers interesting observations concerning the process of canonization. Recognizing the process of canonization is an ongoing one, Professor Davies cautions against the automatic use of fixed lists to judge the status of works at particular points in the process.

Lucretius, On the Nature of Things
gopher://gopher.vt.edu:10010/02/60/1

English translation by W. E. Leonard.

Lutheran Church-Missouri Synod
http://www.lcms.org/

The Lutheran Church-Missouri Synod site offers a fairly complete selection of materials for members of the Synod on both organizational and theological subjects. Links from the main page lead to resources on the Missouri Synod, opportunities for missionary work, directories of churches and schools, and links to other resources.

Lutherans.Net
http://www.lutherans.net/

A very complete web site devoted to Lutherans and issues related to the Lutheran Church. Links are maintained in a number of categories, ranging from bible study and theology to church administration and clip art. This site deserves a bookmark from any Lutheran using web resources as a minister, Sunday school teacher, or interested lay person.

The Madaba Map (Jordan)
http://198.62.75.1/www1/ofm/fai/FAImadmn.html

Madaba, a village south of Amman, is the site of the Madaba Mosaic Map, an important Byzantine map of the Holy Land. Based on the locations represented and the content of its captions the map is thought to be based on the Onomasticon of Biblical Locations by Eusebius (IV century). Dating from the sixth century CE. the map would have been seen by Christians making a pilgrimage to the Holy Land. This website offers background information on the map, images of the map and other information placing it in historical context.

Magic Bibliographies and Resources
http://www.rdg.ac.uk/~lkpbodrd/Academic/magbib/.

A primarily academic bibliographies and Web resources on magic. It concentrates on the use of magic in Classical Greece, and other areas in the ancient world, although some references to anthropological studies of magic in general.

Malina, Bruce J.: Publications 1967-1996
http://www.stolaf.edu/people/kchanson/malbib.html

This is a useful bibliography of the publications of Bruce J. Malina between 1967 until 1996.

Manchester Museum (University of Manchester)
http://www.mcc.ac.uk/~mellorir/museum/index.htm

The homepage for the Manchester Museum offers information on artifacts in its collection as well as other important projects sponsored by the museum. Those projects include: The Manchester Egyptian Mummy Research Project, which is developing non-destructive techniques for the examination of Egyptian mummies; The International Mummy Database, which holds information from scientific studies of mummies from museums around the world; The Centre for Biomedical and Forensic Studies in Egyptology, which offers facilities for postgraduate studies and studies in this area; Schistosomiasis in Ancient and Modern Egypt, a study in palaeoepidemiology; and, the Mummy Tissue Bank, which holds tissue samples from mummies around the world.

The M.A. Mansoor Amarna Collection
http://www.amarna.com

A WWW site devoted to the M.A. Mansoor Amarna Collection. Includes a history of the collection, general information on the collection and images of artifacts, such as portraits of Pharaoh Akhenaten, Queen Nefertiti and their daughters.

Mantovano
http://www.virgil.org/mantovano/

Mantovano is the website for the discussion list of the same name focusing on Virgil and his influence. Subscriptions to the mailing list are possible from the website or in the usual fashion by email. The postings to the mailing list are archived and can be browsed or searched from the website.

Manuel de Codage
http://www.ccer.ggl.ruu.nl/codage/codage.htm

The Manuel de Codage is the standard system for encoding hieroglyphic texts for use with computers. Hans van den Berg traces the origins of this standard and gives valuable pointers on the use of this system with the program WinGlyph.

The Epistle of Mathetes (Believer/Disciple) to Diognetus
gopher://ccat.sas.upenn.edu:3333/00/Religious/ChurchWriters/ApostolicFathers/Diognetus

English translation by J. B. Lightfoot.

Maps of the Near East
http://pubweb.parc.xerox.com

Maps of the Near East that can be viewed using the Xerox PARC Map viewer over the Internet. It is possible to increase the magnification of certain features and to control the features that are displayed.

Marking Systems in the Ancient Near East: The Origins of Punctuation
http://soho.ios.com/~arobe/index.html

This website both acts as a publication of the author's work on marking systems in the ancient Near East as well as providing a place for discussion of such marking systems. Useful information is included for non-specialists who are interested in such marking systems.

The Master's Seminary Journal
http://www.mastersem.edu/journal.htm

The online companion to the print version of the Master's Seminary Journal. Full texts of articles are available for the first six volumes of the journal (1990-1995) but abstracts only for the most recent three volumes (1996-1998).

The Master's Seminary On-Line
http://www.mastersem.edu/home.htm

This is the online presence of a conservative Christian seminary. It will be of interest to either conservative Christians or those studying modern religious movements. A rather well done other resources page that leads to both conservative as well as other academic resources.

Museum Applied Science Center for Archaeology (MASCA)
http://masca.museum.upenn.edu

Information on the activities of the sections of MASCA, part of the University of Pennsylvania Museum of Archaeology and Anthropology, including archaeobotany, archaeological ceramics and chemistry, archaeometallurgy, and dendrochronology. A Roman glass exhibit can also be found at this site, which has general information on the exhibit and eight images of glasswork drawn from this exhibit.

Ancient Palestine Gallery with Biblical References
http://philae.sas.upenn.edu/ANEP/ANEP.html

This site contains images and information drawn from the University of Pennsylvania Museum's excavations at Beth Shan, Gibeon, Sarepta and Tell es-Sa'idiyeh, as well as Haverford College's excavation at Beth Shemesh. The information is well organized and the use of image maps to depict burial sites, for example, allows the user to view objects in the context of the burial site. Users can choose to enlarge the image of the artifact. For those with the appropriate software, there are virtual walk-throughs of the Beth Shan Temple VII and the Sarepta Shrine.

History of Mathematics
http://aleph0.clarku.edu/~djoyce/mathhist/mathhist.html

David E. Joyce, Department of Mathematics and Computer Science, Clark University, maintains this WWW site devoted to the history of mathematics. While not restricted to the Ancient Near East, this site does provide a number of useful links for scholars interested in the history of mathematics in that area.

Medicine in Ancient Egypt
http://www.indiana.edu/~ancmed/egypt.HTM

This essay is part of a course on ancient medicine taught by Professor Nancy Demand at Indiana University Bloomington and focuses on the practice of medicine in Ancient Egypt.

Medicine in Ancient Mesopotamia
http://www.indiana.edu/~ancmed/meso.HTM

This essay is part of a course on ancient medicine taught by Professor Nancy Demand at Indiana University Bloomington and focuses on the practice of medicine in Ancient Mesopotamia.

Index of Medieval Latin texts in the MALIN archive
http://kufacts.cc.ukans.edu/ftp/pub/history/Europe/Medieval/latintexts

This is a listing of Medieval Latin texts for retrieval in the MALIN archive at University of Kansas.

Medieval Glossators of the Corpus Iuris
http://kufacts.cc.ukans.edu/ftp/pub/history/Europe/Medieval/articles/lucas.art

A short article on the Medieval Glossators of the Corpus Iuris by Lucas De Penna.

Megiddo (Tel Aviv University)
http://www.tau.ac.il:81/~archpubs/megiddo.html

This is the main website for the cooperative excavation of Megiddo undertaken by Tel Aviv University and Pennsylvania State University. Other materials related to this site accompany a short history of Megiddo and its importance in the study of the history of the ANE.

Mediterranean Oceanic Data Base
http://modb.oce.ulg.ac.be/

Extremely useful site with advanced data products for oceanographic research on the Mediterranean Sea. Data sets include: Historical hydrographic Data Base (online extraction), Seasonal gridded Data Sets, Climatological charts generator in the Mediterranean (online), World

Ocean gridded Bathymetry (online extraction). Data analysis and visualization software for Unix (X-Windows), DOS and Windows platforms is also available at this site. The physical science community generally makes data sets freely available to all researchers, a stark constrast to the practices of most museums and libraries holding rare manuscripts and artifacts.

Memory of Asia
http://xlweb.com/heritage/asian/palmleaf.htm

The Memory of Asia site details a project to preserve the palm-leaf manuscripts of Asia. With the advent of Western style printing in Asia, the cycle of copying works recorded on palm-leaf manuscripts was broken and now many of these manuscripts are nearing the end of their natural lifetimes. Without sustained preservation efforts, these manuscripts, written primarily in Tamil, and the information they contain will be lost beyond recall. This site details the importance of these manuscripts and their place in documenting Indian culture as well as the techniques that are being employed to preserve these texts.

Mesopotamian Law, Bibliography
http://www.law.pitt.edu/hibbitts/meso.htm

A useful bibliography on Mesopotamian and legal practices prepared by Professor Bernard J. Hibbitts in for courses taught at the University of Pittsburgh School of Law.

Mesopotamian Year Names Neo-Sumerian and Old Babylonian Date Formulae
http://www.mpiwg-berlin.mpg.de/Yearnames/yn_index.htm

A list of more than 2,000 year names spanning the time period from the empire of Sargon to the end of the dynasty of Babylon. The list can be accessed through a list of cities and kings, a list of words and a list of word in English translation. This resource is the result of a collaborative effort spanning more than ten years and will be useful for the dating of cuneiform tablets and for identification of incomplete date formulas. The project continues and scholars should contribute Mesopotamian year names, particularly as readings and translations improve.

United Methodist Church
http://www.netins.net/showcase/umsource

Extensive resources related to the United Methodist Church of a denominational variety. It also includes links to other denominations on the Internet, ministry resources and other Christian resources.

Miami University, Classics Dept.
http://www.muohio.edu/~clscwis

Homepage for the Miami University (Ohio) Classics Department, with current information on the faculty and programs offered. Additional links are available to course materials and other links of interest to classicists. Of particular note are the links to the MiamiMoo: The Virtual Antiquity Project.

MiamiMoo: The Virtual Antiquity Project
http://MiamiMOO.MCS.MUOhio.Edu/moodesc.html

Pilot environments currently constructed at the MiamiMOO are: The Athena Pronaia Sanctuary at Delphi, constructed by Susan Wallrodt of the University of Cincinnati; The Sanctuary of Asklepios at Epidauros, constructed by Amy Deeds Barr of the University of Cincinnati; and, the South Asian Pilgrimage Environment. Online papers describe the experiences of the scholars using the MiamiMOO to reconstruct these environments.

Middle East
http://jfa-www.bu.edu/Indices/MidEast.html

Indexes for the journal Middle East along with search capacity for locating particular authors or articles. Links from article titles reveal an abstract of the article.

The Middle East-North Africa Internet Resource Guide
http://www.cc.utah.edu/~jwr9311/MENA.html

Joseph W. Roberts of the Department of Political Science, Middle East Center, the University of Utah has compiled this guide to Internet resources on the Middle East-North Africa. It is updated on a regular basis and now appears in four parts on the gopher site referenced above.

Middle East Studies at the University of Texas at Austin
http://menic.utexas.edu/mes.html

The Center for Middle Eastern Studies, University of Texas at Austin, maintains this extensive listing of resources from and about the Middle East. There are subject menus as well as a listing of Internet servers by country, and it is possible to search the server if the exact category or name of a resource is unknown.

The Middle East Studies Association
http://www.mesa.arizona.edu/

Information from the Middle East Studies Association includes tables of contents from the MESA Bulletin, indexes to books received, essays and other materials in the MESA Bulletin from 1987-

1996, teaching/research resources, recent books and conferences on Middle East Studies, and other Internet resources.

Mikra
http://www.ktf.uni-passau.de/bibel/mikra.html

Mikra is a mailing list hosted by Franz Böhmisch for the discussion of the bible. This site offers access to archives of the list and guides to other resources of interest to list participants.

Missale Romanum
http://www.cs.cmu.edu/Web/People/spok/mass-parallel.txt

This site offers the text of the Latin Mass (Old Rite) with parallel English translation.

Mission Churches of the Sonoran Desert
http://dizzy.library.arizona.edu/images/swf/mission.html

An interesting presentation by the University of Arizona Library of images of mission churches built in what is now called the Sonoran Desert. Brief historical comments concerning the missionary activity of both the Jesuits and Franciscans set the background for these images, with suggested readings for those wishing to pursue the subject.

Models for Ancient Israel
http://www.creighton.edu/~rsmkns/IndexHand.html

Handouts for classes on Ancient Israel lead by Ronald A. Simkins at Creighton University. These cover such topics as the distinction between models and methods, social models for Ancient Israel, application of social models to Ancient Israel, literary models for the Bible and essays on class topics. A useful starting point for professors preparing for such topics in a survey course or those exploring the use of social models in this context.

MOinfo-I: Platform t.b.v. discussie en info omtrent het Midden Oosten
http://www.leidenuniv.nl/nino/moinfo.html

Information about MOinfo-I, a discussion list for Arabic and Middle East Studies (in Dutch).

Montet,Pierre, Scenes de la Vie Privee dans les Tombeaux Egyptiens de L'ancien Empire Paris : Strasbourg University, 1925
http://eos.lib.uchicago.edu/cgi-bin/LIB_preserve_title.sh?CALL_NUMBER=DT61.M8

A scanned copy of this work by the Electronic Open Stacks project at the University of Chicago Library. The work can be viewed by chapters or a reader can "jump" to a particular page in the work. These image-based texts avoid the expense of creating full text searchable versions and yet provide usable access to materials too fragile for regular use.

Monumenta Musicae Byzantinae
http://www.igl.ku.dk/MMB/Welcome.html

The University of Copenhagen sponsors this site, which includes an inventory of microfilms of medieval Byzantine chant manuscripts and an index to the standard abridged version of the Sticherarion liturgical book. Links to other sites concerned with medieval chants are also available.

Mount Zion Books / Sifrei Har Tzion
http://www.zionbooks.com

The Mount Zion website is rare find among bookstores on or off the Web. Users will find subject catalogs for works in English, French, Hebrew and Russian as well as links to other sites such as the Judaic Archival Project. The site also offers a downloadable catalog of books for viewing offline.

Multilingual Egyptological Thesaurus
http://www.ccer.ggl.ruu.nl/thes/default.htm

The Multilingual Egyptological Thesaurus is a very useful tool that allows terms in Egyptology to be viewed in any of several modern languages. The Thesaurus is divided into 15 categories ranging from Present Location and Category to Royal Names and Acquisition. It is also possible to download the entire Thesaurus as DBase III files.

Museo Archeologico Nazionale di Cagliari
http://www.crs4.it/HTML/RUGGIERO/MUSEO/mus_ind.html

This site presents a special exhibit called "La radici della memoria," a history in text and images of Sardinia from the Stone Age to the early Middle Ages.

Musée du Louvre
http://www.louvre.fr
http://www.paris.org:80/Musees/Louvre

The second site contains many images from the official Louvre site, which is listed first. The Louvre, and other research quality collections, should be encouraged to make images of their holdings, suitable for scholarly use, available on the Internet.

Musei Vaticani (via Christus Rex)
http://www.christusrex.org/www1/vaticano/0-Musei.html

The Vatican museums, which include the Gregorian Egyptian Museum (22 images) and the Gregorian Etruscan Museum (129) images.

Museums (WWW Virtual Library)
http://www.comlab.ox.ac.uk/archive/other/museums.html

This is a very extensive and helpful listing of museums and related organizations with a presence on the Internet. Johnathan Bowen, the maintainer of this resource notes that more than one museum is being added per day, forcing the lists to be split between the U.S., U.K. and the rest of the world. At that rate of expansion, a weekly visit would seem to be a bare minimum.

Music of the Ancient Near East
http://members.aol.com/ricdum/mane.htm

A site dealing with the recovered musicology of the Ancient Near East. There are links to a "comprehensive" Sumerian-French word list, a hypothetical transcription of Hurrian Hymn H6, and articles dealing with *The Morphology of the Babylonian Scale, Gotterzahlen and Scale Structure,* and, *The Uruk Lute.*

Muslim Students Association Islamic Server
http://www.usc.edu/dept/MSA/

The Muslim Students Association sponsors this collection of original materials and links to WWW resources of interest to Islamic scholars. Those resources include links to Islamic organizations, texts relating to Islam and other topics such as Islamic architecture and software for Muslims.

Mythology in Western art
http://www-lib.haifa.ac.il/www/art/mythology_westart.html

This site offers scanned images of mythological characters used in Sonia Klinger's course in Mythology in Western Art. Fourteen images of the most prominent figures in classical mythology and links to other resources for mythology on the Internet.

Mythtext
http://www.the-wire.com/culture/mythology/mythtext.html

A rather popular treatment of mythology but it does have links to resources that may be of interest to classicists.

Nadler, Sonia and Marco, Institute of Archaeology
http://www.tau.ac.il:81/~archpubs/excs.html

The homepage for the Sonia and Marco Nadler Institute of Archaeology offers brief reports on excavations at: Aphek, Har Haruvim, Malhata, Megiddo, Nahal Qana, Qitmit, Qumran, Tel Gerisa, Tel Hadar and the Golan Project, Tel 'Ira, Tel Jezreel, Tel Kabri, Tel Lachish, Uza, and Zippori. Contents and abstracts from recent issues of the Tel Aviv journal are available with subscription information for the journal.

The Nag Hammadi Library
http://www.gnosis.org/naghamm/nhl.html

Sponsored by the Gnostic Society Library, this site offers translations of all the texts found in the Nag Hammadi Library, an alphabetic index to the library, a codex index and the ability to search all the files in the Nag Hammadi Library. The search interface allows the user to specify an allowance for spelling errors, the type of display for results and whether the search should be case sensitive.

National Archaeology Database
telnet://cast.uark.edu or telnet://130.184.71.44

Log in as nadb. The National Archeological Database (NADB) Online System has approximately 100,000 records relating to archaeological excavations in the United States. It is a system that should serve as a model for the construction of such databases in other geographic areas of archaeological interest. The Departmental Consulting Archeologist/Archeological Assistance Program of the National Park Service is responsible for administering the NADB Online System. The development, operation, and maintenance of the system is carried out by the Center for Advanced Spatial Technologies (CAST) at the University of Arkansas, Fayetteville, through a cooperative agreement with the National Park Service. Expanded data coverage and database access has made possible through cooperative agreements with the U.S. Army Corps of Engineers and the U.S. Department of Defense Legacy Program.

National Endowment for the Humanities
http://www.neh.fed.us

The National Endowment for the Humanities sponsors this homepage with important information for those seeking information for grant applications or the status of projects funded by NEH grants. Look for links to archaeology project guidelines, archaeology projects online and information on dissertation grants.

National Greek Exam
http://acs.rhodes.edu/~nle/grkex.html

The National Greek Exam site offers ordering information for the 1998 Exams along with a key for practice purposes, information concerning registration for the exam and other helpful information for Greek educators or students.

National Junior Classical League
http://snafu.mit.edu/njcl/njcl.html

The National Junior Classical League is sponsored by the American Classical League and is composed of approximately 54,000 high school students who are interested in Latin or classical studies. This homepage has links to other classical resources on the Internet as well as information about the NJCL and its members. There are also homepages at this site for a few high school chapters of the NJCL, listing their favorite sites and downloads. A site to be commended and emulated as broadening the appeal of the humanities among the young will strengthen the traditional role of humanities departments in the colleges and universities they will someday attend.

National Latin Exam
http://acs.rhodes.edu/~nle/

The National Latin Exam site offers copies of the 1997 Latin Exams along with a key for practice purposes, information concerning registration for the exam and other helpful information for Latin educators or students.

Navigating the Bible
http://bible.ort.org/

Navigating the Bible is one of the best study tools on the Web for the Hebrew Bible. The Hebrew text is presented in both pointed and unpointed text (and English translation) with sound files that can be downloaded or played over the Web. Commentaries, a glossary and atlas are available for consultation.

Nazereth Resource Library
http://www.cin.org/users/james/

This is an information site on the Catholic Church that addresses a number of typical questions asked by both Catholics and others. Oriented towards a general audience with few links to more academic material.

Near Eastern Archaeology
http://www.asor.org/NEA/NEAHP.html

Biblical Archaeologist has changed its name to Near Eastern Archaeology. (To avoid confusion it has been listed under both names herein.) This site offers the table of contents from recent issues for viewing. The full text of some back issues of this journal are being placed online as part of the SELA project.

Neeley, P.S.
http://ourworld.compuserve.com/homepages/PSNeeley/

P.S. Neeley has developed a number of computer versions of ancient games, including 'The Royal Game of Ur' (Sumerian) and Senet (Egyptian). While not traditional academic resources these games may be useful in interesting the next generation of scholars in ANE studies.

Neo-Assyrian Text Corpus Project
http://www.helsinki.fi/science/saa/cna.html

A long term project undertaken by the Department of Asian and African Studies, University of Helsinki, to create an electronic database of all published and unpublished Neo-Assyrian texts. An example of a database entry and full description of the project and its publications are accessible from this homepage. The State Archives of Assyria is one of the series published by this project. Contact information is also given for this international project under the direction of Simo Parpola.

Nestor
http://ucaswww.mcm.uc.edu/classics/nestor/nestor.html

Nestor is a bibliography of Eastern Mediterranean and southeastern European prehistory, Homeric society, Indo-European linguistics and related fields, published by the Department of Classics, University of Cincinnati. The current editor is Eric H. Cline. Suggestions for inclusion in the bibliography should be addressed to nestor@ucbeh.san.uc.edu. The bibliography from 1957 to 1996 can be downloaded from ftp://cica.cica.indiana.edu/pub/archaeology as tab delimited ASCII files. Online searching of the bibliography is available from this website and covers the time period from 1957 to 1996. The online bibliography links reviews to materials cited in the bibliography and the site provides a listing of links of interest to Agean prehistorians.

Netherlands Institute for the Near East (NINO)
http://www.leidenuniv.nl/nino/nino.html

This page contains information concerning NINO and its publications, Internet resources for Near East studies in the Netherlands and links to other Internet resources are found at this site. It is one of the sponsors for the important Annual Egyptological Bibliography project reviewed separately herein.

The New England Classical Newsletter and Journal
http://www.circe.unh.edu/classics/necn&j.html

Homepage of the New England Classical Newsletter and Journal with a listing of its table of contents and links to the University of New Hampshire Classics department homepage and the homepage for the Classical Association of New Hampshire. Under development by Maria Pantelia, the author of the Electronic Resources for Classicists: The Second Generation, noted above.

The Newsletter for Anatolian Studies
ftp://oi.uchicago.edu/pub/research/nas

The Newsletter for Anatolian Studies is a semi-annual bibliographic publication for linguistic, historical, archaeological and philological research into pre-Hellenistic Anatolia. The NAS was founded in 1985 and has grown rapidly over the past ten years. It contains the following bibliographic categories: research in progress (esp. dissertations), work in press, work recently published (usually within the past six months), and a list of reviews. In addition, the NAS provides a forum for brief excavation reports, book reviews, and announcements of future and past conferences. The newsletter for 1994, NAS_10_1994.ascii.txt, and the first issue for 1995, NAS_11-1_1995.ascii.txt, are currently available at this location.

Newsletter for Targumic and Cognate Studies
http://www.uwyo.edu/a&s/relstds/ts/ntcs.htm

Bibliographic information, useful libraries and a listing of scholars engaged in Targumic and cognate studies can be found on the Newsletter's homepage.

New Advent
http://www.sni.net/advent/

A Catholic website that hosts such resources as the Catholic Encylopedia (1913 edition), an English translation of the Summa Theologica of St. Thomas Aquinas (1947 translation by English Dominicans,) and English editions of some of the Church Fathers (Edinborough edition). Additional resources include a listing of books on the Catholic faith and an "FAQ" on Catholicism.

New York Public Library
http://catnyp.nypl.org/

The online catalog for the New York Public Library contains all catalog records beginning in 1972 and earlier titles as they become available from ongoing recataloging projects. The search interface is easy to use and the depth of the collection makes it a good choice for quick bibliographic reference even in areas not found at the local university library.

The Carsten Niebuhr Institute, University of Copenhagen
http://dorit.ihi.ku.dk/cni/papcoll/index.html

Extensive information concerning the Carlsberg Papyrus Collection which includes a very helpful inventory of published papyri with bibliography. A concordance of joins to texts in other collections and images of some of the papyri make this a useful site for scholars working on texts from Tebtunis, and to a lesser extent texts from Hawara and Edfu.

Nippur: Sacred City of Enlil
http://asmar.uchicago.edu/OI/PROJ/NIP/PUB93/NSC/NSC.html

Professor McGuire Gibson (Oriental Institute, University of Chicago) details the importance of Nippur as a Mesopotamian holy city in this article. Outlining the importance of finds from Nippur in shaping our understanding of Mesopotamian culture Professor Gibson argues for continued attention to this importance religious center of the Mesopotamia.

Nippur Expedition
http://www-oi.uchicago.edu/OI/PROJ/NIP/Nippur.html

Annual reports for 1991 to 1995 excavation seasons at Nippur, led by McGuire Gibson of the Oriental Institute. There are several articles on Nippur available, including McGuire Gibson's Nippur, Sacred City of Enlil, Supreme God of Sumer and Akkad, which originally appeared in Al-Rafidan 14 (1993).

Nitartha International
http://www.nitartha.org/

Nitartha International is the sponsor of the Tibetan teachings preservation project which is seeking to preserve Tibetan culture. This site details its effort to convert Tibetan texts into electronic format and to deliver the same over the WWW. Nitartha maintains a listing of text entry projects at this site to avoid duplication of effort.

Noncanonical Homepage
http://wesley.nnc.edu/noncanon.htm

A site devoted to apocryphal and pseudepigraphal literature and its relationship to biblical interpretation. For the Old Testament the texts of the Apocrypha and pseudepigrapha are reproduced. The New Testament Apocrypha is divided into Acts, Apocalypse, Gospels, Church Fathers, and Writings. A variety of sources was relied upon for the translated texts, including the Revised Standard Version for Old Testament Apocrypha, The Apocrypha and Pseudepigrapha of the Old Testament, R.H. Charles, Oxford: The Clarendon Press, 1913, and, The Apocryphal New Testament, M.R. James-Translation and Notes, Oxford: Clarendon Press, 1924, and others. Presenting this material in translation will reach the larger non-specialist audience and should form the framework for a linking of original source materials to these translations.

NOTITIAE CANTUS
gopher://olymp.wu-wien.ac.at:7121/hGET%20/h/pub/earlym-l/Notitiae.Cantus/local.html

Guido Milanese edits this newsletter on Gregorian Chants and Internet resources for the same. This is a good source of information about ongoing projects on Gregorian chants and Web resources on such chants.

Northwest Semitic Philological Data Bank
http://www.labherm.filol.csic.es/ConsultaBD2_us.html

A very impressive effort by the CSIC, Laboratorio de Hermeneumática, to bring its Ugaritic database onto the Internet. Formally known as the "Generador de Segmentaciones, Restituciones y Concordancias," users are required to use special fonts with their Internet browser to use the search interface. The required fonts are available free at this site.

Not Just Bibles
http://www.iclnet.org/pub/resources/christian-resources.html

Not Just Bibles has one of the most extensive listings of various Christian resources on the Internet. It also includes a large number of denominational specific resources.

Novum Testamentum et Orbis Antiquus (NTOA)
http://www.unifr.ch/bif/ntoa/ntoa.html

This is the homepage for the series Novum Testamentum et Orbis Antiquus (NTOA) which focuses on New Testament scholarship. A listing of forthcoming volumes and a backlist of all volumes in print are available for browsing.

Nubia Salvage Project Reports
http://www-oi.uchicago.edu/OI/PROJ/NUB/Nubia.html

Report concerning the UNESCO international salvage excavation project in the reservoir area of the Aswan High Dam. Includes links to two exhibitions by the Oriental Institute, "Nubia - Its glory and its people" (1987 Exhibition Brochure) and "Vanished Kingdoms Of the Nile: The Rediscovery of Ancient Nubia" (1992 Exhibition Brochure), which were based on artifacts and information recovered during these excavations.

Karel C. Innemee's Handlist of Nubian Wallpaintings
http://132.229.192.124/www.let.data/arthis/Nubian/intro.htm

This handlist gives basic information on wall-paintings from Christian Nubia. The list includes paintings saved during the UNESCO campaign to salvage Nubian monuments, paintings which remain in situ and paintings that have been lost, but for which documentation has been preserved.

At present, images from the central church located at Abdallah-n-Irqi are available at this site, with a bibliography.

O'Donnell, James J.
http://ccat.sas.upenn.edu/jod

James J. O'Donnell of the University of Pennsylvania is one of the leaders in the use of the new tools offered by the Internet for teaching and research. As noted elsewhere in this resource listing, O'Donnell has offered several graduate level courses for credit over the Internet and has made a large body of material available in electronic format. While his homepage has links to material that reflects his interest in Augustine, Boethius and late antiquity, it is an interactive WWW exploration and demonstration of practical applications of Internet technology for teaching that is the most notable item. If after four years of using the Internet I had to choose one link to make the case for use of the Internet in teaching or research, it would be this demonstration by O'Donnell.

Odyssey in Egypt - Week by Week
http://www.website1.com/odyssey/

A site designed for virtual participation in an archaeological dig in Egypt over the Internet. Sponsored by the Scriptorium, this site is primarily focused on the use of technology to in K-12 educational settings. The principles used in this presentation could be easily adapted to more advanced educational settings.

Odyssey Online
http://www.emory.edu/CARLOS/ODYSSEY/

An educational site sponsored by the Carlos Museum at Emory University, Odyssey Online offers the opportunity to explore ancient Near Eastern, Egyptian, Greek and Roman cultures. Images of objects are drawn from the collection at the Carlos Museum and the Memorial Art Gallery of the University of Rochester in Rochester, New York. This is primarily an educational site for K-12 or non-specialist audiences. The site does suggest accessing the site with at least a 28.8 modem and installing a QuickTime plugin.

Offline Column
http://shemesh.scholar.emory.edu/scripts/offline.html

Robert Kraft edited the Offline column in *Religious Studies News* for ten years. This site offers access to all of Kraft's columns (Offline 1-44, plus the pivotal pilot article "In Quest of Computer Literacy"), as well as the more recent columns. James Adair and Patrick Durusau are the present editors of the Offline column.

The Ohio State University Excavations at Isthmia
http://www.acs.ohio-state.edu/history/isthmia/isthmia.html

Ohio State University conducts archaeological research and publication at the Sanctuary of Poseidon at Isthmia. This WWW site contains more information on the Sanctuary of Poseidon at Isthmia, the Roman Bath, a preliminary report on the 1994 field season and other information concerning this site.

Ohtfrid's Letter To Liudbert on translating the Gospels
http://kufacts.cc.ukans.edu/ftp/pub/history/Europe/Medieval/latintexts/ohtfrid.txt

James Marchand provides the Latin text of Ohtfrid's Letter to Liudbert on translating the Gospels. The Latin text is followed by some brief comments by Marchand and then his English translation of this work.

Okeanos
http://weber.u.washington.edu/~snoegel/okeanos.html

This is one of the very best collections of Web resources on biblical, Classical and Ancient Near Eastern Studies. The resources are grouped in categories that range from Archaeology: Sites and Reports to Useful Course Material. The site is well maintained and its organization makes it a pleasure to use for research.

The Old Catholic Homepage
http://www.maths.tcd.ie/hyplan/thomas/oldcath.html

This is primarily a collection of historical and confessional documents for the Old Catholic Church movement. It would be of some interest to those teaching a history of religion in Europe course.

Old Testament Pseudepigrapha Web Page
http://www.st-andrews.ac.uk/~www_sd/otpseud.html

Dr. James R. Davila, Lecturer in Early Jewish Studies, St. Andrews University, created and maintains this page in connection with his course The Old Testament Pseudepigrapha. The course examined writings excluded from the canons of both Judaism and Christianity and included use of an email discussion list as part of the discussion segment of the course. A reading list, detailed syllabus and instructions for obtaining the email discussions held during the course are available here. The course will be offered again in the spring of 1999 focusing on texts composed and transmitted in Greek.

Old Testament Pseudepigrapha: Annotated Basic Bibliography
http://www.st-andrews.ac.uk/~www_sd/bibliog.html

Compiled by Dr. James R. Davila for the Old Testament Pseudepigrapha course listed above, this annotated bibliography merits separate mention. The bibliography focuses primarily on basic works in English but includes editions of primary texts in other modern languages. Of particular note is the effort by Dr. Davila to give full references for lesser-known or fragmentary documents.

Old World Archaeology Newsletter
http://www.wesleyan.edu/classics/OWAN.html or
gopher://weserve.wesleyan.edu:70/11/Classics/OWAN

The Department of Classical Studies at Wesleyan University publishes the Old World Archaeology Newsletter three times per year. The 1994, 1995, and 1996 issues are currently available.

On Loving God by St. Bernard of Clairvaux
http://www.cs.pitt.edu/~planting/books/bernard/loving_God/loving_God.html

Part of the Christian Classics Ethereal Library, translator and source text unspecified.

Online Archaeology
http://avebury.arch.soton.ac.uk/Journal/journal.html

An experimental electronic journal to gauge technical difficulty and reader's responses to electronic publication. This issue includes "Neolithic Houses in Mainland Britain: A Sceptical View" by Julian Thomas; "On Electronic Publication in Archaeology" by William Kilbride; and "The Borges Matrix: A Serendipitous Bibliographical Narrative" by Paul Graves-Brown. Sponsored by the Department of Archaeology, University of Southhampton.

Online Bible
www.online-bible.com/

The Online Bible site offers software and electronic texts for Windows and Macintosh computers. There is free viewing software and electronic texts that include popular translations of the Bible as well as Hebrew and Greek texts. Cross Country Software also offers at this site CD-ROMs on the Bible, Reformation, John Calvin and the Master Christian Library (330 resources) for sale at very modest prices.

Online Book Initiative
ftp://ftp.std.com

The Online Book Initiative is an offering of public domain electronic texts. As of the end of 1994, there were almost 600MB of compressed text in the collection. The primary directories of interest are obi/Religion and obi/Classics, although the archive does repay some random wandering through other directories. It contains for the most part public domain texts and other similar material, although under obi/Classics there is a compressed copy of Wheelock's Latin grammar, an older but useful resource. From the OBI ftp site, there are directories for the Gutenberg Project and the Oxford Text Archive.

On-line Dictionaries
http://www.bucknell.edu/~rbeard/diction.html

The On-line Dictionaries site has links to over 500 dictionaries covering over 140 languages. In addition to the links to dictionaries, the site also collects links to on-line grammars, thesauri and multilingual dictionaries. While the quality of the dictionaries may be somewhat uneven, this is an excellent demonstration of the Web's ability to provide access to materials that are not needed on a regular basis.

Online Reference Book (ORB): Medieval Studies
http://orb.rhodes.edu/

ORB is the starting point for any serious inquiry into web based resources for medieval studies. ORB contains original articles (2 peer reviewers), bibliographies and syllabi, software and links to other resources for medievalists. Of particular interest is the Medieval Sourcebook (edited by Paul Halsall) which offers online access to electronic versions of medieval texts or references to assist in locating such text for teaching or study purposes. Designed from the outset as an academic site with institutional support, ORB maintains traditional academic standards for quality in a new medium of communication.

Online Study Bible
http://www.goshen.net/bible/

This site is most notable for the user-friendly search interfaces for its bible collections. A user can select a particular translation, including the Authorized Version (AV/KJV), the Darby translation (DBY), the New Revised Standard Version (NRSV), or one of five others and begin searching by reference or the more sophisticated word or phrase search interface. Additional resources at this site include a multi-translation concordance, Hebrew and Greek lexicons, and shareware for biblical studies.

OPAC 97
http://opac97.bl.uk/

A free online service for researching materials held in the major Reference and Document Supply Collections of the British Library. Copies of documents can be requested from the Library's Document Supply Centre (BLDSC) in most cases.

Orbis Biblicus et Orientalis (OBO)
http://www.unifr.ch/bif/obo/obo.html

Homepage for the series Orbis Biblicus et Orientalis (OBO) published by Othmar Keel and Christoph Uehlinger. OBO concentrates on publication of studies in the Hebrew Bible, ANE iconography, Egyptology, Assyriology, history of the ANE and all topics concerning the Levant. A listing of forthcoming volumes and a backlist of all volumes in print are available for browsing.

Ordinance Survey of Jerusalem
http://www.templemount.org/wilson1.html

A web republication of excerpts from the Ordinance Survey of Jerusalem conducted by Captain Charles W. Wilson in 1886.

Oriental Institute
http://www-oi.uchicago.edu/OI/default.html

James Breasted founded the Oriental Institute, a part of the University of Chicago, in 1919. This WWW homepage is one in a history of pioneering projects of the Institute, as it adapts new technology to its work in the archaeology, philology, and history of early Near Eastern civilizations. Links to information on the museum, archaeology projects, philology projects, individual scholarship, departments of the Institute, and a phone directory for all departments are present on this page. Links also lead to numerous other resources on the Internet.

Oriental Insitute - FTP Server
ftp://oi.uchicago.edu

The FTP server maintained by the Oriental Institute has a variety of resources such as the Oriental Institute Research Archives (pub/oi/resarch), which includes The Oriental Institute Research Archives Acquisitions List (RAAL), numbers 3-4, 5-6, and 7-8 (all issues are available in plain ASCII, Macintosh Microsoft Word 5.1 format, and a tab delimited, ASCII text file suitable for importing to a database); Oriental Institute Demotic Dictionary Project files (pub/oi/demotic); Oriental Institute Cushitic and Omotic Etymological Database Directory (pub/oi/cushlex); Ancient Near East (ANE) discussion list digest files (pub/ane); American Schools of Oriental Research information files (pub/asor); Archaeological Institute of American information files (pub/aia); Comprehensive Aramaic Lexicon Project information files (pub/cal); Individual research projects at the Oriental Institute (pub/research); Achaemenid Studies (pub/research/achaemenid); and Contributions by Individuals to the FTP server (pub/stuff).

The Oriental Institute Museum: Highlights from the Collections
http://www-oi.uchicago.edu/OI/MUS/HIGH/OI_Museum_Highlights.html

This virtual museum reflects the depth of the collections of the Oriental Institute Museum and the skill used in making these items available to a wider audience. The artifacts can be viewed by region, reaching from Anatolia to Egypt, or by subjects ranging from animals and boats to tools and women. The collections are suitable for browsing or serious classroom use by secondary schools lacking direct access to such collections.

Orientalia Ab Argentina: Journal of Ancient Near East History And Biblical Studies
http://www.geocities.com/Tokyo/Temple/7042/ORABARG.HTM

An entirely electronic journal devoted to articles on the history, society, economy, anthropology, philology or ecology of the Ancient Near East. Submissions can be in English, French, Italian, Spanish or Portuguese. The journal has a fairly diverse board of editors but few articles at this point in time.

Order of St. Benedict
http://www.osb.org/osb/index.html

The Order of St. Benedict WWW site is a well-organized and informative homepage with resources related not only to the Order of St. Benedict. Links to other, primary monastic, resources are also maintained at this site.

Orion Center
http://orion.mscc.huji.ac.il/

The Orion Center for the Study of the Dead Sea Scrolls and Associated Literature is part of the Institute of Jewish Studies at Hebrew University of Jerusalem. The Center website provides information on the Center and scholarly as well as educational resources. Extensive information on Center activities, a bibliography on the Dead Sea Scrolls, educational opportunities and other information on activities concerned with the Dead Sea Scrolls are available either at this site or through links to other resources.

Orthodox
http://www.forthnet.gr/hellas/Orthodox-Page/Orthodox.html
http://www.ocf.org:80/OrthodoxPage

Includes sections on Holy Scripture, Divine Liturgy, Orthodox Reading (including Texts by Orthodox Christians, Orthodox Church and Sacraments), Orthodox News, Icons, Information and Resources (including Mount Athos Greek Manuscripts Catalog, Orthodox subscriber list log files, FTP site information, and a pointer to MIT Orthodox Christian Fellowship WWW page).

Orthodoxy by G. K. Chesterton
http://www.cs.pitt.edu/~planting/books/chesterton/orthodoxy/orthodoxy.html

HTML version of Orthodoxy offered by the Christian Classics Ethereal Library. Text is also available in RTF, PDF, text, and HyperCard formats.

OsirisList
http://www.geocities.com/Athens/Olympus/1011/

This website is the home of the ancient Egyptian mailing list OsirisList. The archives of the mailing lists, conventions for the representation of the Egyptian language, the Mariannes List of Ancient Egyptian quotations, and reconstructions of the faces of the Pharaohs by Marianne Luban can be accessed at this site.

OSSHE Historical & Cultural Atlas Resource
http://darkwing.uoregon.edu/~atlas/europe/maps.html

A stunning resource with maps that detail natural resources in Europe, political changes in Ancient Mesopotamia 3000-1000 BCE, to The Jewish Diaspora: in the 1st Cent. CE and Spread of Christianity: 2nd-4th Cent. CE.

Osten, Hans Henning von der Ancient Oriental Seals in the Collection of Mr. Edward T. Newell Chicago : The University of Chicago Press, 1934 The University of Chicago Oriental Institute Publications; Vol. XXII
http://eos.lib.uchicago.edu/cgi-
bin/LIB_preserve_title.sh?CALL_NUMBER=CD5348.N54

A scanned copy of this work by the Electronic Open Stacks project at the University of Chicago Library. The work can be viewed by chapters or a reader can "jump" to a particular page in the work. These image-based texts avoid the expense of creating full text searchable versions and yet provide usable access to materials too fragile for regular use.

Ovid, Metamorphoses
gopher://gopher.vt.edu:10010/02/128/1

The full text of Ovid's Metamorphoses, approximately 950K size file, noted at the beginning of the text as "Translated into English verse under the direction of Sir Samuel Garth by John Dryden, Alexander Pope, Joseph Addison, William Congreve and other eminent hands ...."

Ovid im WWW
http://www.phil.uni-erlangen.de/~p2latein/ovid/start.html

A very complete collection of links to resources on Ovid found on the Web. The main page is in German but cites resources on a global basis.

Recent Ovidian Bibliography
http://www.nyu.edu/classes/latin2/rob/ovidbib.html

This is a bibliography on Ovid from 1990 to the present. The bibliography is searchable by author, title, or full text, which increases the usefulness of this resource. There is also a searchable database of books relating to Ovid, which are currently available from online bookstores.

Oxford Radiocarbon Accelerator Unit
http://sable.ox.ac.uk/departments/rlaha

Background information and general information on the submission of samples for dating to the Oxford Radiocarbon Accelerator Unit.

Papyrology Home Page
http://www-personal.umich.edu/~jmucci/papyrology/home.html

This site is one of the major resources in the area of papyrology. Links are included at this site to all major university projects worldwide dealing with papyri, images of papyri and ostraca on the Internet, a table of contents and index to Zeitschrift Für Papyrologie, and other papyrological resources.

PAPY-L discussion list
http://www.urz.uni-heidelberg.de/subject/hd/fak8/papy/logs/

Archives for the PAPY-L discussion list, which focuses on issues of interest to papyrologists.

The Papyrus-Collection at The Institute of Greek and Latin University of Copenhagen.
http://adam.igl.ku.dk/~bulow/PHaun.html

The Copenhagen papyrus collection is described at this web site with brief publication information.

The Papyrus of Ani (The Egyptian Book of the Dead)
http://www.sas.upenn.edu/African_Studies/Books/Papyrus_Ani.html

The translation of the Papyrus of Ani as one long file by E. A. Wallis Budge. This is apparently the same English text that is used for the Dover reprints of his translation, without the hieroglyphic text, transliteration, critical notes, etc., of the original. However dated and/or inaccurate Budge's translation, it is only made worse by presentation without any apparatus at all.

The Papyrus of Ani
http://www.lysator.liu.se/~drokk/BoD

Budge's translation of the Book of the Dead converted into hypertext by Mathias Hansson. See also preceding comments on the reproduction of out-dated translation without their original apparatus.

The Papyrus of Ani
http://www.teleport.com/~ddonahue/papy.html

A total of twenty-one image files, the first ten of which lead to larger JPEG images of the depicted scene from this papyrus. This site is an excellent illustration of the ability of the WWW to distribute images of original primary materials.

Papyrus Westcar
http://www.ccer.ggl.ruu.nl/texts/ael/westcar/index.html

Middle Kingdom text translated by Geoffrey Graham and typeset by Mike Dyall-Smith.

The Paths of History
http://almashriq.hiof.no/lebanon/900/930/930.1/ph/ph.html

A listing of archeological projects in the Beirut Central District by the Ministry of Culture and Higher Education and the Directorate General of Antiquities and SOLIDERE. The site includes a clickable map of archaeological sites in the Beirut Central District.

Peeters Publishers
http://193.75.142.2:62/

Peeters Publishers offers an online catalog that can be searched or browsed over the WWW. Searching is the best choice as the organization of the catalog requires traversing several links before reaching information on actual publications.

The Peloponnesian War
http://www.mygale.org/~sdelille/gdpa.html

A very large collection of both local resources and links to other web resources on the Peloponnesian war. Major sections include local resources, ancient sources (links to historical texts), Thucydides, the war in general, particular points, inscriptions, reviews, bibliographies and discussion lists.

Peloponnesian War (431-404 B.C.)
http://www.cfcsc.dnd.ca/links/milhist/pelo.html

Approaching the Peloponnessian War from the standpoint of military history this site offers a contrast to the usual classical view this event. Links are included to most of the major Peloponnesian War sites but resources describing the military aspects of the conflict take precedence.

Pelusium: Gateway to Egypt
http://www.archaeology.org/online/features/pelusium/

This is a detailed report on the danger to archaeological sites from the construction of the Peace Canal from the Nile east to El Arish. Grzymski carefully documents what is known from prior finds in this area in constructing a case for preserving the sites that could be lost or damaged by the construction of this canal.

Pennsylvania Sumerian Dictionary Project
http://ccat.sas.upenn.edu/psd/

The homepage for the Pennsylvania Sumerian Dictionary Project offers links to the Index to Sumerian Secondary Literature and information on a mailing list for the dictionary.

The Perseus Atlas Project
http://perseus.holycross.edu/PAP/Atlas_project.html

As part of the Perseus Project, the Perseus Atlas Project is developing a geographic information system (GIS) which focuses on classical Greece. Currently available resources include Landsat satellite data, a gazetteer of archaeological sites, and, perhaps of greatest importance, a linking of references in classical texts to actual geographic features in the GIS. At present there is a database of ancient geographic names that provides the entire text of Stephanus of Byzantium's Ethinica, which returns the name of the site, the type of site, the region, and the full text of Stephanus' description.

Perseus Project
http://www.perseus.tufts.edu

Perseus is a teaching and research tool that combines in a multimedia database environment resources for the study of ancient Greek literature, history, art, and archaeology. The material currently available is a result of the cooperative effort of a large team of specialists, including archaeologists, classicists, historians, and philologists. The Greek text of Aeschylus' Agammemnon is available, for example, but unlike other Greek texts on the Internet, each word has a morphological link to the appropriate section in the Intermediate Liddell-Scott-Jones Greek Lexicon, which itself has hypertext links to the usage of a particular word in other Greek texts in the database. In addition to its own unique contributions in this rapidly developing area, Perseus maintains searchable links to well over one hundred other sites of interest to classicists. Perseus is based at the Classics Department, Tufts University and is supported by a number of public as well as private sponsors.

The Perseus Project and Beyond: How Building a Digital Library Challenges the Humanities and Technology
http://www.dlib.org/dlib/january98/01crane.html

Gregory Crane's article "The Perseus Project and Beyond" appeared in the January 1998 issue of D-Lib magazine (http://www.dlib.org/dlib/). D-Lib is one of the leading journals addressing issues of technology in both libraries and the humanities. Professor Crane's article provides important insights into the role that technology can play in developing academic resources and generating broad support for areas of academic study. In his introduction he notes, "Even now, as our modest digital library on ancient Greek culture finds its way into homes, schools and offices where traditional scholarly publications have not reached, we can see by the patterns of use and the mail that we receive the stirrings of a vast audience, hungry for ideas and for that practice of thought to which we, professional academics, have been privileged to dedicate our lives." This article deserves close study and discussion by academics seeking to use technology to advance the study of humanities in every field.

The Persian Expedition
http://www-oi.uchicago.edu/OI/PROJ/PER/Persian_Ex.html

A recounting of the Oriental Institute's excavations in Persia, including a site plan of the terraces of Persepolis, a brief account of work at Naqsh-I Rustam and Tall-I Bakun, an aerial view of Persepolis, and information on the Holmes expedition to Luristan. A short bibliography of Oriental Institute publications on these excavations completes this resource.

Petrie, W. M. Flinders, Naukratis London : Trubner and Company, 1886 The Egyptian Exploration Society
http://eos.lib.uchicago.edu/cgi-bin/LIB_preserve_title.sh?CALL_NUMBER=DT57.E28_vol3,6

A scanned copy of this work by the Electronic Open Stacks project at the University of Chicago Library. The work can be viewed by chapters or a reader can "jump" to a particular page in the work. These image-based texts avoid the expense of creating full text searchable versions and yet provide usable access to materials too fragile for regular use.

Petronian Society Ancient Novel Web Page
http://www.chss.montclair.edu/classics/petron/PSNNOVEL.HTML

The Petronian Society webpage offers a number of interesting resources for scholars interested in ancient novel or related genres. Two issues of the Petronian Society Newsletter are available (1996 and 1997) both of which contain extensive references to secondary literature and reviews. A bibliography of over 2,000 items relating to ancient novels and other genres and summaries of ancient novels are also available.

The Philistine Homepage
http://home.uleth.ca/geo/philhp.htm

Maps and other information on important Philistine sites such as Ashkelon, Ashdod, Tell Qasile and Ekron. Also offers background information on the Philistines.

Philo Alexandrinus's De Somniis
http://www.hivolda.no/asf/kkf/marindex.htm

An abstract of the author's dissertation El De Somniis de Filón de Alejandría, defended in Madrid (Universidad Complutense), September 12th. 1995.

Philo Concordance Project
http://proffen.avh.unit.no/rel/Filon.htm

The University of Trondheim sponsors this Web site detailing their Philo Concordance Project. It is the aim of this project to produce a complete Greek concordance to the texts of the Greek-Jewish philosopher and exegete, Philo of Alexandria. This Web page offers online examples of this ongoing project.

The Philotheou Monastery Project
http://abacus.bates.edu:80/~rallison/

The Philotheou Monastery Project is being conducted under the direction of Robert W. Allison of the Department of Philosophy and Religion, Bates College. This is the primary site for information concerning the Philotheou Monastery catalog project (which is related to the Mount Athos Greek Manuscripts Catalog Project of the Patriarchal Institute for Patristics Studies). It includes general information on the Patriarchal Institute for Patristic Studies, a summary catalog of Greek manuscripts of the Philotheou Monastery (summary information on approximately 100 codices at present), description of the method used for full description of Akolouthies, a history of the Philotheou Monastery and its manuscript library. Access is also provided to the an electronic archive of paper types and watermarks preserved in Philotheite manuscripts.

Pindar, Commentaries on Individual Odes of
http://classics.rutgers.edu/pindar.html

Lowell Edmunds constructed this bibliography of commentaries on the odes of Pindar. Primarily limited to more recent material with directions for finding nineteenth-century commentaries.

Pirqe Rabbi Eliezer Electronic Text Editing Project
http://www.usc.edu/dept/huc-la/pre-project/

Lewis Barth has made images of a first edition (Constantinople, 1514) and two manuscripts (HUC MS.75 HUC MS.2043) of this work available as part of his text editing project. The images were made available with the permission of the Hebrew Union College-Jewish Institute of Religion and bear a digital watermark.

Pirradazish: Bulletin Of Achaemenian Studies
ftp://oi.uchicago.edu/pub/research/achaemenid

Edited by Charles E. Jones, Pirradazish focuses primarily on materials related to the Achaemenian Empire. Bulletins 5-8, containing primarily bibliographical material, are currently available.

Pitts Theology Library, Emory University
http://www.pitts.emory.edu

The Pitts Theology Library homepage provides a useful guide to computing resources for students of religion both at this library and on the Internet. Of particular note under the Reference link, is a set of bibliographies by the staff of the Pitts Library on a variety of religious studies topics.

Plato, Works
gopher://gopher.vt.edu:10010/11/131

The complete works of Plato, translated by Benjamin Jowett.

Plotinus, The Six Enneads
gopher://gopher.vt.edu:10010/02/132/1

English translation of Plotinus' The Six Enneads by Stephen MacKenna and B. S. Page.

Ploutarchos
http://www.usu.edu/~history/plout.htm

The website of the International Plutarch Society, Ploutarchos offers information on the society as well as an extensive link collection to texts of Plutarch on the Web. A lengthy bibliography of Plutarch (approximately 227K) is another important resource at this site.

The Pluralism Project
http://www.fas.harvard.edu/~pluralsm/

Diana L. Eck of Harvard University began the Pluralism Project to study and document religious diversity in the United States. Of special interest to the project were immigrant religious communities that had arisen in the last thirty years and the impact of pluralism on American society. The project has amassed a large amount of materials from a wide range of immigrant religious communities and interested researchers should contact the project for further information on accessing these materials. Research data and papers from scholars are accepted for inclusion into the archives of this project and the project administers small grants to further studies of immigrant religious communities. An online database is maintained of over 3,000 religious centers in the United States representing many of the religious communities that are the focus of this project.

Plutarch
gopher://gopher.vt.edu:10010/11/133

The complete writings of Plutarch, translated by John Dryden.

Political Change and Cultural Continuity in Eshnunna from the Ur III to the Old Babylonian Period
http://www-oi.uchicago.edu/OI/DEPT/RA/DISPROP/Reichel_diss.html

This is the dissertation proposal of Clemens Reichel to the Department of Near Eastern Languages and Civilizations at the University of Chicago. A good step towards sharing information over the WWW that is of interest to other graduate students and specialists in particular fields.

The Epistle of Polycarp to the Philippians
gopher://ccat.sas.upenn.edu:3333/00/Religious/ChurchWriters/ApostolicFathers/Polycarp

The Epistle of Polycarp, translated by J. B. Lightfoot. Adapted and modified in an unspecified manner by Athena Data Products.

The Martyrdom of Polycarp
gopher://ccat.sas.upenn.edu:3333/00/Religious/ChurchWriters/ApostolicFathers/Martyrdom_Polycarp

The Martyrdom of Polycarp, translated by J. B. Lightfoot. Adapted and modified in an unspecified manner by Athena Data Products.

Polyglot Bible (The Gospel of St. Luke)
http://138.87.135.33/bibl-eng/bible.htm

This is a very able demonstration by Mark Davies of the use of hypertext to create a polyglot version of a biblical text. In this case, Davies used the Gospel of St. Luke in Old English, Middle English, Early Modern English and Present Day English to create this polyglot version of St. Luke.

Polyglot Bible (1 Samuel)
http://138.87.135.33/bibl-span/samuel.htm

This is the site of another polyglot rendition of a biblical text, in this case, 1 Samuel, by Mark Davies. The text of 1 Samuel is presented in Latin, Old Spanish and Modern Spanish for this hypertext.

Pomoerium. Studia et commentarii ad orbem classicum spectantia
http://pomoerium.com

Pomoerium is an electronic journal publishing articles in classical studies with a particular emphasis on ancient history and classical philology. The journal is composed primarily of solicited materials but suggestions and ideas for articles are welcome. Articles are accepted in English, German, French or Italian. The journal is currently free but at some unspecified future time users will need to be registered to view the journal contents.

Pompeii Forum Project
http://jefferson.village.virginia.edu/pompeii/page-1.html

This is a collaborative project between several departments at the University of Virginia that focuses on the remains of Pompeii and its Forum in particular. The project has made images and reconstructions of the site available for viewing over the Internet. This type of project spans specialties and institutions in a way that is possible only with the advent of the Internet.

Papal Documents
http://listserv.american.edu/catholic/church/papal/papal.html

This site offers a listing of encyclicals and other papal documents by the reigning Pope. The following popes are represented: Boniface VIII (1294-1303), Paul III (1534-1549), Benedict XIV (1740-1758), Gregory XVI (1831-1846), Pius IX (1846-1878), Leo XIII (1878-1903), Pius X (1903-1914), Benedict XV (1914-1922), Pius XI (1922-1939), Pius XII (1939-1958), John XXIII (1958-1963), Paul VI (1963-1978), John Paul II (1978-). This collection includes such important works as Unam Sanctam, Sublimus Dei, Pacem in Terris, Populorum Progressio, and Puebla and Beyond, All of the documents are provided in English translation.

The Portrayal of God's Absence in the Book of Ezekiel
http://shemesh.scholar.emory.edu/scripts/SBL/ezekiel/block.html

A paper presented at the Society of Biblical Literature Seminar Theological Perspectives in the Book of Ezekiel by Dr. Daniel I. Block, The Southern Baptist Seminary.

Postmodern Bible: Amos
http://www.auckland.ac.nz/acte/pmb/index2.htm

To view the Hebrew text at this site the user must download and install Hebrew fonts from ftp://ftp.snunit.k12.il/pub/fonts/pc/ (webfont.exe and webfont.txt). This site is limited to the text of Amos although it does a very credible job with both the text and commentary.

Processing Pottery in the Field: The First Step Toward Publication
http://www.cla.umn.edu/cnes/pottery/

A discussion of both practical and theoretical aspects of processing excavation pottery during and after an excavation season.

Project Genesis
http://www.torah.org

A Jewish education project that has used cyberspace to bring information about Jewish philosophy, kabbalah, ethics and law to an international audience. There are online classes that focus on various areas of Jewish studies and are free of charge.

Project Gutenberg Etext of Plutarch's Lives
ftp://ftp.prairienet.org/pub/providers/gutenberg/etext96/plivs10.txt

This is an etext collection of A.H. Clough's English translation of Plutarch's Lives.

Project Runeberg
http://www.lysator.liu.se:7500/runeberg/Main.html

A voluntary initiative to create and collect free electronic editions of classic Nordic literature and art. At present there are fifty titles, including the Elder Edda, which are available for downloading.

Project Libellus
gopher://wiretap.spies.com/11/Library/Classic/Latin/Libellus

A fairly extensive collection of Latin classics on the Internet Wiretap site. Includes works by Caesar, Catallus, Cicero, Holmes' Commentary on De Bello Gallico, Horace, Livy, and others. The texts are in the TeX format.

Prosopographia Aegypti
http://www.ccer.ggl.ruu.nl/names/names.html

A database of Egyptian names based upon the archives of the Wörterbuch der Agyptischen Sprache (Berlin-Brandenburgische Akademie der Wissenschaften). At the time of writing, the database contained only names from the first half of the Egyptian alphabet (A-H). This is n important resource for Egyptologists and an excellent demonstration of the delivery of Egyptian language material over the Internet. The database is courtesy of Jochen Hallof, of Berlin and the interactive features that make the database so useful by Hans van den Berg of the Centre for Computer-Aided Egyptological Research.

Proto-Cuneiform Texts from Archaic Babylonia
http://early-cuneiform.humnet.ucla.edu/

This site has a prototype database for cuneiform texts from Babylon. At present the database has only ten texts and some 17 signs in the database but it is estimated that upon completion it will hold 5,000 texts and some 1,500 signs. Scholars interested in proto-cuneiform texts are should review this work and contact its participants with comments and suggestions.

Prudentius' Liber Peristephanon
http://ccat.sas.upenn.edu/jod/wola.html

The text of Purdentius' Liber Peristephanon is part of James J. O'Donnell's Worlds of Antiquity homepage. The text is a working tool and is not presented as an authoritative critical edition.

Ptahotep's Australian Egyptology Page
http://www.zeta.org.au/~ptahotep/

Most notable for a collection of texts, some onsite and other by hypertext link, composed of English translations of Egyptian material. The texts include excerpts from the Maxims of Ptahhotep, the Inscription of Harkhuf, the Biography of Ineni and others. Unlike some Internet text collections it is noted that these translations date from 1906 and may have been superceded by advances in the study of ancient Egyptian language.

Pylos Regional Archaeological Project
http://rome.classics.lsa.umich.edu/projects/prap/prap.html

A preliminary report on the Pylos Regional Archaeological Project in southwest Messenia, Greece for 1993. This report includes a number of images and other information from this site.

Pyramids: The Inside Story
http://www.pbs.org/wgbh/nova/pyramid/

Based on a Nova program by the same name this website offers rarely matched educational materials on Ancient Egypt, the pyramids generally and the tombs of Khufu, Khafre, Menkaure, as well as the Sphinx. An excavation in Giza is followed in detail and the user is provided with maps and transcripts of the original broadcasts.

Quran

The Quran is available from a number of sources as listed below. Translations of the Qur)an have been listed in the hopes that exposure to even a "translation" will inspire some to learn Arabic and read the original text. The work by Abdullah Ysufali listed below represents a tradition that considers "translations" to be commentaries and not translations in the sense accepted in Western traditions.

Arabic
ftp://cs-ftp.bu.edu/amass/Islam/Quran/arabic-by-eyler.hqx (must be downloaded and viewed on Macintosh)
http://www.wam.umd.edu/~lilsistr/Quran/quran.html (online Arabic image files, non-searchable)

These links lead to copies of the Quran in its original Arabic text.

Translations

gopher://ccat.sas.upenn.edu:3333/11/Religious/Islam/Quran (trans. M. H. Shakir)
ftp://cs-ftp.bu.edu/amass/Islam/Quran/trans-pickthal.text.gz
ftp://cs-ftp.bu.edu/amass/Islam/Quran/trans-yousufali.text.gz
ftp://ftp.wustl.edu/systems/mac/info-mac/Old/app/quran-arabic-english-one.hqx
ftp://ftp.wustl.edu/systems/mac/info-mac/Old/app/quran-arabic-english-two.hqx

These links lead to translations of the Quran into English.

Quran Browser

http://goon.stg.brown.edu/quran_browser/pqeasy.html

The Quran Browser allows searches of three English "translations" of the Quran by passage, word or word-part. This browser is another scholarly tool from Richard Goerwitz, who is now with the Scholarly Technology Group, Brown University.

Rangjung Yeshe Tibetan-English Dharma Dictionary

http://www.nitartha.org/dictionary.html

This is an online version of the Rangjung Yeshe Tibetan-English Dharma Dictionary, which contains over 65,000 entries. Tibetan terms should be entered in Wylie format for proper searching. (Example given at web site was karma would be entered kar ma.) The dictionary returns English translations of the term entered.

Rassegna degli Strumenti Informatici per lo Studio dell' Antichita Classica

http://ecn01.economia.unibo.it/dipartim/stoant/rassegna1/intro.html

This is one of the more complete collections of resources on the Web for Classical Antiquity. An alphabetical index of sites lists some 1,000 resources, while those awaiting addition to the main list or verification number over 800.

The Raphael Stanze and Loggia (via Christus Rex)

http://www.christusrex.org/www1/stanzas/0-Raphael.html

This is a very impressive collection of 226 images from the Raphael Stanze and Loggia at the Vatican in Rome. Highly recommended for viewing on a high-resolution screen and a fast Internet connection. Viewing on a computer screen is no substitute for being in the presence of such works of art, but if the choice is between no knowledge of the work at all and this pale imitation, then the latter seems an attractive choice.

Reading Lists for the MA (MAT) in Classics
http://classics.rutgers.edu/mareading.html

The reading lists for the Master's degree in Classics at Rutgers University provide prospective graduate students in the classics guidance to the texts that will be required as part of their program. It can also serve as a reading list for those pursuing classical studies independently or who wish to refresh their knowledge of the classics in a systematic way. Separate reading lists are given for both Latin and Greek.

Reading Lists for the Ph.D. in Classics
http://classics.rutgers.edu/phdreading.html

The reading lists for the Ph.D. in Classics at Rutgers University provide prospective graduate students in the classics guidance to the texts that will be required as part of their program. It can also serve as a reading list for those pursuing classical studies independently or who wish to refresh their knowledge of the classics in a systematic way. Separate reading lists are given for both Latin and Greek.

Recommended Reading on the Ancient Near East: A Guide to Introductory Readings on the Ancient Near Eastern World
http://www-oi.uchicago.edu/OI/DEPT/RA/RECREAD/REC_READ.html

This is a collection of basic bibliographic references on the Ancient Near East from the Research Archives of the Oriental Institute at University of Chicago. Hyperlinks connect to basic resources that are available over the Internet. An excellent resource for those studying or teaching on the many topics related to the Ancient Near East.

The Relationship Between Exegesis and Expository Preaching
http://www.mastersem.edu/journal/j2th2.htm

Robert L. Thomas, Professor of New Testament at the Master's Seminary explores the use of expository preaching to convey the results of biblical exegesis. Recognizing that the parishioners almost always lack the ability to work in the original biblical languages or with traditional exegetical tools, it is the minister's job to convey readings found in exegesis in a way that can be understood by his audience.

Religion in South Asia Archives
http://www.acusd.edu/~lnelson/risa/

The Religion in South Asia Archives (RISA) project was formed by the Religion in South Asia Section of the American Academy of Religion. These archives were designed to give all scholars of religion in South Asia easy access to the archives of the mailing list for this section (see RISA-L under mailing lists) and to other resources of interest to scholars in this field. Other resources at this site include a document archive, bibliographies, teaching resources, video and multimedia resources, religion in South Asia links and instructions on obtaining the list of subscribers to RISA-L.

Religion on the Web
http://www.stolaf.edu/people/kchanson/relweb.html

An extensive collection of links organized by religious traditions such as: Baha'i, Buddhism, Christianity: General, Christianity: Eastern Orthodox, Christianity: Protestant, Christianity: Roman Catholic, Hinduism, Islam, Jainism, Judaism, Mormonism, Native American Religions, Shamanism, Sikhism, and, Ancient Religions: Roman. A very good starting place for web related research on primarily extant religions or their predecessors.

Religion, Society and Culture in Newfoundland and Labrador
http://www.ucs.mun.ca/~hrollman/

Dr. Hans Rollmann has created a set of web pages that address the social and cultural interaction of religious faiths over time in Newfoundland and Labrador. The religions documented at this site include native religions, Anglicanism, Roman Catholicism, Methodism, Moravian, Congregationalism, Salvation Army, Pentecostal and others. The site also makes local documentation available for all the religious movements examined.

Religious and Sacred Texts
http://www.marshall.edu/~wiley6/index.html

A useful gathering of links to sacred texts, organized by religious traditions. Links are provided to the following groups of texts: Apocryphal Texts, the Analects of Confucius, Bahai, Egyptian Book of the Dead, Ethiopian, Gnostic, Hindu, Islamic, Mormon, Sikh, Taoist, Zen, and Zoroastrian.

Resource Pages for Biblical Studies
http://www.hivolda.no/asf/kkf/rel-stud.html

Extensive collection of links for resources related to biblical studies. The links are gathered under the general categories of texts and translations, linguistic resources, lexica, libraries and publishers.

Resources for the Study of East Asian Language and Thought
http://www.acmuller.gol.com/index.html

This site offers an extensive and current listing of resources for the study of East Asian languages and texts. Resources at the site include a CJK-English Dictionary Database, a dictionary of East Asian CJK Buddhist Terms, CJK character lexicons, a directory of on-line CJK E-texts, annotated links to significant textual resources on the Web, and classic texts offered in English translation.

Restoration Movement
http://www.mun.ca/rels/restmov/index.html

The homepage for the Restoration Movement documents the history of the Churches of Christ, the Christian Churches, and the Disciples of Christ, and the efforts of the Restoration Movement to unite those distinct traditions.

Restoring ancient Egyptian artifacts... by computer.
http://131.211.68.206/ccer/restore.html

Hans van den Berg demonstrates at this homepage the use of photo editing software for the restoration of archaeological artifacts. As photo editing involves only the manipulation of an image of the original, there is more freedom to experiment with possible reconstructions. Images presently available include prince Amerherkhopshef (son of Ramesses III) from his tomb in the Valley of the Queens and, from the tomb of general Horemheb in Saqqara, an image of scribes. Work is currently in progress on an image from the tomb of Menna.

Retiarius: Commentarii Periodici Latini
http://www.uky.edu/ArtsSciences/Classics/retiarius/

Retiarius is a solely electronic journal published in Latin concerned with the study of Latin language and literature. A variety of articles on the Latin language and texts are currently available for viewing.

Revelations From Megiddo
http://www.tau.ac.il:81/~archpubs/newslett.html

A newsletter from the Megiddo excavations containing articles on: Egyptians at Early Bronze Megiddo, Thutmose III & the 'Aruna Pass Survey, Faunal Remains from Megiddo, Megiddo's Charms Capture Student, Plus: Megiddo Up-and-Comers and New, and, Publications of the Megiddo Staff. This newsletter dated November 1997 (Number 2) reveals that Egyptian pottery has been confirmed at Megiddo, raising important questions concerning Egyptian influence on the culture in Canaan. These artifacts (pots) were found in an abandoned monumental EBI (fourth millennium BCE) temple compound.

Revival of the Ancient Library of Alexandria
http://www.unesco.org/webworld/alex/alex.htm

Sponsored by the Egyptian government and UNESCO this site offers a virtual tour of the historic Ancient Library of Alexandria. Perhaps just as importantly this site showcases the ongoing construction of a new Library of Alexandria to honor this important historical and contemporary city.

Revue Internationale des Droits de l'Antiquite
http://www.ulg.ac.be/vinitor/rida/

Beginning with 3e Serie, Tome XLIII, 1996, the Revue Internationale des Droits de l'Antiquite has begun placing articles from the journal online for free viewing. The journal focuses primarily on ancient Greek and Roman law issues but occasionally has articles of specific interest to biblical scholars.

RK Ancient Fonts 1
http://www.geocities.com/Athens/9145/index.html

R. Kainhofer has developed fonts for Symbol accentuated Sanskrit, Meroitic, Ugaritic, and Old Persian cuneiform that are freely available at this site. The fonts are TTF Windows fonts and are available with or without an installation program.

Roja Muthiah Research Library
http://www.lib.uchicago.edu/LibInfo/SourcesBySubject/SouthAsia/RMRL.html

A mirror of the Roja Muthiah Research Library in Chennai (formerly Madras), India located at the University of Chicago. The library has one of the largest collections of research materials for Tamil studies in existence. A searchable interface to the library collection with notes on the transliteration scheme used is available.

Roman Law, Bibliography
http://www.law.pitt.edu/hibbitts/rome.htm

A useful bibliography on Roman law and legal practices prepared by Professor Bernard J. Hibbitts in for courses taught at the University of Pittsburgh School of Law.

Roman Law Resources
http://www.jura.uni-sb.de/english/

Available in English, Latin, German and Italian, the site of the Roman Law section of the Law-related Internet Project at the University of Saarbrücken will interest classicists and legal scholars. The core of the project seeks to link fragments of the Corpus Iuris (Emperor Justinian) with the glosses of Accursius. The site also provides background information on Roman law and its medieval commentators that form the basis for many modern legal systems.

ROMARCH: A Resource for the Art and Archaeology of Ancient Italy and the Provinces of Rome
http://www.umich.edu/~pfoss/ROMARCH.html

ROMARCH is the companion of the ROMARCH Internet discussion list sponsored by the Interdepartmental Program in Classical Art and Archaeology at the University of Michigan. The focus of the list and this WWW site is the art and archaeology of Italy and the Roman provinces, 1000 B.C. to A.D. 600. The site offers access to the archives of the discussion list, an index to more than 150 links of interest, and information on the operation of ROMARCH.

Romulus Project: An Electronic Library of Latin Literature with Virtual Commentary
http://ccat.sas.upenn.edu/~romulus/romulus.html

Dr. William Harris first wrote the Romulus Project paper in 1996 and it was placed on the Web some months later. The Romulus Project is a call for the creation of an electronic corpus of Latin texts with hyperlinked commentaries. Dr. Harris establishes the need for electronic versions of Latin texts with commentary and outlines a program to create such texts.

Rosenbaum, David Myriad
http://members.tripod.com/~davidmyriad/myriads.font.page.html

David Myriad has created Moabite, Phoenician and Ugaritic fonts for Macintosh computers which can be downloaded from this site.

Routledge
http://www.routledge.com/

The Routledge site offers access to a searchable database of all its published titles and information concerning its many books and other products. One of the more notable resources is the "The Philosophy Resource Center" which is a guide maintained by Routledge to philosophy resources and guides on the Internet. There is also a Current Awareness Service for philosophy that offers updates as new philosophy materials appear on the Internet.

Royal Inscriptions of Mesopotamia (RIM)
http://www.chass.utoronto.ca/nmc/rim/

Homepage for the Royal Inscriptions of Mesopotamia project which is in the process of publishing standard editions of the inscriptions of rulers of ancient Mesopotamia. This site contains general information on the project, a listing of its publications and its personnel.

St. Shenouda Center for Coptic Studies
http://www.stshenouda.com

The premier site for Coptic Studies on the Internet, which includes information on the vast resources assembled for the study of Coptic and the Coptic Christian religious heritage.

Sanskrit Home Page
http://reality.sgi.com/employees/atul/sanskrit/sanskrit.html

The Sanskrit home page is an extensive collection of resources for the study of Sanskrit. Links lead to collections of Sanskrit songs, short-stories, word games, sentences used in common conversation as well as excerpts from modern publications in Sanskrit. One primary resource of interest is an online Sanskrit dictionary that permits searching for exact matches to Sanskrit words, matching prefixes of words, substrings of words and searching for all Sanskrit words that have certain English words in one of their definition fields. A list of books for beginners and a listing of bookstores that carry Sanskrit materials are listed along with other relevant sites on the WWW.

Sanskrit manuscript of Isa Upanishad
http://www.ucl.ac.uk/~ucgadkw/isa-upanisad.html

Drawn from the library of the Wellcome Institute for the History of Museum, bearing shelf mark Sanskrit MS alpha 37, this site presents scanned images of a manuscript of Isa Upanishad. Dominik Wujastyk, who is responsible for this presentation, welcomes comments on this experiment in providing Web access to Sanskrit manuscripts. Issues include the adequacy of the resolution, type of image (TIFF, JPEG, etc.), color vs. black and white images, for what purposes are the images useful?

Sanskrit manuscript of Patañjali's Yogasûtras
http://www.ucl.ac.uk/~ucgadkw/yogasutras.html

Drawn from the library of the Wellcome Institute for the History of Museum, bearing shelf mark Sanskrit MS alpha 997, this site presents scanned images of a manuscript of Patañjali's Yogasûtras. Dominik Wujastyk, who is responsible for this presentation, welcomes comments on this experiment in providing Web access to Sanskrit manuscripts. Issues include the adequacy of the resolution, type of image (TIFF, JPEG, etc.), color vs. black and white images, for what purposes are the images useful?

Sanskrit Manuscripts (Upenn)
http://www.library.upenn.edu/etext/sasia/skt-mss/

The University of Pennsylvania has created an electronic archive of South Asian (Sanskrit) manuscripts that can be viewed over the WWW. Some eighteen manuscripts are already available and more are to be added from the collection of manuscripts at the University of Pennsylvania. Despite holding the largest collection of such manuscripts in North America, the University of Pennsylvania has made these images freely available to all interested scholars. This is a far cry from the practices of other manuscript collections both in the U.S. and abroad where limiting access seems to be a cardinal virtue.

SARAI: South Asia Resource Access on the Internet
http://www.columbia.edu/cu/libraries/indiv/area/sarai/

Sponsored by Columbia University, the Sarai offered access to a collection of links on all matters pertaining to South Asia. Resources are listed by country of interest, by subject area and ultimately are searchable in a database maintained by Sarai. For scholars working in any area of South Asian studies it would be difficult to find a better starting place for finding Internet resources.

SAGAR: South Asia Graduate Research Journal
http://asnic.utexas.edu/asnic/sagar/sagar.main.html

The Center for Asian Studies at the University of Texas at Austin sponsors SAGAR, a biannual journal composed of articles by graduate students and young scholars in South Asia studies. The journal is available in print, over the WWW, and by email subscription.

Sakhr
http://www.sakhrsoft.com/

This is one of the most comprehensive sites on the Web for software for displaying Arabic text. It is also an important site for materials relating to the study of Arabic and Islam.

Scholarly Societies Project
http://www.lib.uwaterloo.ca/society/overview.html

A listing of Internet resources of 533 Scholarly Societies that forms part of the Scholarly Societies Project's effort to provide greater access to information about scholarly societies.

Scholia Reviews(update entry)
http://www.und.ac.za/und/classics/scholia.html

The Scholia website offers electronic, pre-publication versions of reviews that may appear in the printed version of the journal. The Scholia journal focuses on studies in classical antiquity.

Science, the Occult, and Religion
http://www.library.upenn.edu/etext/occult/

This is a collection of images of 15th and 16th century treatises on the subjects of science, the occult and religion. These works include: Under the heading of Science: Miscellany of Scientific Treatises: manuscript, ca. 1450-1475, John French's Art of Distillation (1651), Edgar Fahs Smith Memorial Collection: Images of Philosophers, Scientists and Scientific Apparatus; Under the heading of Occult: Sindon euangelica, by Emanuele Filiberto Pingone (1581), Tractatus duo (de sortilegiis and de lamiis et excellentia) by P. Grillandus and G. Ponzinibio (1592), Aqua philosophica atque occulta, in Miscellany of Scientific Treatises.

SCRIPTA
http://www.univ.trieste.it/scripta/scripta.html

Paolo Tosolini is responsible for this experimental project on the study of Palaeography. The software for this project has been developed using Multimedia Toolbook 3.0 for Microsoft Windows.

Scriptorium Center for Christian Antiquities
http://www.scriptorium.org/scriptorium/

A non-sectarian research center that focuses on the Van Kampen Collection of ancient artifacts, manuscripts and rare printed materials. This website offers information on the activities of the Center and its academic initiatives. The Odessey in Egypt project for K-12 educators and interdisciplinary seminars in textual and codicological analysis for advanced scholars are representative of the activities of the Center.

Scottish Egyptology
http://wkweb4.cableinet.co.uk/iwhawkins/egypt/scotland.htm

A very good guide to the resources for Egyptologists held by Scottish museums. Listings of all known Scottish museums and galleries with Egyptian exhibits, images from the National

Museums of Scotland Gallery, news from the N.M.S. Mummy Project and Amarna objects in the N.M.S. are some of the resources found here.

A Scribe of Kmt
ftp://newton.newton.cam.ac.uk/pub/ancient/egypt/kmt.sea.hqx

A HyperCard stack for the Macintosh, by Mike Dyall-Smith. This consists of a set of linked stacks designed to introduce the beginner to hieroglyphs to signs, phonetics, and simple principles of writing.

The Search for Ubar
http://observe.ivv.nasa.gov/nasa/exhibits/ubar/ubar_0.html

This is a detailed and entertaining account of the use of remote sensing to find the lost city of Ubar. Mentioned in the Koran, the Arabian Nights and Bedouin folklore the city of Ubar remained unknown until discovered using search techniques developed by NASA. These techniques have relevance for scholars seeking evidence for settlements and travel routes in the Ancient Near East.

The Secrets of the Dead Sea Scrolls
http://www.edf.fr/html/en/mag/mmorte/intro.htm

An interesting site that focuses on the Copper Scroll of the Dead Sea Scrolls and provides a good account of the restoration process by EDF-Valectra Laboratory on the Copper Scroll. Images include a facsimile of the Copper Scroll by the process of galvanoplasty.

SELA Journals Project
http://shemesh.scholar.emory.edu/scripts/SELA/SELA.html

The SELA Journals Project is a cooperative venture between Scholars Press and the Emory University Libraries to distribute four of the journals published by Scholars Press in electronic format. The project began with the 1996 issues of each journal: the *Journal of the American Academy of Religion, Semeia, Biblical Archaeologist* (now called *Near Eastern Archaeology*), and *Critical Review of Books in Religion*. Back issues of *Semeia* were included as part of this project as well as the appearance of proposed *Semeia* articles as electronic preprints. While the texts are delivered over the web as HTML files for the convenience of most users, the actual archive files are held in TEILite (SGML) format and converted for web delivery.

Semantics of Ancient Hebrew Database
http://www.ed.ac.uk/~dreimer/SAHD/

An international cooperative project to develop a database of ancient Hebrew, with references to secondary literature. A preliminary version of the entry for the lexeme TFPEL is available.

Seminary Co-op
http://www.semcoop.com/

The website for the Seminary Co-op lists recent titles stocked by the bookstore, prior issues of The Front Table, an announcement of new titles, special discounted titles and information on ordering books from the Co-op.

Semitic Museum
http://fas-www.harvard.edu/~semitic/museum_semitic.html

The Semitic Museum located at Harvard University houses important collections of Near Eastern artifacts, sponsors the publication of the Harvard Semitic Series and Harvard Semitic Monographs and is a participant in ongoing excavations in the Near East. This website offers information on the activities of the museum but does not currently offer access to its collections over the Internet. It is hoped that improvements in technology and changes in norms of access will lead to greater access to the collections in the near future.

Glass Finds From Sepphoris (1983-1991): A Preliminary Report
http://www.colby.edu/rel/Glass.html

This is Professor Longstaff's preliminary report on glass finds at Sepphoris, 1983-1991. The report takes full advantage of the ability of the WWW to link images of artifacts to particular references in the text. The Sepphoris Project is the work of the University of South Florida.

Sepphoris, Report of the Excavations
http://www.colby.edu/rel/Sep93.html
http://www.colby.edu/rel/Sep94.html
http://www.colby.edu/rel/Sep95.html

These are the excavation reports of James F. Strange on the University of South Florida activities at Sepphoris, Israel.

Service Informatique et Recherches en Archeologie
http://silicon.montaigne.u-bordeaux.fr:8001/HTML/SIRA/SIRA1000.html

This site, sponsored by the Institut de Recherché sur l'Antiquiteacute; et le Moyen-âge, contains quite a bit of useful information, including a database of more than 1000 images from late 19th century Egypt, a virtual reconstruction of the temple of Akhenaten from Karnak, images of Roman obelisks, and a collection of images from El-Jem, Tunisia. Bibliographies of several of the members of the Institut are also available.

Morphologically Analyzed Septuagint
gopher://ccat.sas.upenn.edu:3333/11/Religious/Biblical/LXXMorph

A morphologically analyzed version of the Septuagint by the Computer-Assisted Tools for Septuagint Studies (CATSS) staff.

Shareware game of Senet
http://www.newton.cam.ac.uk/egypt/ad/senet.html

A historically accurate version of the Egyptian game Senet, written as a Windows Program. Programmed by P. S. Neeley.

Sheshadrivasu Chandrasekharan(Vasu)
http://members.tripod.com/~sheshadrivasu/

Sheshadrivasu Chandrasekharan (Vasu) has created two very interesting software packages for using Kannada script both on and off the Web. Maathu-kathe is a video conferencing Windows environment that allows users to chat over the Web in Kannada script. The second package, Baraha1.1 allows for the entry of Kannada text in English transliteration and then coverts the text into Kannada script. Both of these applications are freely available for download over the Web.

The Shipwrecked Sailor Papyrus Leningrad 1115
http://home.prcn.org/~sfryer/Hieratic/papyrus/index.html

The complete text of the Story of the Shipwrecked Sailor in hieratic (images) with linked hieroglyphic transcription. This is an excellent resource for those teaching or learning Hieratic and the Middle Egyptian language.

The Shipwrecked Sailor: Manual de Codage Format
http://webperso.iut.univ-paris8.fr/~rosmord/hieroglyphes/naufrage.hie

This site offers an encoded version of the Shipwrecked Sailor, following the version of Blackman in *Middle Egyptian stories*, Bibliotheca Aegyptiaca, and using the Manuel de Codage.

Shin Buddhism
http://www.aloha.net/~rtbloom/shinran

This site is focused on Shin Buddhism and provides access to articles in English and Japanese related to Shin Buddhism, as well as a bibliography of works related to Shin Buddhism. It also has links to sites concerning Buddhism generally.

A Short Introduction to Hieroglyphs
http://webperso.iut.univ-paris8.fr/~rosmord//Intro/Intro.html

This is Serge Rosmorduc's introduction to the study of Egyptian hieroglyphics. This is the type of resource needed to interest both undergraduates and non-traditional students in taking more formal instruction in Middle Egyptian.

Shroud of Turin
http://www.cais.com/npacheco/shroud/turin.html

This site offers a collection of resources on the Internet relating to the Shroud of Turin. It includes links to bibliographies on the shroud and current investigations concerning the shroud.

Silver Mountain Software
http://rampages.onramp.net/~jbaima

This homepage of Silver Mountain Software offers shareware and information on its commercial products. Silver Mountain produces commercial products for use with the TLG and PHI CD-ROMS, and fonts for Coptic, Greek, Hebrew and Latin.

Sinuhe
http://staff-www.uni-marburg.de/~aegypt/sinlit.htm

Orell Witthuhn has prepared this bibliography of the Story of Sinuhe which is known to all beginning and seasoned students of Egyptology. The bibliography is organized into hieroglyphic and hieratic editions, grammars and handbooks (using Sinuhe), discussions/explanations of the text and translations.

The Sistine Chapel (via Christus Rex)
http://www.christusrex.org/www1/sistine/0-Tour.html

Three hundred twenty-five high quality images of the Sistine Chapel for display on a computer screen.

SKT-series Devanagari font
http://www.ucl.ac.uk/~ucgadkw/wikner.html

A high quality TeX font for devanagari and transliteration. Documentation and samples can be found at: ftp://ftp.nac.ac.za/wikner/sktdoc.ps600, ftp://t.ms.uky.edu/incoming/sanskrit/sktdoc.ps600.

Smithsonian Institution
http://www.si.edu
http://www.si.sgi.com/sgi.htm

The Smithsonian houses artifacts and exhibits of interest to scholars in all fields of study. This WWW homepage is well organized and has the ability to search its Web site for items of interest. For example, a search for the term Egypt led to information on an exhibit for the ancient Nubian City of Kerma, which is composed of items from the Museum of Fine Arts, Boston.

Snunit
http://www1.snunit.k12.il

Sponsored by the Hebrew University of Jerusalem, Snunit offers a wide variety of resources for scholars. The Hebrew Bible, Mishna, Tosefta, and the Babylonian and Jerusalem Talmuds are offered in their original languages for web viewing. A variety of other resources for educational use are also available. A Hebrew font is necessary to make full use all the resources at this site.

Society for American Archaeology Bulletin
http://www.sscf.ucsb.edu:80/SAABulletin

This is an important source of information on American archaeology and the SAA Bulletin. The issue for September/October 13(4), includes articles on the use of computers in the recording and visualization of archaeological information.

Society for Egyptology
http://www2.ipcku.kansai-u.ac.jp/~horus/

Homepage for the Society for Egyptology based at Kansai University in Japan. Note that the site is written in Japanese only and requires Japanese fonts for proper viewing.

The Society for Hindu-Christian Studies
http://www.acusd.edu/theo/hcs-l/

This site offers information on the Society for Hindu-Christian Studies, its mailing list (HCS-L), the Hindu-Christian Studies Bulletin, and other resources for Hindu-Christian studies. An index to past discussions on the HCS-L mailing list and the table of contents for the Hindu-Christian Studies Bulletin are two of the more important resources located at this site.

Society for Late Antiquity
http://www.sc.edu/ltantsoc/

The website for the Society for Late Antiquity offers convenient access to a number of resources on the WWW for scholars interested in Late Antiquity. Links are offered to archives for the LT-ANTIQ discussion group as well as ANCIEN-L, BYZANS-L, CLASSICS, NUMISM-L, and

ROMARCH. A very complete listing of web sites of interest to Late Antiquity studies is broken into subject groupings that facilitate consulting related web sites.

The Society for the Study of Egyptian Antiquities (SSEA)
http://www.geocities.com/TheTropics/1456/

The homepage of the Toronto based The Society for the Study of Egyptian Antiquities (SSEA) which was established to increase public interest in Egyptology. Notices of public lectures, grants by the society and membership information are offered at this site along with links to other Egyptology resources on the WWW.

Society of Biblical Literature
http://www.sbl-site.org/

The Society of Biblical Literature is one of the oldest organizations based in the United States for scholars engaged in biblical studies. Organizational, membership information, and links to other resources are available from this page. One important addition to this site is the *Review of Biblical Literature* (RBL) which is a collection of book reviews of important monographs in biblical and related studies such as reference works, commentaries, dictionaries and biblical translations. A new service that will present a searchable database of books received (prior to reviews being posted) is also under construction at the SBL site.

Software Directory for the Classics
http://www.centaursystems.com/soft_dir.html

This site offers a very complete listing of software for DOS, Mac and Windows computers of interest to classicists. The software runs from drill programs for Greek or Latin to multilingual wordprocessors and classical texts on disk. A version with descriptions is available in hard copy for $10 from the American Classical League.

Software for Theologians
http://crane.ukc.ac.uk/cprs/rel_studs/theoltxt.htm

Another useful resource from Michael Fraser, who has compiled information on Greek and Hebrew font and word processing software, Bible software tools, text databases and other search software, computer assisted language learning, and a bibliography of computing in theology.

Some Dictionaries of Literary Theory and Related Areas
http://classics.rutgers.edu/theory.html

This compilation of dictionaries of literary theory and related areas will be useful for both undergraduate as well as graduate students facing modern literary theory.

Some Methodological Considerations on the Rabbis Knowledge of the Proverbs of Ben Sira
ftp://ftp.lehigh.edu/pub/listserv/ioudaios-l/Articles/bwsira

An interesting treatment of the proverbs of Ben Sira by Benjamin Wright in Ioudiaos-l. Raises important questions concerning the stability of the text at a time when the Hebrew Bible is viewed as becoming more stable.

The South Asia Gopher
gopher://gopher.cc.columbia.edu:71/11/clioplus/scholarly/SouthAsia

David Magier of Columbia University maintains this gopher site, which focuses on all matters relevant to the study of South Asia. Of particular note are the links to electronic texts archives of Sanskrit texts and software for the display and printing of South Asian languages.

Space Speaks Volumes: Quantifying Spatial Characteristics of 3rd Millennium B.C. Houses at Tell Melebiya, Syria
http://cctr.umkc.edu/user/fdeblauwe/StLouis.html

A paper presented at the Archaeological Institute of America, St. Louis Chapter, Symposium, At Home in the Ancient World (April 25-26, 1997, St. Louis, MO) by Francis Deblauwe (University of Missouri-Kansas City).

A Specific Application of the Proverb in Ecclesiastes 1:15
http://www.ualberta.ca/ARTS/JHS/jhs-article.html#A6

An interesting examination of the interpretive context of Ecclesiastes 1:15.

A Spiritual Canticle of the Soul and the Bridegroom Christ by St. John of the Cross
http://www.cs.pitt.edu/~planting/books/john_of_the_cross/canticle/canticle.html

A translation by David Lewis, this text is offered in a variety of formats, RTF, PDF and HyperCard. A part of the Christian Classics Ethereal Library.

Spiritual Exercises by St. Ignatius of Loyola
http://www.cs.pitt.edu/~planting/books/ignatius/exercises/exercises.html

This edition of the *Spiritual Exercises* were translated from the autograph by Father Elder Mullan, S.J. The text is available as RTF, PDF and compressed postscript files.

Sri Lanka Tripitaka Project
http://jbe.la.psu.edu/ibric.html

This is the first public domain version of the Pali Canon and is being distributed by the Journal of Buddhist Ethics. The texts consist of an estimated 35 million characters and have been entered as transliterated Pali. While proofreading of the texts is not yet complete, this site offers links to the necessary fonts, concordance and text analysis programs to allow scholars to begin working with these preliminary texts.

Splendors of Ancient Egypt (Museum of Fine Arts, Houston)
http://www.chron.com/content/interactive/voyager/egypt/tour/index.html

An excellent collection of 67 images of Egyptian artifacts held by the Museum of Fine Arts in Houston. The images include false doors, scenes from tombs and representations of gods and pharaohs.

The State of the Arts: Archaeology in Israel 1995
http://www.israel-mfa.gov.il/mfa/ariel/archeol.html

Ronny Reich examines both the history of archaeological research in Israel and the political challenges facing archaeologists. Originally published in Ariel, the Israel Review of Arts and Letters, Number 99-100, July 1995, this review continues to be of relevance even though the political landscape has continued to evolve since its publication.

Steinschneider, Moritz Judische Schriften zur Geographie Palastina's (X-XIX. Jahrh.) Jerusalem : A. M. Lunez, 1892 "Jerusalem" Bd. III, IV Rosenberger 293-175
http://eos.lib.uchicago.edu/cgi-bin/LIB_preserve_title.sh?CALL_NUMBER=293-175

A scanned copy of this work by the Electronic Open Stacks project at the University of Chicago Library. The work can be viewed by chapters or a reader can "jump" to a particular page in the work. These image-based texts avoid the expense of creating full text searchable versions and yet provide usable access to materials too fragile for regular use.

Storytelling, the Meaning of Life, and The Epic of Gilgamesh
http://eawc.evansville.edu/essays/brown.htm

This essay by Arthur A. Brown is part of the Exploring Ancient World Cultures site at University of Evanston. Part recounting of the tale of Gilgamesh and Enkidu and part literary analysis of the story, Brown's essay will awaken interest in a text often read in stiff translation.

Strudwick, Nigel, Report on the work of the University of Cambridge Theban Mission 1993
http://www.newton.cam.ac.uk/egypt/tt99.report.93/report.tt99.93.ht

Nigel Strudwick needs no introduction to Egyptologists, either on the Internet or off. His report on the Theban Mission of the University of Cambridge, 1993, is cited here as another example of how Egyptologists are beginning to use the Internet as a means of effective and efficient communication.

Studium Biblicum Franciscanum
http://198.62.75.1/www1/ofm/sbf/SBFmus.html

A guide to the collections held by the Studium Biblicum Franciscanum museum in Jerusalem. Although only a part of the collection is displayed over the Website, the images are excellent and descriptions of the collections illustrate the breath of items to be found at the museum.

Stylistic Analysis of Latin Prose: A Checklist
http://ccwf.cc.utexas.edu/~tjmoore/stylechecklist.html

A useful checklist for stylistic analysis of Latin prose covering topics such as morphology and orthography, diction, syntax and others. While focused on the analysis of Latin prose, the checklist illustrates the range of issues to be considered in stylistic analysis of any text.

Sumerian Language Page
http://www.primenet.com/~seagoat/sumerian/sumerian.htm

An interesting site that offers a lexicon of Sumerian logograms; essays on the development of Proto-Sumerian, counting tokens in the Ancient Near East; a map of Sumerian Neolithic and Chalcolithic archaeological sites; links to Mesopotamian or language web sites; and, proverbs in Sumerian cuneiform.

The Sumerian Lexicon Project
http://www-oi.uchicago.edu/OI/PROJ/SUM/SLA/SLA1.html

This site exists as both a forum and an archive for discussions of the Sumerian lexicon. Information on current entries, transliteration systems, abbreviations, and the contribution of addition material is available. Special fonts are required to properly view both Sumerian and Akkadian transliterations from this site.

Sumerian Mythology FAQ
http://pubpages.unh.edu/~cbsiren/sumer-faq.html

This resource is similar to the Assyro-Babylonian Mythology FAQ and is a rather colloquial rendition of Sumerian mythology and its principal characters. It does cite scholarly sources and gives full bibliographic information for the works cited.

Sumerian Text Archive
http://www.leidenuniv.nl/ub/sta/sta.htm

The Sumerian Text Archive is a collection of transliterated Sumerian texts. The texts have been translitered using only ASCII characters so the files can be used on any computer. The text fall into the following categories: administrative texts from the Ur III period, administrative texts from the Old-Sumerian and Old-Akkadian periods, and royal inscriptions.

SUNY Press
http://www.sunypress.edu

A current listing of publications by SUNY Press in Buddhist Studies, Jewish Studies, Muslim Studies, Religion, as well as other areas. Within subject divisions books are listed by author with links to a short description of the work.

University of Wales Swansea
http://www.swan.ac.uk/classics/HomePage.html

Information for the Department of Classics and Ancient History, including undergraduate and postgraduate courses offered, email addresses for staff, and other information concerning the department and a list of electronic resources for classicists.

The Swedish Jordan Expedition 1989-1997: Tell Abu al-Kharaz, Tell Ain Abda, Sahem
http://www.lls.se/~fischer/

The Swedish expedition to Jordan is described in some detail at this site. Information on the excavations at these sites as well as a paper examining the possible identification of Tell Abu al-Kharaz as the biblical town of Jabesh Gilead can be found here.

The Sword Project
http://www.crosswire.org/

The Sword Project is seeking to create a body of freely accessible software and bible texts for students and researchers. All the software is produced under the GNU General Public License (GPL) which allows changes, improvements and the like to be added to the software but such changes must be freely passed onto the others using the software. The basic software is complete for viewing and searching texts on a PC, along with several electronic text modules.

The Synoptic Problem
http://www.mindspring.com/~scarlson/synopt/

A very useful site that collects and organizes diverse resources found on the Web dealing with the Synoptic problem. It is also the source for materials not previously available in electronic format.

The Syriac Computing Institute
http://www.acad.cua.edu/syrcom/index.html

A non-profit institute led by George A. Kiraz, St. John's College, Cambridge, which is working in the area of Syriac computing. Syriac computing is relevant to Syriac studies and other areas, such as biblical research and classics. The home page has information on current projects and contact information for volunteers who wish to work on any current or proposed projects.

Tacitus
gopher://gopher.vt.edu:10010/11/147

Texts of the Histories and Annals of Tacitus, translated by Alfred John Church and William Jackson Brodribb.

Talmud Appreciation Society
http://jumper.mcc.ac.uk/~tas

This is the homepage for the Talmud Appreciation Society, which includes volume 3 of their newsletter. Some links to other material of interest to Talmudic scholars.

Tanach Directory from Shamash
http://shamash.org/tanach/tanach.html

Includes the Hebrew text of the Tanach and links to all the known Divrei Torah on the Internet. It is possible to search the archives that are maintained locally at the Shamash site.

Taoism Information
http://www.cnu.edu/~patrick/taoism.html

Offers two translations of the Tao Te Ching in English, one by Peter Merel and the other by Stan Rosenthal, which includes an introduction with background material. Also available are an English translation of Sun Tzu's The Art of War and Richard Le Mon's translation of the I Ching.

Taylor-Schechter Genizah Research Unit
http://www.cam.ac.uk/Libraries/Taylor-Schechter

The discovery of manuscripts hidden in a forgotten storeroom of the synagogue in old Cairo created a great deal of excitement in the late 19th century. The Taylor-Schechter Genizah Research Unit is now making many of these texts available to scholars with Web access. Still in its early stages, the project promises to be a boon to scholars interested in Judaism, the Hebrew Bible, medieval history, and other areas.

TC: A Journal of Biblical Textual Criticism
http://purl.org/TC

An electronic, peer-reviewed, journal focusing on biblical textual criticism. Submissions, the editorial process and publication are accomplished without the delays and costs associated with traditional print journals. The ease of electronic communication allows TC to number editors from geographically diverse locations such as Australia, Belgium and South Africa. The journal contains full-length articles, shorter textual notes, project reports, and book reviews.

The Tebtunis Papyri Collection and the Advanced Papyrological Information System project at The Bancroft Library
http://sunsite.berkeley.edu/APIS/index.html

This project is cataloging the over 21,000 separate fragments of papyri gathered at the ancient site of Tebtunis, Egypt. As part of the Advanced Payrological Information System (APIS), the papyri are being cataloged and imaged for exhange with other papyrologists. This site offers a wide variety of information concerning this important collection including information on the cultural context of the documents, images of some of the papyri, and list of the contents of the papyri as well as other information.

The Tech Classics Archive
http://the-tech.mit.edu/Classics

This archive of classical authors in English translation offers 375 works by 30 classical authors. The texts in the archive can be listed by author, title, date, or translator. It is also possible to search a group of texts for a particular word or phrase.

TELA: The Electronically Linked Academy
http://shemesh.scholar.emory.edu

Scholars Press took the initiative to establish this WWW site for scholars working in the areas of archaeology, classics, papyrology, and religious studies in August of 1994. The Scholar's Corner is the focus of resources of interest to the scholarly community, including pages on archaeology, languages and literature, diversity of religious expression and computer tools. TELA also hosts an electronic directory of scholars in these fields. *TC: A Journal of Biblical Textual Criticism* and Offline Online! can also be found at this site.

Tel el Amarna Collection of M.A. Mansoor
http://www.amarna.com/

This WWW page reflects the breath of this collection of Amarna Era art. In addition to information on the collection and its history, with images of some of its more important pieces as noted in the first edition of HP, the site now offers access to scholarly reports on the collection. A useful selection of links to other Amarna and Egyptology sites makes this good starting point for tracing Amarna information on the Web.

Tall-e Bakun Project
http://www-oi.uchicago.edu/OI/PROJ/BAK/Bakun.html

Background report on Tall-e Bakun excavations and ongoing excavations at the site. Accompanied by a short bibliography of publications relating to the site.

Tell Beydar
http://users.skynet.be/lebeau/pages/engl/enbint.htm

The Tell Beydar website offers a short introduction and background information for the excavations at Tell Beydar. A joint Syrian and European mission, this project has found architecture from the Early Dynastic III period and some cuneiform tablets. Basic contact information for the project participants is also listed.

Tel Dor Archaeological Expedition
http://www.qal.berkeley.edu/~teldor/

This excavation focuses on a site that was a major Phoenician, Jewish, Persian, Greek and Roman city. A history of the site, an extensive bibliography of the site, site plans showing areas of excavation, a summary of finds for particular areas of excavation as well as a map of other excavations by participating universities can be found on this web site.

Tel Hazor
http://unixware.mscc.huji.ac.il/~hatsor/hazor.html

The Hazor excavation webpage offers a narrative history of the site, short excavations reports (1991-1997), a basic bibliography for Hazor and information for volunteers wishing to join the excavation. The narrative history traces references to Hazor in the Hebrew Bible and other ANE texts onto the archaeological record found at the site.

Tell Mashnaqa
http://dorit.ihi.ku.dk/cni/mashnaqa/

A summary of the activities of the Danish expedition to Tell Mashnaqa and related research projects. This site offers information on architecture and stratigraphy, burials, pottery, stone tools, and terra cotta objects, along with images of some of the finds. Research projects of the participants include field methods for ancient DNA, biological anthropology, building materials, databases and pottery fragmentation. This group takes the futuristic (and scholarly) step of presenting all drawings and images to the international community for use with citation of their origin.

The Tell en-Nasbeh Research Project
http://www.people.cornell.edu/pages/jrz3/

This presentation of the state of the Tell en-Nasbeh excavation offers both information on artifacts found and interpretations based upon those findings. In addition to an article evaluating the identity of Tell en-Nasbeh in the Hebrew Bible, Tell en-Nasbeh: Biblical Mizpah of Benjamin, a bibliography of the site and a site plan can also be found at this site. The site map is useful but would be more useful if the user had the ability to zoom in on particular squares and follow links from those squares to artifacts found in that location.

Tel Rehov
http://www.Rehov.org/

This excavation web site offers magnetic survey maps, detailed topographical maps, preliminary dig reports and other resources. A few images of artifacts are available but far less than one would like or expect. As is common for most excavations, information is available for volunteers who want to work at the dig.

Tell Tuneinir, Syria
http://www.stlcc.cc.mo.us/fv/tuneinir/

Michael Fuller and Neathery Fuller of the St. Louis Community College report on their excavations at Tell Tuneinir, Syria. Investigations have focused on Islamic commercial structures, a church and monastery used by a Syriac speaking congregation and various pre-Islamic strata. Maps with links to strata and further information on each area of excavation are available.

The Temple Mount in Jerusalem
http://www.templemount.org/

An extensive collection of both original material and links to other sites concerned with the Temple Mount and its history. This site presents evidence and arguments for various locations of the First and Second Jewish temples on Temple Mount as well as discussions of the latest scientific evidence.

The Temple Palace of Rameses III at Medinet Habu 1175 BC
http://archpropplan.auckland.ac.nz/People/Motlib/rameses/rameses.html

A computer reconstruction of the temple palace of Rameses III at Medinet Habu by Mohammed Motlib and Matiu Carr of the University of Auckland, School of Architecture Property and Planning. An interesting demonstration of reconstructive technique, if somewhat overdone by the addition of computer generated images of people in period dress.

Text - Reader -Author. Towards a Theory of Exegesis: Some European Views.
http://www.ualberta.ca/ARTS/JHS/jhs-article.html#A1

An excellent article by Helmut Utzchneider in the Journal of Hebrew Scriptures that examines the current approaches to academic biblical exegesis and the possibility of dialogue with non-academic contextual approaches to the same materials. The article can be downloaded in Word, WP or .pdf formats for either pc or mac computers.

Texts on the Verdun Altar
http://kufacts.cc.ukans.edu/ftp/pub/history/Europe/Medieval/latintexts/verdun.txt

James Marchand provides the Latin text and English translation for the text of the Verdun Altar of Klosterneuburg, which has been said to be an early version of the Biblica pauperum.

Theban Mapping Project
http://www.kv5.com/intro.html

Established after the publicity surrounding the discoveries in KV5, this site offers excellent images of the Theban Necropolis, the Valley of the Kings and KV5. Recent news from the KV5 excavations, extensive bibliographies on Egyptology (30,000+ references), and other resources make this one of the most important Egyptology sites on the Internet.

Thebes Photographic Project
http://www-oi.uchicago.edu/OI/TVE_TPP/TVE_TPP.html

A selection of panorama images made by Tom Van Eynde at Thebes. The Oriental Institute displays selected images from a larger collection of images that was exhibited at the Gibson Gallery Exhibition, State University Of New York, College At Potsdam: October 13 - November 11, 1995. The images are primarily of an artistic nature although they do show the relationship between various structures and the landscape.

The Theban Desert Road Survey
http://www-oi.uchicago.edu/OI/AR/95-96/95-96_Desert_Road.html

The 1995-1996 Annual Report on the desert route exploration by John Coleman Darnell and Deborah Darnell. This project has found evidence linking the system of routes discovered to the ascendancy of Thebes during the Middle Kingdom and New Kingdom. (Previously known as: The Luxor-Farshut Desert Road Survey.)

THEOLDI: Documentation of Theological and Interdisciplinary Literature School of Theology at University of Innsbruck
http://starwww.uibk.ac.at/theologie/theologie-en.html

A collection of searchable databases in the areas of biblical literature (60,000 titles), Girard-Documentation (Mimetic Theory of René Girard) (3,000 titles), systematic and fundamental theology (3,000 titles), and canon law (2,000). These databases are composed of titles gleaned from periodicals and annuals, collected works and Festschriften as well as listing monographs. The search interface is powerful but easy to use and its creators deserve high marks for creating useful user guides.

Theological Perspectives in the Book of Ezekiel
http://shemesh.scholar.emory.edu/scripts/SBL/ezekiel/index.html

Homepage for the Society of Biblical Literature Seminar Theological Perspectives in the Book of Ezekiel. The seminar lists its future topics, grants access to papers presented at previous Annual Meetings, lists other information concerning the seminar composition and membership. This webpage is part of a growing trend by established scholars to use the World Wide Web to disseminate scholarly discussions and publications.

Theology on the Web
http://www.vpm.com/thawes

A useful collection of links relating to Christianity, rather than the more general field of theology as indicated by its title.

Thesaurus Indogermanischer Text- und Sprachmaterialien
http://watson.rz.uni-frankfurt.de/home/ftp/pub/titus/public_html

A variety of projects concerning Indo-Germanic languages are accessible at this site.

Thesaurus Linguae Grecae
http://www.uci.edu/~tlg/

Basic information about the TLG and a list of the texts which are presently available are listed at this site.

Thesaurus Musicarum Latinarum
http://www.music.indiana.edu/tml/

Located at Indiana University, this site has texts of medieval treatises on music theory ranging from the 4-5th to the 17th century. Each section of texts has an index and a search option. An important resource for those interested in medieval music theory and another illustration of the usefulness of electronic publication.

Thesaurus Precum Latinarum (Treasury of Latin Prayers)
http://www.catholic.net/RCC/Indices/subs/tlp.html

A very complete collection of Latin prayers compiled by Michael W. Martin. The prayers are divided into various subjects and if used as part of religious services the context of use is indicated.

Thucydides, Short Bibliography on
http://classics.rutgers.edu/thuc.html

A bibliography of Thucydides that includes primarily monographs. The bibliography is arranged by topics such as commentaries, text, speeches, style, etc., which facilitates finding material of interest.

Thureau-Dangin, F., Les Cylindres de Goudea Paris : Librairie Orientaliste Paul Geuthner, 1925
http://eos.lib.uchicago.edu/cgi-bin/LIB_preserve_title.sh?CALL_NUMBER=PJ3711.P2

A scanned copy of this work by the Electronic Open Stacks project at the University of Chicago Library. The work can be viewed by chapters or a reader can "jump" to a particular page in the work. These image-based texts avoid the expense of creating full text searchable versions and yet provide usable access to materials too fragile for regular use.

Tibetan Book of the Dead: Literature and Artwork on Prayer, Ritual, and Meditation from the Religious Traditions of Tibet, India and Nepal
http://www.lib.virginia.edu/exhibits/dead/

This virtual exhibit is based upon an actual exhibit at the Alderman Library at the University of Virginia on the Tibetan Book of the Dead. A number of the artifacts from the exhibit are available for viewing online and explanatory materials place these items in their cultural context.

Tibetan Studies WWW Virtual Library
http://coombs.anu.edu.au/WWWVL-TibetanStudies.html

Tibetan Studies is edited by T. Matthew Ciolek, and like Buddhist Studies, it is one of the leading WWW sites in its area. There are links to well over one hundred sources of information of interest to those in Tibetan Studies.

TOCS-IN: Tables of Contents of Journals of Interest to Classicists
gopher://gopher.lib.virginia.edu/11/alpha/tocs
ftp://ftp.epas.utoronto.ca/pub/tocs-in/Search.html
ftp://ftp.epas.utoronto.ca/pub/tocs-in

This important project is composed of volunteers who scan journals and send in the table of contents from each new issue. As of July 1996, TOCS-IN covered 12,933 articles from 154 journals, starting with the first issue of 1992. The second URL listed above allows online searching of this resource.

Tomb of Senneferi (TT99)
http://www.newton.cam.ac.uk/egypt/tt99/

The homepage for all activities of the University of Cambridge archaeological fieldwork project at Theban Tomb 99. In addition to the report noted above, this site offers detailed image maps of areas of excavation that lead to further information on particular artifacts or tomb locations. Finds from the site have been summarized by year and location with representative items available as images. This site offers very complete information concerning this excavation and includes QuickTime VR movies of the tomb. A very good example of how excavations can be documented and information made available over the WWW.

Tools of the Trade for the Study of Roman Literature
http://classics.rutgers.edu/tools.html

This Tools of the Trade... bibliography is an excellent guide to the materials available for the study of Roman literature. While obviously not exhaustive, it provides an excellent starting point for any student in the following areas: databases, dictionaries and lexicographical works, encyclopedias, fragments, grammars, history of literature, inscriptions, linguistics and etymology, metrics, religion, roman social life and customs, special vocabularies, style, texts and transmission, and the topography of Rome.

Tracce
http://www.geocities.com/RainForest/3982/karak.html

The Tracce site offers information on rock carvings and inscriptions found on the Karakorum highway (Pakistan). Prof. Karl Jettmar (Heidelberg, Germany) and Prof. A.H. Dani (Quaid-i-Azam University Islamabad, Pakistan) have lead efforts that have discovered ca. 30,000 petroglyphs and 5,000 inscriptions in more than 10 writing systems.

Traditio
http://ccat.sas.upenn.edu/jod/traditio/traditio.html

Traditio is a journal of ancient and medieval history, thought, and religion published by Fordham University. Its website offers an index by subject and author to the first fifty volumes of the journal and the introductory essay from the fiftieth anniversary volume.

Transcribing New Testament Manuscripts for Computer Collation
http://www.entmp.org/entmp/papers/trans.html

In a companion article to his treatment of computer assisted collation of New Testament manuscripts Tim Finney sets forth a method for unambiguous transcription of New Testament manuscripts. Finney details sources of manuscripts for transcription and the difficulties of working with photographic reproductions before turning to his system of transcription. Highly recommended for its detailed treatment of problems that will confront scholars who are interested in preparing transcriptions for use with computerized collation software.

Tridentine Latin Mass in Latin and English
http://www.cs.cmu.edu:8001/Web/People/spok/ mass-parallel.txt

Latin text of the Tridentine Mass (1962 edition) with parallel English translation.

Tutorial on Gregorian Chant
gopher://osiris.wu-wien.ac.at:7121/11/pub/earlym-l/gregorian.chants

Donald J. Casadonte, of the University of Vienna, wrote this tutorial on the Gregorian Chant for non-professionals.

Ugaritic Cuneiform
http://www.informatik.uni-stuttgart.de/ifi/bs/lagally/ugarit.html

A sample of Ugaritic cuneiform script produced using TeX. The sample file is in postscript format.

UK Buddhist Studies Association
http://www.sunderland.ac.uk/~os0dwe/bsa.html

Primarily information concerning the Buddhist Studies Association, but this site also includes links to other resources of interest to Buddhist scholars.

Uniformity with God's Will by St. Alphonsus de Liguori
http://www.cs.pitt.edu/~planting/books/alphonsus/uniformity/uniformity.html

Part of the Christian Classics Ethereal Library and available in text, RTF, postscript and PDF formats, in addition to the HTML version at this site.

Union Seminary Quarterly Review
http://www.cc.columbia.edu/~pm47

USQR is a journal of theology and religion edited by graduate students at Union Theological Seminary/Columbia University in the City of New York.

United Church of Christ
http://www.ucc.org/

The United Church of Christ site offers a wide range of information of interest to members of the United Church of Christ or those interested in its theology. In addition to the usual organizational information and links to other resources it includes an online chat facility for discussions of issues of interest in the UCC.

University of Chicago Libraries, The Classics and Ancient Near East Department
http://www.lib.uchicago.edu/LibInfo/SourcesBySubject/CANE

This is the origin of useful resources for classics and the Ancient Near East, with links to other resources on the Internet.

University of Edinburgh, Department of Archaeology
http://www.geo.ed.ac.uk/arch/homepage.html

This site is sponsored by the Department of Archaeology, University of Edinburgh, and provides information on the department. It also provides information on courses and degrees, excavations at Pinarbasi, and a listing of current research projects by students and staff at Edinburgh.

University of Illinois Mummy Project
http://www.grad.uiuc.edu/departments/ATAM/mummy.html

Excellent presentation of information derived from a Roman period (second century CE) mummy owned by the World Heritage Museum at the University of Illinios. All the techniques used were non-invasive and the results are reported under topics such as: Age and Sex of the Mummy, Embalming Procedures, Textile Analysis, the Mummy's Diet, and 3-D Imaging. Unfortunately, like too many ancient artifacts, the provenience of this object is unknown.

University of Kentucky, Lexington, The Classics Department
http://www.uky.edu/ArtsSciences/Classics

The Classics Department sponsors this home page, which contains information about the department and its activities. Links to other resources of interest to classicists are also provided.

The University of Melbourne North Eastern Turkey Project
http://adhocalypse.arts.unimelb.edu.au//Dept/Arch/NETurkey/home.html

Antonio Sagnona has led the University of Melbourne excavations in NorthEast Anatolia since 1988. Further information on the Bayburt plain survey and the Buyuktepe Hoyuk excavations can be found here.

University of Michigan: Papyrus Digitization Project
http://www.lib.umich.edu/pap/HomePage.html

The University of Michigan, through the Papyrus Digitization Project, is leading the scholarly community in the exploration of ways to make papyri more accessible to scholars. As the holder of the fifth or sixth largest collection of papyri in the world, it has taken a leadership role in using technology to advance the accessibility of its collection to scholars.

University of Pennsylvania African Studies Program Home Page
http://www.sas.upenn.edu/African_Studies/AS.html

The African Studies Program at University of Pennsylvania, Professor Sandra T. Barnes, Director, sponsors this home page with resources of interest to scholars of African Studies and such items as materials related to ancient Egypt.

Department of Religious Studies
http://ccat.sas.upenn.edu/rs

The home page for the Religious Studies Department of the University of Pennsylvania, which, with the Classical Studies Department, is responsible for the work of CCAT since its beginning. CCAT (Center for Computer Analysis of Texts) has produced many of the electronic texts, both classical and religious, that are noted in this book. Their work is a good example of electronic texts and computer analysis being used as tools by traditional scholars in the furtherance of scholarship. Links to the archive of texts maintained on the CCAT Gopher and other significant resources are present at this site.

University of Pennsylvania Museum
http://www.upenn.edu/museum/

Interesting virtual exhibits that include Greece and a fly-by of Corinth. Some images drawn from the museum collection but a meager number considering the holdings of the museum. There are useful links to information on the Museum Applied Science Center for Archaeology (MASCA); The Pennsylvania-Yale Excavations at Abydos, Egypt; The Gordion Archaeological Project at Gordion, Turkey; and, The University Museum-Museum of Fine Arts, Boston Expedition to Saqqara, Egypt.

University of Saskatchewan, Department of Classics
http://www.usask.ca/classics

A welcome departure from departmental home pages that merely recite the names and addresses of current faculty and course schedules. The Department of Classics has made available sample syllabi and related material, sample examinations and study guides, course notes, departmental translations and bibliographies, in addition to more traditional information. This site offers a number of resources that will be helpful to its own students as well as students of the classics at other institutions.

University of Sheffield Library
http://library.shef.ac.uk/www-bin/www_talis?

The WWW interface for the University of Sheffield Library is well-organized and easy to use. The suggestions for searching will help researchers make good use of this online catalogue. The library homepage found at: http://www.shef.ac.uk/~lib/ offers a number of subject guides and other effective use of the library type materials.

University of Warwick, Department of Classics and AncientHistory
http://www.warwick.ac.uk/WWW/faculties/arts/Classics/index.html

In addition to departmental and course information, includes links to the Centre for East Roman Studies and the rescue operation at Coftlik (Sinop), Turkey. The Sinop excavation page includes one image and one drawing of recovered mosaics.

Using Hypertext Courseware to Teach the New Testament
http://info.ox.ac.uk/ctitext/publish/comtxt/ct13/ford.html

A detailed account of the use of Hypertext courseware on 'Graeco-Roman Culture and the Rise of Christian Faith' in a first year New Testament course at Department of Theology at the University of Durham. (Computers & Texts No.13)

Vanderbilt Divinity Library
http://www.library.vanderbilt.edu/divinity/homelib.html

The home page of the Vanderbilt Divinity Library contains links to Internet resources for religious and theological research, a guide to the Divinity Library with photo tour, guides for research in religion, bibliographies for religious and theological research, and, most notably, a guide to Library of Congress Classification in Hypertext. While the Library of Congress Classification guide does not go into extreme detail, it will definitely improve casual browsing of the library stacks.

Vatican City (via Christus Rex)
http://www.christusrex.org/www1/citta/0-Citta.html

As mentioned for other collections of images from Christus Rex, a high-resolution monitor and fast Internet connection will definitely improve the enjoyment of this site. This site contains 255 images.

Documents of Vatican II
http://listserv.american.edu/catholic/church/vaticanii/vaticanii.html

This site contains many of the documents produced by the Vatican II council (1962-1965), including Ad Gentes, Dignitatis Humanae, Gaudium et Spes, and Unitatis Redintegratio.

Vatican Library exhibit
http://sunsite.unc.edu/expo/vatican.exhibit/Vatican.exhibit.html

A virtual exhibit that is a mirror of the actual exhibit that appeared at the Library of Congress. Actually, the virtual exhibit includes not only the items from the actual exhibit, but alternate items brought to take the place of primary objects should the need arise, as well as items later omitted from the exhibit. The exhibit rooms off of the main entrance include the Vatican Library, Archaeology, Humanism, Medicine and Biology, Music, Nature Described, Orient to Rome and Rome to China.

Vergilius
http://vergil.classics.upenn.edu/vergilius/index.html

Vergilius is the Journal of the Vergilian Society of America. Only the table of contents for volume 42 (1996) is available at the site and article links lead to brief abstracts.

Vergilius Bibliography Index
http://ccat.sas.upenn.edu/~joef/vergil/vergilius/finger.html

The bibliography of Vergilian scholarship for the years 1986-88, 1990-93 is currently available at this site. This bibliography is a witness to the current health of studies in the classics in general and Vergil in particular.

Vergil, Works
gopher://wiretap.spies.com/11/Library/Classic/Vergil

The works of Vergil, including the Aeneid, in TEX format.

The Vergil Project
http://ccat.sas.upenn.edu/~joef/courses/project.html

The Vergil Project, under the direction of Joseph Farrell, Department of Classics, University of Pennsylvania, is seeking to develop an on-line hypertext database of all materials related to the study of Vergil. The project will offer texts drawn from particular manuscripts, texts of Vergil of particular historical significance (for Dante, Milton, etc.), all with traditional critical apparatus and every word in a text linked to a menu of interpretive resources. It is worthy of note that the project intends to generate what is termed a Communal Text of Vergil. In essence, each user of this resource can choose among variants and textual traditions, which can then be tallied to produce the text preferred by the largest number of users. This Communal Text would never become fixed and would continue to evolve with resources and users. The project is seeking the assistance of all persons interested in Vergil, of whatever skill level, to contribute to this truly collaborative enterprise. An innovative and thoughtful plan to fully utilize hypertext and the Internet in the presentation of scholarly information.

Vergil's Home Page
http://vergil.classics.upenn.edu/home/

Vergil's Home Page is part of the Vergil Project at the University of Pennsylvania being directed by Professor Joseph Farrell. Links are available to texts and commentaries, bibliography, teaching materials, discussion lists and other materials.

The Virtual Mummy: Unwrapping a Mummy by Mouse Click
http://www.uke.uni-hamburg.de/Institutes/IMDM/IDV/Projects/Mumie/mumieEN.html

A delightful presentation that makes the unwrapping of a mummy an experience that can be shared with an entire classroom with no danger to an archaeological artifact. The user downloads a QuickTime (VR) movie and can unwrap the mummy's head on screen. The mummy used for this virtual reconstruction is of a female approximately 30 years of age and the mummy is approximately 2,300 years old. Suggested further reading on the techniques used to reconstruct the mummy: R. Drenkhahn und R. Germer: Mumie + Computer, Kestner Museum, Hannover, 1991, ISBN 3-924029-17-2.

Virtual Nimrin
http://www.cwru.edu/affil/nimrin/

This web site, Virtual Nimrin, is a virtual presentation of the findings at Tell Nimrin. When the site is completed it will "...will include electronic versions of all field books, selected photos, and publishable drawings, as well as a comprehensive collection of reports, including materials that have been published in hardcopy elsewhere." Tell Nimrin is located in Shuna South Jordan, north of the Dead Sea and in the Jordan Valley. It is hoped that efforts such as this one will lead other scholars to make complete materials from excavations available over the WWW.

VRoma
http://vroma.rhodes.edu

VRoma has been designed to function as a gathering place for live interaction, sharing of resources, courses and lectures as well as a collection of and filter for Internet resources on the ancient world. Some of the resources at this site include: VRoma image collection, A collection of lexica and search engines front end for many on-line resources, Ross Scaife's LUPA: Subsidia interretialia quae ad Romanos antiquos pertinent, The Roman Forum (allows users to view various parts of the Forum and use links to further information), Plautus, Aulularia (a very impressive hypertext edition of this text with links to English translation and other resources keyed to the text), Syllabus for the Spring 1998 Aulularia course at Miami University, The Riley Collection of Roman Sculpture and Syllabus for Women in Antiquity at Cornell College.

Vulgate Bible of St. Jerome
gopher://ftp.std.com/11/obi/book/Religion/Vulgate

The text of Jerome's Latin translation of the Bible available as separate books.

Vulgate
gopher://ccat.sas.upenn.edu:3333/11/Religious/Biblical

Choose the To Search Biblical Files menu option, and the next menu will offer the ability to search the text of the Vulgate, a morphologically analyzed Hebrew Bible, a morphologically analyzed Septuagint, and the KJV and RSV translations of the Bible.

Wadi Araba: Archaeological Research Project
http://www.wam.umd.edu/~amsii/

This is the webpage for the Wadi Araba project to investigate the cutural environment of this site for all historical and prehistoric periods.

Walter de Gruyter
http://www.deGruyter.de/index.html

This homepage offers access to both recent titles and the complete catalog from Walter de Gruyter in both English and German. The catalog allows the selection of works for inclusion in a "shopping cart" and ordering of these works online by credit card or by mailing the order to the publisher.

Walther Library of Concordia Theological Seminary
http://www.palni.edu/~cosmithb/concordia.html

The Walther Library sponsors this home page, which has a number of useful links for scholars of religion. Most notably, there is an ILL form which can be executed by those with a forms capable browser, which is then confirmed by email. There are also links to the Walther Library, Lutheran Electronic Texts (Project Wittenberg) and Internet Tools for the Study of Theology.

Waseda University Egyptian Expedition
http://www.waseda.ac.jp/projects/egypt/index-E.html

This site appears in both English and Japanese and details the activities of the Egyptian Culture Center at Waseda University from 1966 to present. The topics range from the Interim Report on the Re-clearance at the Royal Tomb of Amenophis III (KV 22) to Excavations at the Islamic City al-Fustat.

The Way of Perfection by St. Teresa of Avila
http://www.cs.pitt.edu/~planting/books/teresa/way/way.html

Translated and edited by E. Allison Peers from the critical edition of P. Silverio De Santa Teresa, C.D. Unfortunately, only a few of approximately 1200 footnotes are reproduced in this electronic edition.

WebAcropole
http://atlas.central.ntua.gr:8080/webacropol
http://www.atkinson.yorku.ca/exhibits/webacropol

A virtual guided tour of the Acropolis with useful historical comments and numerous images. The thumbnail images that link to larger images range in size from 25K to almost 30K so use of the Canadian mirror site and/or a fast connection is recommended for non-European users.

Webcats
http://www.lights.com/webcats/

This is a very comprehensive listing of library catalogues that are accessible over the Internet via the WWW, telnet or Z39.50 clients. Libraries are organized by geographic location as well as the type of library. A collection of links to vendors (library resources) and publishers catalogues add to the usefulness of this site. Highly recommended as a source for scholars wishing to consult library catalogues in particular locations in preparation to travel or for general bibliographic purposes. Librarians should note this site as the home of archives for the Webcat-L mailing list archives and the Biblio Tech Review, a web publication focusing on library automation.

Web Torah Library
http://www.etzion.org.il/Torah.htm

For those seeking Jewish religious texts in Hebrew, this site offers both guides to adding the ability to display Hebrew as well as links to a large selection of religious texts. From this page, access is available to the Tanach, the Babylonian and Palestinian Talmud, the Mishna and other texts in Hebrew. The Sefrot Kodesh site, http://www1.snunit.k12.il/kodesh/kodesh.html, is the principal location for the Hebrew texts found at this site.

West Semitic Research Project
http://www.usc.edu/dept/LAS/wsrp/index.html

The history of the West Semitic Research Project and the importance of high resolution images for serious academic work are both addressed in an excellent article by one of the founders of the project, Bruce Zuckerman. In addition to the history of the project, the site offers low resolution images of ancient documents with commentary for classroom use and a catalog of images that can be ordered in high-resolution formats. The images range from cuneiform tablets to the Leningrad codex and include a variety of other important materials.

What Happens in Qohelet 4:13-16.
http://www.ualberta.ca/ARTS/JHS/jhs-article.html#A4

Michael Fox examines Qohelet 4.13-16 in this early article in the Journal of Hebrew Scriptures. A notable article in its own right it serves to prove that scholarship is not determined by the medium of delivery (paper or electronic) but by the skill and intelligence of the scholar.

The Malcolm and Carolyn Wiener Laboratory for Aegean and Near Eastern Dendrochronology at Cornell University
http://www.arts.cornell.edu/dendro/

A web site devoted to the use of dendrochronology (tree-ring dating) as an archaeometric technique in the Agean and the Ancient Near East. This project is developing a master tree-ring chronology from the present to the seventh millennium B.C.E. for this area. Project reports are available from 1990-1997 and links point to other web sites with information on this topic. Guidelines on the collection and submission of samples for dating are available on the main page. This is an important site for anyone interested in the use of dendrochronology as part of their archaeological work.

Who Was Who Among the Royal Mummies
http://www-oi.uchicago.edu/OI/IS/WENTE/NN_Win95/NN_Win95.html

Edward F. Wente's article is ostensibly concerned with the identification of royal mummies and does summarize all the known information in that regard admirably. It should be noted, however, that it also provides a fascinating account of the methods used to probe the identities of royal mummies and the problems and difficulties associated with the same. It is a good example that scholarly writing need not be dull or lifeless, either on or off the Net.

Why Study Ancient World Cultures?
http://eawc.evansville.edu/

An interpretive essay by Bill Hemminger addresses the broad question of the relevance of ancient world cultures augmented with links to further information on such cultures. The use of hypertexting makes it possible to readily illustrate the arguments made in favor of studying ancient cultures. Non-specialists should be aware that some of the translations on the Internet for older materials, such as Hammurabi's (sic) Code of Laws, are seriously outdated and do not reflect current grammatical or semantic understandings of the relevant languages.

Wilbour Library, Brooklyn Museum
ftp://newton.newton.cam.ac.uk/pub/ancient/egypt/wilbour

Recent acquisitions by the Wilbour Library in ASCII format files. At present, the only file available is dated April of 1995.

Wiretap collection of Catholic source documents
gopher://wiretap.spies.com:70/11/Library/Religion/Catholic

Documents from the reigns of the following Popes: Boniface VIII, John Paul II, John XXIII, Leo XII, Paul VI, Pius XI, and Pius XII. There are also texts from Vatican II, and the menu option labeled rituals leads to materials on the Rosary and the Holy Saturday Mass.

Project Wittenberg
http://www.iclnet.org/pub/resources/text/wittenberg/wittenberg-home.html

Project Wittenberg seeks to make available over the Internet the works of Martin Luther and others important figures in the history of Lutheranism. Works by Luther currently posted include The Augsburg Confession, The Small Catechism of Martin Luther, Treatise on the Power and Primacy of the Pope, and the Smalcald Articles of Martin Luther. Selected historical works from Philip Melanchthon and Paul Gerhardt are also available.

Wittern, Christian
http://www.gwdg.de/~cwitter/

Christian Wittern's homepage offers access to KanjiBase, a Chinese Character Dictionary on the Web with over 48,000 characters, the WWW Database of Chinese Buddhist texts, and an article on the development of that database, Taming the masses: A practical approach to the encoding of variant and rare characters in premodern Chinese texts. The techniques developed by Wittern could well be applicable to the encoding of variant characters found in historical texts in other languages.

Women and Gender in Ancient Egypt: From Prehistory to Late Antiquity
http://www.umich.edu/~kelseydb/Exhibits/WomenandGender/title.html

This is an online version of a Kelsey Museum exhibition mounted from March 14 through June 15, 1997, and curated by Terry G. Wilfong. The topics treated in this series of essays range from gender ambiguity and gender in the archaeological record to gender, mortality and demographics to gender in archaeology. This is an important source for anyone pursuing gender studies in the Ancient Near East.

Women in the Ancient Near East
http://www-oi.uchicago.edu/OI/DEPT/RA/WOMEN.HTML

Terry G. Wilfong has compiled an excellent bibliography focusing on Women in the Ancient Near East from materials acquired by the Oriental Institute between 1988-1992.

The World Archaeological Congress
http://wac.soton.ac.uk/wac

This is primarily a source of information on the World Archaeological Congress and its activities. Choose the index image at the lower part of the page to access a table of contents for this site. A number of other links are available from the contents page, including the table of contents from World Archaeological Bulletins.

World Art Treasures
http://sgwww.epfl.ch/BERGER

A series of programs based upon the 100,000 slides belonging to the Jacques-Edouard Berger Foundation that create a unique viewing experience. The programs include First program: Art from Egypt, China, Japan, India, Burma, Laos, Cambodia and Thailand; Second program: Pilgrimage to ABYDOS - Egypt; and Third Program: Portraits Romains d'Egypte. René Berger is the director of this project, which has opened the archives of images from the Jacques-Edouard Berger Foundation to the Internet. Pages are available in both English and French. The site continues to add images and programs which merit frequent visits to this site.

World Mythology
http://www.artsmia.org/mythology/

Sponsored by the Minneapolis Insitute of Arts the World Mythology site is an welcome educational tool for teachers seeking to interest secondary level students in the Ancient Near East. Extensive commentary accompanies the images offered by this site along with suggested questions designed to provoke both thought and comment from the viewer. In recounting the story of Nebuchadnezzar, the presentation begins with a color print by William Blake of Nebuchadnezzar. Following this attention getting image is are sections covering the key ideas, the story from mythology, background information (on Nebuchadnezzar as well as William Blake) and a list of discussion questions.

World Scripture: A Comparative Anthology of Sacred Texts
http://rain.org/~origin/ws.html

The complete text of World Scripture: A Comparative Anthology of Sacred Texts, edited by Adrew Wilson, which was published by the International Religious Foundation, Paragon House, New York, 1991. This work is incorporates 4,000 passages drawn from 268 sacred texts and 55 oral traditions organized around 165 separate themes.

World Wide Study Bible
http://ccel.wheaton.edu/wwsb/

Organized by the books of the Old and New Testament this site links a large number of resources around the world under each book. For example, the Genesis link leads to a page offering such diverse resources as the entry for Pentateuch in the Catholic Encylopedia (1913 edition) and the Julius Manuscript (Oxford, Bodleian Library, MS Junius 11). Individual chapters for Genesis represent hyperlinks that when followed lead to other link collections that include nine English translations of that chapter (ranging from the American Standard Version to the New Revised Standard Version), five commentaries (mostly older materials, including an 1847 translation of John Calvin's commentary) as well as links to other related materials. A very good example of the level of hypertext linking that could be achieved by scholars of more academic materials and not a bad starting place for divinity students seeking to compare translations of biblical texts. It should be noted that the translation of the Calvin commentary has been rendered almost useless by the person scanning the text for Internet access who notes: "The footnotes of the Editor, and the Latin translation of the Bible-text, are omitted. Thus you have the most pure form of Calvin's Commentary." It is uncertain how an English translation qualifies as the pure form of a German language work and certainly the omission of footnotes may ease the scanner's task but it deprives the reader of the benefit of an editor's comments and references. This unfortunate practice has been followed in other online editions of otherwise classic works of scholarship.

WWW Database of Chinese Buddhist texts, Release 2.0 (updated Feb 1st, 1998).
http://134.76.129.21/kb/query.htm

The Database of Chinese Buddhist texts is offered in both Chinese (BIG5 encoding) and Japanese (Shift-JIS encoding) versions. The database contains records on some 4418 texts by 1513 authors/translators/compilers and is part of the foundation for future development of an online archive of Buddhist texts. The texts were encoded following the TEI Guidelines to provide a means of linking texts to other relevant materials.

World Wide Web Sites Relating to the Ancient Mediterranean
http://www.stolaf.edu/people/kchanson/websites.html

This is a catalog of World Wide Web sites relevant to the ancient Mediterranean. The categories are: Ancient World Searches, Museums with Significant Ancient Art and Artifact Collections, Archaeology, Ancient Document Collections (searchable), Papyrology and Epigraphy, Ancient Near East, Egypt, Canaan, Israel & Judah, and the Hebrew Bible, Greece and the Hellenistic Empires, Roman Empire, Qumran and the Dead Sea Scrolls, Palestine, the New Testament, and Early Christianity, Professional Societies and Journals, and Miscellaneous.

Chogye Zen
http://oac11.hsc.uth.tmc.edu/zen/index.html

Primary Zen Buddhist texts and links to other sites of interest to students of Buddhist Studies.

7. Searching for Internet Resources

Thousands of resources are available on the Internet and more are added each day. But the Internet resembles a library that collects anything and everything, lists items in no consistent way, and maintains no complete index of what is available or where it is located. Works such as this one are one answer to finding resources on the Internet of interest to scholars. Unfortunately, it cannot list every available resource even in fairly narrowly drawn categories or direct the reader to new resources that appear after its publication.

Rapid Internet growth created the need for some mechanism for discovery of new resources or those not listed in print or online resource collections. Search engines were developed to visit sites on the Internet and to index the resources found at each site. Each search engine differs from the others in the scope of its searching of the Internet, the information stored as a result of its search and the underlying indexing of its search results. Like any other technology, the usefulness of a search engine depends upon the skill of its user. The following sections outline common aspects of search engines, details the search logic used by most search engines and conclude with an examination of several specific search engines.

Search Engine Overview

Search engines, despite their name, do not search the Internet in response to a search request. A database of search results compiled by other programs is consulted by the search engine and the results of that query is given to the user. Search engine databases are constructed from the findings of web robots or spiders that follow links on the Web. A web robot can start with a single web page and follow all the links it finds on that page and then examine the results of that search to extract links found on the pages visited and then follow those links. The results provided by the web robot depend upon site accessibility (sites can block well-behaved robots), the computer resources devoted to running the search program, the search criteria used by the robot program and other factors.

Once the results of a robot search have been received, the results are then processed for use in the database queried by the search engine. Some of the indexes contain more information concerning the resources than others. Most of the better search engines (including all of those treated in **Common Search Engines**) retain metadata contained in document headers as part of their databases. The more complete the set of information contained in the database the higher the likelihood of a successful search for a particular resource.

Search engines vary in the number of pages indexed in their databases, the frequency of updates to the database, and the methods used to gather information for the database. Within the top five search engines the differences are more of a concern for information theorists than casual users. It is more important to learn the specifics of two or three search engines and their requirements than seeking a new search engine with the latest advances in searching or indexing theory.

The Art of Good Questions (Search Logic)

Very often a searcher will enter a one-word search, such as "bible," "Paul," or "John," only to be confronted with a massive listing of "hits" on documents that might be relevant. (On June 27, 1998, AltaVista returned 2,424,950 hits for "bible," 8,154,520 hits for "Paul," and 19,150,910 hits for "John.") A "hit" is a document that contains the word that was entered in the search request. For the examples mentioned, the researcher would need to be very lucky for the resource sought to be in the first ten or twenty hits or extraordinarily patient to make any use of these search results.

Part of the searching process is constructing queries that will find a particular resource or a small group of likely candidates. For more familiar resources such as a library catalog or Religion Index One: Periodicals, searchers are constructing queries but probably not consciously. Years of use develop into searching habits that hide the explicit process of formulating the query. Search engines index a very diverse body of material and require greater assistance from searchers to isolate the resources of interest.

Constructing successful searches depends in part on the searchers familiarity with the subject under investigation. Phrase searches that enclose several words within double quotation marks have a high chance of success if created by someone familiar with the subject matter of the search. As with any field, classics, religion and archaeology have set phrases or terms of art that are unlikely to be found outside the field. For example, a search for the Greek word "doxa" and "new testament" returned 139 hits, which with relevancy ranking is a manageable number. A search with the common English translation "glory" and "new testament" results in 29,480 hits, a rather large number of documents. The **AND** in the search query is an example of using Boolean operators to modify the scope of a search query.

Searchers can use Boolean operators to narrow the number of resources that match the search query. Boolean operators commonly available at most search engines include: **AND**, **OR**, and **NOT**. (Web trivia: Boolean operator is a term used to describe a logical operator that includes or excludes a term from a set. The term "Boolean" operator recognizes the foundational work of George Boole in the application of algebraic methods to logic.) These operators are most often used with parentheses to group terms together. The following examples illustrate the operation of each of these operators.

AND: If the search request is for: Julius **and** Caesar, the query will return all documents containing Julius and Caesar but not necessarily as a phrase. Phrase searching is generally performed by enclosing a phrase in double quotation marks, in this case "Julius Caesar." **AND** is the default for keyword searching on Lycos but **OR** is the keyword default on AltaVista.

OR: If the search request is for: Julius **or** Caesar, the query will return all documents containing either Julius or Caesar anywhere in the document. With keyword searches the **or** operator is probably most useful when separating two phrases, two fairly unique terms or more complex expressions created with the use of parentheses.

NOT: If the search request is for: "Julius Caesar" **not** Shakespeare, the query will return all documents including "Julius Caesar" as a phrase and exclude those that also include the name

Shakespeare. This operator is sometimes written out as **AND NOT** but its operation in search engines is the same as **NOT**.

Common Search Engines

Some of the more important search engines on the Web are listed below with any particular features that should be noted by newcomers to Web searching. The absence of any search engine from this listing is not a commentary on its usefulness or accuracy. This listing was developed to aid new Web users to begin searching the Web and to develop their own preferences for search engines and searching techniques. These search engines and many other call all be accessed from the All-in-One Search page located at: **http://www.albany.net/allinone/**

AltaVista

AltaVista, **http://www.altavista.com**, is one of the largest keyword indexes to the Web. It indexes the full text of all the files contained in its database. The Boolean default for simple searches with AltaVista is **OR** which may result in largely irrelevant search results. Using a service known as Babelfish the AltaVista can provide translations of web pages in foreign (for the user) languages. The syntax and features of AltaVista searching can be summarized as follows:

AltaVista: Simple Search

AND or + : Requires two or more terms to appear in a document

NOT or - : Excludes a term or phrase from the query

OR : Default, does not need to be specified

( ) : Parentheses are used to gather terms for operators

* : Truncation of term (stemming). Ex. rid* returns rides, riding. Internal truncation also supported. Ex. colo*r returns both color and colour.

" " : Phrases must be enclosed in double quotation marks.

Case : AltaVista supports full case sensitivity, i.e., distinguishes "Park" from "park", but lower case "park" will also return hits for the upper case "Park."

AltaVista: Advanced Search

AND or & : Note the + operator does not work for advanced searches.

OR or | : Note no default operator between terms in advanced search mode.

NOT or ! : AltaVista syntax requires this operator be used as: **AND NOT** followed by the excluded search term.

NEAR or ~ : The **NEAR** operator requires that the terms or phrases in the query occur within ten words of each other. Note the **NEAR** operator is system dependent and it behavior will vary depending upon the search engine where it is implemented.

Date : The advanced search page offers the opportunity to set a range of dates for documents otherwise meeting the criteria of the query. If the month or year is omitted from the range it will be supplied as the current month or year.

Boolean Expression : The Boolean expression box allows for the entry of a Boolean search query and the results of the search as not ranked by the search engine. It is also possible to have a simply count of documents matching the Boolean expression returned.

AltaVista Field Searches

anchor:text : Matches an anchor in any page containing specific text. Ex. anchor:"SPIonic" will find all pages with a link to the SPIonic Greek font as a hyperlink.

applet:class : The applet class field searches for pages that use particular Java applets. Ex. applet:babble (Returns one site that plays a Nixon snippet on a loop.)

domain:domainname : A domain field limits a search to a particular domain. The number of pages within any domain limits its usefulness unless combined with another term. Ex. egyptology domain:de returns 126 hits.

host:name : The host field matches the query against the pages of a specific site. May be misleading if the site is behind a firewall or otherwise not indexed.

image:filename : Useful for finding pages that contain images with particular filenames.

link:URLtext : This field answers the question of "who has links to my site?" (If a site uses absolute links to pages this field will also return those pages as well.)

text:text : This field limits the query to the specified text in a page outside an image tag, link or URL. Useful when searching for terms that may also appear in links or URLs in particular.

title:text : The title field limits the query to words or phrases found in the title element of the page. Assuming that only the most significant terms would be included in the title, this field offers a useful way to narrow a search for most terms.

url:text : The URL field searches for pages containing a specific word or phrase in a URL, which consists of the host name, path or filename.

Excite

Excite, **http://www.excite.com**, reflects a different strategy from AltaVista in terms of how it indexes sites and the type of searching available for its database. Excite uses "Intelligent Concept Extraction (ICE)" to develop links between words and concepts. Instead of searching for keywords (AltaVista) terms describing ideas or concepts can be entered and Excite will return what it considers to be the best matches. The results of a search are returned with options to narrow the search, which can be helpful for most researchers. For example, when simply "Paul" is entered as a search on Excite, it note some 1,021,905 hits and suggests limiting the search by saint, mccartney, prudhomme, and apostle, among others. Adding "apostle" to the search phrase returns more limited search results and further suggestions for words to add to the search such as: epistle, truthfulness and gentiles. Excite also offers a subject guide to various topics on the Web for browsing or use in developing search strategies for areas not familiar to the searcher.

The principal drawbacks to Excite are a lack of case sensitivity, searches limited by fields and truncation. Despite these limitations its concept extraction technology and ease of use for beginning users make it an excellent web search engine. The syntax and features of Excite searching can be summarized as follows:

Excite: Simple Search

AND or + : Requires two or more terms to appear in a document

NOT or - : Excludes a term or phrase from the query

OR : Default, does not need to be specified

( ) : Parentheses are used to gather terms for operators

" " : Phrases must be enclosed in double quotation marks.

More Like This : Once a useful resource has been found, choosing "More Like This" (an icon next to the item on the search results) will use that page as the basis for a new search for other items most closely matching that one.

List by Web Site : Most searches on the Web will return several pages from the same website although the matching items are listed separately on the results. Choosing "List by Web Site" after completing a search will compress the results to show the website only once and list relevant pages under the website.

Excite: Advanced Search (Templates)

CAN contain : The search results can contain the specified words or phrases. (**OR**)

MUST contain : The search results must contain the specified words or phrases. (**AND**)

MUST NOT contain : The search results must not contain the specified words or phrases. (**NOT**)

HotBot

HotBot, **http://www.hotbot.com**, has one of the largest search engine databases on the Web with over 110 million files. Unlike AltaVista, HotBot defaults to **AND** when searching for individual terms. The search will return pages that contain all the terms listed. Boolean logic for searches can be used via templates or entered in all CAPS in the search phrase. Hotbot offers extensive facilities for searching for different types of media found on web pages such as audio, video and others. The syntax and features of HotBot can be summarized as follow:

HotBot Menu Search

Look For (Drop Down Menu)

All the Words : Search words are entered in the template and the search returns pages with all the words. **(AND)** This setting can be changed in drop down menu.

Any of the Words : The search returns pages that contain any of the words entered in the search window. **(OR)**

Exact Phrase : HotBot returns pages that contain the words entered in the search window as a phrase. The phrase can also be enclosed in parentheses for the same purpose.

The Page Title : The search queries only the title element of pages in the database and returns those matching the request.

The Person : Oddly named "The Person" is actually a proximity operator for the terms entered in the search window.

Links to the URL : This search option returns pages containing a URL entered in the search window.

Boolean Phrase : The Boolean Phrase option supports the use of **AND, OR, NOT** and **( )** in the construction of complex search requests.

Word Filter (Drop Down Menu)

Must Contain the Words : The "Must Contain" option under "Word Filter" allows the searcher to require certain words to be found in the pages selected to answer the query.

Must Not Contain the Words : The "Must Not Contain" option under "Word Filter" allows for the exclusion of certain words from the search results.

Date : The data menu allows the searcher to select pages found on the Web during certain time periods or at anytime. Dates can be selected by day, month and year.

Pages Must Include : The pages returned under a search query can be required to use certain technologies or contain certain media types. At present the media/technology selection options are: Acrobat, ActiveX, Audio, Extension (specify .gif, .txt, etc.), Image, Java, JavaScript, Shockwave, VB Script, Video and VRML.

Location/Domain : The location menu allows entry of domains or continents to limit the sites searched in response to the query.

Page Depth : One of the more interesting features of HotBot is the ability to control the depth of the pages searched in response to the search request. When searching for primary sites on a subject it is helpful to exclude sites where the target words or phrase is found in a page of links several layers from the primary page for the site. Searchers can choose to search anypage, the top pages only or set a page depth.

Return Results : The display of the search results can be set both by the number of responses shown and the length of the descriptions given.

HotBot Advanced Searching (Not Using Menu Options)

Boolean Operators (Enter as all CAPS)

AND or & : A page must contain all terms joined by **AND** to meet the terms of the query.

OR or | : A page must contain at least one of the terms separated by **OR** to meet the terms of the query.

NOT or ! : A page cannot contain the terms following **NOT** to meet the terms of the query.

( ) : Parentheses can be used to group Boolean expressions to permit more complex search queries.

Query Modifiers

: Quotation marks are used to indicate an exact phrase. Words will be found in the order indicated and not in alternative sequences.

+ : The plus operator indicates that the word or phrase following it must be found in the pages returned from the query.

- : The minus operator indicates that the word or phrase following it in the search expression must not be contained in the pages returned for a query.

Meta Words

domain:name : Domain restricts searches to particular domains. Domains can be specified up to three levels deep. Ex. domain:edu, domain:emory.edu, domain:scholar.emory.edu

depth:[number] : Depth: is followed by a number to set the depth of pages to be included in answering the search request.

feature:acrobat : Finds Acrobat files in the pages searched.

feature:applet : Finds Java applets embedded in web pages.

feature:activex : Finds ActiveX controls or layouts in pages.

feature:audio : Finds various audio formats available on web pages.

feature:embed : Finds pages that require plugins.

feature:flash : Finds pages that use the Flash plugin in HTML.

feature:form : Finds pages that contain forms in HTML.

feature:frame : Finds Pages that contain frames in HTML.

feature:image : Finds a variety of image formats used on web pages.

feature:script : Finds scripts embedded in HTML pages.

feature:shockwave : Finds Shockwave files.

feature:table : Finds pages that contain tables in HTML.

feature:video : Finds a variety of video formats used on web pages.

feature:vrml : Finds VRML files.

linkdomain:[name] : Allows for searching for links to a particular domain.

linkext:[extension] : Limits searches to pages containing files with specific extensions.

newsgroup:[newsgroup name] : Limits searches on Usenet newsgroups to particular newsgroups. The newsgroup must be specified with its full name.

scriptlanguage:[language] : Permits searches for pages where JavaScript or VBScript is used on web pages. Both should be entered in lower-case with the scriptlanguage meta word, i.e., as javascript or vbscript.

title:[word] : Limits the word sought to occuring within the title of the pages searched.

after:[day]/[month]/[year] : Limits the query to documents created or modified on or after the date specified.

before:[day]/[month]/[year] : Limits the query to documents created or modified before teh date specified.

within:number/unit : Used to specify number of time units and unit of measurement. Since all date meta words are special cases the user should be careful to put the within:number/unit as a single term in a Boolean expression.

Lycos

Lycos, **http://www.lycos.com**, offers a very large web database and very useful collections of links organized by subjects known as "Web Guides." Lycos offers very current coverage of the Web and very easy to use menu interfaces to its search options. More importantly Lycos allows searchers to set relevancy rankings for search results and offers excellent proximity operators for search requests. The syntax and features of Lycos can be summarized as follows:

Lycos Main Screen

AND or + : Keyword search defaults to **AND**.

- : Used for Boolean **NOT** in main search window.

" " : Use double quotes to search for exact phrases.

**. or $** : The Lycos search engine automatically stems search terms. To prevent stemming close the term with "." or to specify truncation, use the "$" character. (Truncation and stemming both refer to the practice of removing the endings from words for matching purposes.)

Lycos Pro Search (Drop Down Menu)

Any of the Words

Any of the Words (or Query) : The "Any of the Words (or Query)" setting for Lycos will match any word in the search request that is found in a webpage. That does not mean that all the terms of the search request were matched.

Natural Language Query : This option allows the search request to be phrased as a normal question. A good example of the advances in use of normal language for computer input. It also allows the use of some reserved words such as "Near," "Far" and "Before" in making the natural language search request.

All the words (any order) : This option will find only webpages that contain all the words in the search request but they can appear in any order.

All the words (in order) : This option does not necessarily find words that are adjacent to each other. Such matches would be included in the results of this option but adjacent searches should use the "Exact Phrase" option mentioned below.

All the words (within 25 words, any order) : This option is the same as the "All Words, Any Order" option mentioned above but limits matches to the search words occurring within 25 words of each other. The separation distance allows for some uncertainty on the part of the researcher as to the exact phrase or its order but limits the number of matches to a manageable number (in most cases).

All the words (within 25 words, in order) : A useful option when the order of the phrase is fairly certain but may be found in differing formats. For example, a search for the Chicago Assyrian Dictionary would want to find a page with "The University of Chicago announced today an electronic version its Assyrian Dictionary project." (That is a fictional example but one the author hopes will come to pass in time.)

All the words (adjacent, any order : A very useful option for searches where the exact language of a quote or phrase is known but the searcher is uncertain about its order.

The Exact Phrase The most restrictive option under "Any of the Words" the "Exact Phrase" is a good choice for searching for personal names but the Lycos help guide cautions that it may be too exact for some purposes. Lycos uses the example of an exact phrase search for "Apple Pie" would miss a recipe for "Apple Pecan Pie."

Advanced Options

Look for : The "look for" radio buttons allow searches to be directed to "Any content," "Sounds," "Pictures," "Recipes," "Personal home pages on Tripod.com and Geocities.com," "Lycos City Guides" and "Web Site Reviews (Top 5%)."

Search the : The "search the" radio buttons allows the searcher to specify a particular part of a web site or even a single web site for searching. The search defaults to "entire document" but can be set to "Title only," "URLs only" or "selected website." The last two options allow for entry of a URL or website address in a text box at the "Search for" section.

Select a language : Allows the search results to be limited by the language of the matching results. Available selections are: Danish, Dutch, English, French, German, Icelandic, Norwegian, Portuguese, Slovenian, Spanish, Swedish and Welsh.

Sort your results : The sort results menus allow the results of searches to be sorted by: "Match all words," "Frequency of words," "Near beginning of text," "Close together," "Appear in title" and "In exact order." Each of these can be set to "High", "Medium" or "Low" allowing for a high degree of control over the sorting of the search results.

Boolean Expressions

AND : **AND** and all the Boolean operators for Lycos can be entered as upper or lower case. The **AND** operator is used to force documents to contain the search terms joined by it. **AND** can also be entered with the + sign.

OR : **OR** is used to join search terms when matching any of the terms in the search request will be a successful search. It is probably best used with obscure terms or as part of a larger Boolean expression.

NOT : **NOT** is used to exclude terms from the search request and thereby limiting the documents that will be returned. The - sign can be used in place of **NOT**.

" " : Double quotation marks are used to create phrases from groups of words.

ADJ : **ADJ** is an operator that requires the search terms to be next to each other in any order.

NEAR : **NEAR** requires that the search terms appear within 25 words of each other in any document returned for the query.

FAR : **FAR** is the opposite of **NEAR** in that it requires the search terms to appear at least once more than 25 words apart. To preclude the results from including pages with the terms appearing closer than 25 words in other instances **FAR** must be used with other operators such as **NOT**.

BEFORE : **BEFORE** requires the search terms to appear in the same document as **AND** but also requries that one term appear before the other. This can be useful in searching for phrases or titles that are not known exactly although the order of some of the words are known.

O : **O** is not an independent operator but is used with **ADJ,, NEAR** and **FAR** to force the terms to appear in the order specified in the search request. These operators become **OADJ, ONEAR** and **OFAR** respectively.

/ : **/** can be appended to **ADJ, NEAR, FAR, OADJ, ONEAR** and **OFAR** to set a specific distance between words for these operators. To find all the dictionaries published by

Chicago University, which have the form generally of "Chicago Name_of_Dictionary Dictionary" use the search "Chicago ONEAR/2 Dictionary."

MetaCrawler

MetaCrawler **http://www.metacrawler.com** is a search engine that submits queries to other search engine databases such as Altavista, Excite, Infoseek, Lycos and Yahoo, returning the results in a uniform format. Metacrawler eliminates duplicate hits from the results and ranks the results with confidence scores obtained from the other search engines. The search logic for MetaCrawler is not as complex as some of the search engines since the abilities of the search engines queried by MetaCrawler vary cosiderably. MetaCrawler uses template technology for the entry of the options described below rather than allow users to input Boolean operators. Users can enter double quotation marks to create phrases for use with the "any" or "all" search options. The syntax and features of MetaCrawler can be summarized as follows:

MetaCrawler Main Screen

any : The "any" option operates likes the Boolean **OR** operator seen on other sites. A webpage will match the search request if it has any of the words found in the search request.

all : The "all" selection joins all the words in the search request with the Boolean **AND** operator. All the search terms must be found in a web document for it to be returned for the query.

phrase : The "phrase" option searches the words in the search request as a phrase.

MetaCrawler Power Search

any : The "any" option operates likes the Boolean **OR** operator seen on other sites. A webpage will match the search request if it has any of the words found in the search request.

all : The "all" selection joins all the words in the search request with the Boolean **AND** operator. All the search terms must be found in a web document for it to be returned for the query.

phrase : The "phrase" option searches the words in the search request as a phrase.

Results from : With "Power Search" the geographic location of sites and within the U.S. the type of site, i.e., commercial, educational, government, can be limited to particular areas.

Timeout : The "Timeout" option allows a user to request MetaCrawler to wait longer for results from the search engines queried.

Results per page : The "Results per page" controls the number of results that will be displayed on each page. This does not have any affect on the actual searching or its results.

Results per source : By default MetaCrawler limits the number of hits returned from each source for processing. The default limit is 10 hits which should contain some relevant information in response to a properly constructed query. This option allows the number of results to be increased up to 30 per source, although it will rarely increase the usefulness of the search results in most cases.

Search : The areas to be searched can also be limited to the Web, newsgroups, computer products, files and stock quotes.

In the search window of MetaCrawler it is possible to construct more advanced queries that allowed by the template technology. As with most of the search engines queried by MetaCrawler, the + sign is used for Boolean **AND** with the - representing Boolean **NOT**. Since phrases can be constructed using double quotation marks, it is possible to construct a relatively complex query that will be recognized by most of the search engines contacted by MetaCrawler.

MetaSpy

One of the more entertaining resources on the Web is the MetaSpy (**http://www.metaspy.com** page at the MetaCrawler site **http://www.metacrawler.com**. MetaCrawler is a search engine that consults the databases of several search engines, including AltaVista, Excite, Infoseek, Lycos and Yahoo, returning the results in a uniform format. The search logic for MetaCrawler is not as complex as some of the search engines since it submits its searches to a variety of databases that support different features. MetaSpy shows recently submitted search requests made to the MetaCrawler search engine and by selecting one of these searches the user can view the results of that search.

Yahoo

Yahoo **http://www.yahoo.com** is both a search engine and one of the older subject indexes to the Internet. The first database searched in a query on Yahoo is Yahoo's subject index. The subject index can also be browsed and may be a useful way of discovering information at the listed sites that will help narrow a search request in unfamiliar topics. The usefulness of the search engine is limited by the range of searching options offered and the lack of case sensitivity for search requests. The syntax and features of Yahoo can be summarized as follows:

Yahoo Main Search Screen

AND or + : Requires two or more terms to appear in a document. Default setting for Yahoo.

NOT or - : Excludes a term or phrase from the query

Search Fields

Fields

Title : Forces the search term to appear in the title of the document. Can be specified with "t:" as in "t:clinton".

URL : Forces the search term to appear in the URL of a document returned from the search. Can be specified with "u:" as in "u:sil".

Phrases : Phrases are specified by the use of double quotes to surround the entire phrase.

Truncation : Truncation of words is mandatory and the truncation character is "*".

Yahoo Advanced Search (select Options)

Select a search method

Intelligent default : No explanation offered at site.

An exact phrase match : Forces search query to be treated as a phrase.

Matches on all words (AND) : All words must be found on page.

Matches on any word (OR) : Matches any word in the search query.

A person's name : No explanation offered at site.

Select a search area : Can select Yahoo Categories or Web Sites

Find only new listings : Can select time period limitation for search

After first result page, display : Allows setting the number of results on subsequent pages

8. Creating A Web Resource

The process of creating a Web resource is one that calls upon design and programming skills that are not taught in most graduate programs in the humanities. Despite increasing interest in web technology among both graduate students and professional scholars there has been little movement towards incorporating classes on such technologies in graduate curriculums. This need for information can be partially satisfied with online information resources and numerous books published on each of these topics. To supply the instruction and information needed to use any of the current web technologies herein would over tax the reader's arm as well as their pocketbook. The goal of this chapter is to outline the basic principles of each technology and give one or two examples of its use by a scholarly site. This chapter concludes with a selected set of resource links that will be helpful to both experienced and beginning web resource creators.

When, in the beginning...: Basic Questions of Creation

The ease of publication on the Web has lead more than a few scholars to condemn its contents as little more than vanity publishing at its worst. Readers reaching this section will realize that such characterizations are unfair when applied to any of the resources listed in this work. In all fairness, however, it should be noted that resources were selected for inclusion in this work because of their scholarly nature and that does not mean that less scholarly materials cannot be found on the Web. Like print publications, the development of scholarly norms of conduct for Web "publication" will play an important role in increasing the legitimacy of web based resources. The decision to create a web based resource shares some of the concerns of traditional publications and others that are unique to the new media.

A tentative list of some of the more prominent issues in the creation of a web resource includes:

Web Resource Creation Questions

Content : Is the content to be made available by the resource of significance to the discipline? Does the academic community need another Encyclopedia Britannica from the early 20th century online?

Continuity : Will the resource be sponsored by an academic department or organization that will maintain the resource after its author/creator leaves or moves onto other projects?

Longevity : Will the resource be created in a platform and software independent format that will allow future researchers to reuse the resource in unanticipated ways?

Originality : Does this resource or project offer a new method of manipulating data or new insights into existing material.

Peer Review : What provisions have been made for peer review of the content of the resource? If an online journal is contemplated, does it have an active board of editors that fairly represents the field of study?

Professionalism : Will the resource be freely shared with other researchers or will other, less collegial conventions govern access?

There are not quick or ready anwsers to the questions posed in the foregoing list which will be the subject of debates in academia for the forseeable future. Some mirror traditional academic concerns with the quality of work while others are concerned with the changing norms of access to academic materials.

HTML and Text Resources

HTML (HyperText Markup Language) is the *lingua franca* of the world of web pages. It began as a research proposal by Tim Berners-Lee at the CERN in Switzerland to create a "hypertext system" for communications over a computer network. A revision of that proposal can be found at: **http://info.cern.ch/hypertext/WWW/TheProject.html** It has been revised several times (the latest revision is 4.0) and extended in a number of inconsistent ways by major browser suppliers. The infamous <BLINK> element was an extension of HTML by Netscape and allowed portions of text to be set to blink off and then on again.

HTML is based upon SGML but originally was to some degree a presentational markup language. In version 4.0, users can markup text with HTML 4.0 elements and rely upon stylesheets to impose the proper style on the pages when presented. Due to the rapid advance of technology on the web however, there will be users' whose browsing software will not support stylesheets. To reach the widest possible audience, prospective web authors should adhere to the HTML 4.0 Transitional standard to reach readers who lack the latest browsing software.

HTML has been used for every possible type of text from personal homepages to online journals. It is usually the first experience users have with a markup language and is adequate for many purposes. The advantages and disadvantages of HTML can be summarized as follows:

HTML Advantages

HTML has a very low learning curve. (Albeit higher when using cascading style sheets)

HTML can be created with simple text editors or professional WYSIWYG editors

HTML can be written to be non-browser specific

HTML Disadvantages (Including Version 4.0)

HTML lacks an adequate hierarchy of container elements.

HTML lacks extension mechanisms for adding elements.

HTML lacks sufficient elements for creating textual databases of textual materials

Most of the disadvantages of HTML become apparent only when scholars attempt to create complex textual resources using HTML tagging. It is more than adequate for class syllabi, required reading lists, or short papers that do not form part of some larger textual collection. Materials can also be converted into HTML a presentation format for web delivery.

The **SELA** project noted in the Internet Resource section is a good example of using HTML as a delivery format. While a user views the available issues of *Semeia* or *JAAR* in HTML the text was actually held in TEILite SGML markup and served to the user through a DynaWeb server that converted the SGML markup into HTML markup at the time of the user request. This use of HTML as a delivery format allows maintenance of a textual database that is not limited to use over the web. These texts can be queried and searched in ways not possible if they were held in HTML format. It is this ability to extend the usefulness of a document that is the basis for referring to SGML documents as "intelligent documents."

Intelligent Documents: An Overview of SGML/XML/XLL

SGML (Standard Generalized Markup Language) was developed by Charles F. Goldfarb as a method of divorcing the presentation of a document from its structure. While the implementation of SGML is relatively complex, the insight that underlies it is fairly simple. (After it was discovered by Goldfarb at any rate.) Consider the paragraph that you are now reading in this book. Even at a glance you could identify it as a paragraph due to the space that precedes and follows it as well as its location relative to the right and left margins of the page. The presentation of the material is a visual clue that this is a paragraph and not a block quote or list or some other type of text.

Goldfarb's essential insight was that a paragraph (or other text structure) could be indicated by some means that was not specific to any type of software or hardware. All word processing software marks paragraphs but not always in ways that can be understood by other software. Once a paragraph or quote was indicated in a non-specific way, then any software program could attach its specific way of displaying that particular item. Each of these items are called elements and are defined by a DTD (Document Type Declaration) which defines what elements can appear in a document.

The power of this insight cannot be overstated. For example, each of the URLs in this work were marked as <seg> elements. In the processing to produce the camera ready copy for publication, each of the <seg> elements was printed in **BOLD** face type. For an online edition or set of bookmarks, these same <seg> elements could be extracted from the original document and a new document created that only contained hypertext links to each of these resources. Since the original document has not been changed, there is no need to reproof the content of the new document for errors.

A scholar can use a well-designed DTD to encode a document (or create a new one) that is composed of a hierarchy of containers. The demarcation of the structure of a document makes it possible to reorder the document or search it in ways not readily apparent when it was originally created. A journals database in SGML could be searched for the number of times the authors of articles (one possible element) also cited themselves in bibliographic references (another possible element) or portions of articles or entire articles could be extracted for inclusion in a book of readings for a class.

Actually it is not technically correct to say that a document is encoded using SGML. The document is encoded using a Document Type Declaration (DTD) that conforms to the SGML standard. The **Text Encoding Initiative (TEI)** developed a DTD that was written specifically for use in the humanities. Markup languages based on the original SGML standard have developed and are rapidly changing the exchange of structured information.

XML (eXtensible Markup Language) is a rapidly developing web technology for the delivery of information. It is actually a subset of SGML and should not be considered as a replacement for SGML. The portions of the SGML standard that are not allowed in XML mainly concern shortcuts for entry of markup data and features that were never fully supported by available SGML software. XML documents can either be "valid" or "well-formed" or both. A "valid" XML document conforms to a given DTD. A "well-formed" XML document may conform to a DTD but the XML software merely verifies that it meets the constraints placed on it by the XML standard. Along with XML there are evolving standards for XSL (eXtensive Style Language) and XLL (eXtensible Linking Language) which will specify the use of style sheets with XML documents and the formation of links to and from XML documents respectively.

The Document Style Semantics and Specification Language (DSSSL) standard was developed for the formatting and transformation of documents encoded using a DTD. DSSSL has not yet been fully implemented but there are several free or shareware software tools that rival any commercially available for those wishing to explore the capacities of DSSSL.

HyTime is an evolving standard concerned with the linking of information between components of information. The use of SGML Architectural Forms arose out of the first HyTime standard and is now playing an important role in the development of markup based on both HyTime and the SGML standard.

Interactivity: The Magic of Java and Scripting Languages

Java is a programming language that has achieved some degree of platform independence by use of what is known as a virtual machine. Once Java is installed on a personal computer, it is included with most web browsers, a user can download a Java Applet that will compile and run on their local computer. The same Applet will run on a Windows 95, Macintosh or Unix workstation, without any changes in the underlying program. Applets are meant to be run over the web but Java can also support the use of Java programs as standalone applications on a local machine.

The example programs cited below for the use of Java are the results of years of effort and sophisticated programming skills. There are a number of educational uses of Java that do not require the degree of computer skills evidenced by these programs. These programs were cited as good examples of software that would be of significance to scholars and which could be usefully employed by most scholars (even if the average humanist could not recreate these programs).

One good example of the use of Java is the **Xerox Arabic Morphological Analysis and Generation** site that can be accessed at: **http://www.xrce.xerox.com/research/mltt/arabic/**. Ken Beesley is a Principal Scientist at the Xerox Research Centre Europe in Grenoble, France in the Multi-Lingual Theory and Technology group. This applet accepts a Modern Standard Arabic word and returns a morphological analysis with English gloss. The use of a Java applet permits remote users to enter Arabic words in traditional Arabic script. A paper on this process Arabic Morphological Analysis on the Internet is available at this site. This is a very instructive application of both parsing technology and web access.

Another example of the use of Java for scholarly projects can be found at the Institute for Advanced Technology in the Humanities (IATH) at the University of Virginia. IBabble is a synopic Unicode browser that is SGML aware under development by Robert Bigler. IBabble cannot current run as an applet but can exist as a helper application to another browser program. Written entirely in Java, IBabble can display several multilingual texts in parallel windows. IBabble is available for free downloading from the IATH website under software: **http://www.iath.viginia.edu**.

The ITeach software, also from IATH, is a network based collaborative environment written in Java that could be used for distance instruction or small collaborative meetings of scholars. Basic text and chat facilities are already available and other tools are to be added as the software develops. IATH is currently distributing beta versions of both the server and client software for interested scholars. The ITeach software can be found at the IATH website under software: **http://www.iath.virginia.edu**.

Scripting languages are computer programming languages that are mainly used to write short programs for immediate tasks at hand. Like more traditional programming languages, scripting languages can be used for tasks ranging from simple to complex. The choice of a scripting language and the merits of various candidates is a matter of serious debate between advocates for each language. The best option for beginning users is to ask local computer support staff or fellow users which scripting language they prefer. Scripting languages are responsible for most of the web programs that dynamically generate HTML pages, access simple databases and provide other services on websites. The use of scripting languages for academic purposes is well illustrated at the Language Interactive: A Trailguide to Creating Dynamic Web Pages site (**http://www.vcu.edu/idc/li/interact.html**).

VRML: Virtual Worlds, Sacred Spaces and Recreating Excavations

The VRML (Virtual Reality Modeling Language) standard describes how users can construct 3D objects and worlds that are accessible by others. VRML is actually a specification of a file format that contains all the information necessary to produce an interactive object or world that can link to other objects or worlds. VRML holds a great deal of promise in such diverse areas as scientific visualization, educational tools, multimedia applications and construction of representations of archaeological sites or excavations.

It is possible to construct elaborate models or worlds in VRML with nothing more than a text editor and VRML viewing software. The file format does not require access to expensive authoring tools but the simpler route does require more hand coding than VRML authoring tools. Even with good VRML authoring tools it is no trivial task to create a representation of an archaeological dig or ancient site in sufficient detail to be useful. It is suggested that scholars form teams with graphics designers, computer programmers and VRML practitioners before embarking on substantial VRML projects.

A very good example of the use of VRML for the representation of an ancient site is the Funerary Chapel of Ka(i)pura, **http://www.learningsites.com/Kapure/Kapure_home.htm**. Prepared by Learning Sites, this representation allows students to examine this structure in ways not possible even with an actual physical visit to the site. Scholars should be mindful that this project was crafted by professional site builders who were being advised on content by scholars in Egyptology. Assuming cooperation between VRML professionals and scholars there is a great deal of potential for the use of VRML in both education and professional activities.

References for Resource Creators

The sites listed below are collections of tutorials, resource materials, and software that will be helpful to scholars seeking to create new web resources. Most of these sites maintain or have listings for mailing lists and other forums for discussion of various software packages or techniques. This listing is not exhaustive but should be used as a starting point for further investigation into creating web resources. The development of the web and many of its dominant technologies are the result of informal collaboration and sharing of information and resources. The continuation of this collaborative model depends upon the continued sharing of diverse communities of individuals. Scholars should make opportunities to share both techniques and results from their web projects as their expertise and experience grow.

alphaWorks
http://www.alphaWorks.ibm.com/Home/

IBM's alphaWorks site is a showplace for the latest Web technology. All of the software featured on this site is available for free downloading and anyone can contribute cutting edge software. For researchers interested in the latest software for use on the Web this site deserves regular monitoring.

CGI Resource Index
http://www.cgi-resources.com

The CGI Resource Index is a collection of 1,228 CGI (Common Gateway Interface) related resources which includes over 1,000 scripts for use and modification. The site also has links to tutorials, FAQs and guides to using particular programming languages for CGI programming.

developer.com
http://www.developer.com

Created by the developers of Gamelon, the developer.com site offers links to almost any resource needed by a web developer. The directories section leads to listing of resources on ActiveX, ASP, C/C++, Cold Fusion, CGI, Databases, Distributed Objects, HTML/DHTML, Intranets, Java, JavaScript, Middleware, Perl, Push Technology, Visual Basic, XML, VRML, What's Cool, What's New and Who's Who. It also offers listing of books and software that may be of interest to web developers.

Gamelan
http://www.developer.com/directories/pages/dir.java.html

Gamelan is now a directory of developer.com but merits separate mention simply on the basis of the depth of Java resources offered. The sections available at Gamelan and the number of resources offered (as of July 4, 1998) are as follows: Arts and Entertainment (389), Business and Finance (315), Commercial Java (973), Educational (1238), Games (1838), How-To (97), JavaBeans (129), Miscellaneous (166), Multimedia (767), Network and Communications (830), Programming (1889), Publications (221), Sites (855), Special Effects (1256) and Tools and Utilities (1170). Gamelan is one of the first Java sites to check for recent or innovative Java software.

GNU Documentation
http://www.delorie.com/gnu/docs/

The GNU documentation site offers online access to the manuals for software released as part of the GNU project. The GNU (GNU's Not Unix) project is an effort begun by Richard Stallman to create a complete Unix-compatible software system that would be freely available to all interested users along with the source code for the software. The GNU project has a full range of software packages which are often offered as binaries for a variety of Unix operating systems by third parties. GNU software and a Unix platform are the basis for serious humanities computing efforts.

HTML Goodies
http://www.htmlgoodies.com

HTML Goodies offers over 100 tutorials on HTML and related topics. This is an excellent site for those just learning HTML or who are trying to duplicate special HTML effects they have seen at other website.

Icon Programming Language
http://www.cs.arizona.edu/icon/index.htm

Icon has excellent support for manipulation of data structures and character strings. Icon was designed by Robert Griswold as a successor to the programming language SNOBOL. This site offers access to large amounts of documentation on Icon and sample programs that have been constructed using Icon.

Intel Architecture Labs
http://developer.intel.com/ial/

The Intel Architecture Labs site offers a look at ongoing developments at the very edge of information technology.

Java Goodies
http://www.javagoodies.com

Java Goodies is a repository of JavaScripts and posts between 5 to 10 new scripts each week. There are several JavaScript tutorials also available at this site.

JARS.COM
http://www.jars.com/

JARS.COM is a Java review service that reviews Java applets and applications and then posts the reviews to its website. Submissions are judged on the basis of quality and innovation with no distinction made between commercial, shareware or even student submitted programs. This is a very good site for finding the latest advances in Java based technology.

JavaSoft
http://www.javasoft.com

JavaSoft is the principal website for distribution of Sun's Java software, related documentation and sample code for Java projects.

Mulberry Technologies
http://www.mulberrytech.com/dsssl/index.html

Mulberry Technologies sponsors the DSSSL-L discussion list, the DSSSL Documentation Project and its site offers links to a wide range of DSSSL software. Both beginning and experienced DSSSL users should consider the Mulberry Technologies site a mandatory bookmark for their browsers.

Perl
http://www.perl.com/perl/index.html

Perl is a scripting language written by Larry Wall that is used extensively on the WWW for a variety of purposes. Its excellent string handling abilities make it a good choice for text manipulation programs on or off the Web. This site offers access to the latest releases of Perl in binary packages for many platforms, documentation on Perl, Perl FAQs and links to support and training on Perl.

Python
http://www.python.org/

Python is the official Python programming language website. Python is described at this site as "a portable, interpreted, object-oriented programming language." It has been ported to a number of platforms and can be used for a variety of applications both on and off the Web. This site offers binaries for most platforms, extensive tutorials and other documentation for the Python language.

Snobol4 and Spitbol
http://www.snobol4.com

Snobol4 is a programming language that emphasizes complex pattern matching and text manipulation. Spitbol is an optimized implementation of Snobol4. Professor Burhard Meissner of the Institut fuer Klassische Altertumswissenschaften, Martin-Luther-Universitaet Halle-Wittenberg, has posted his article SPITBOL Programming by/for Classicists: Accessing and Analyzing Classical Texts at **http://mlucom6.urz.uni-halle.de/altertum/v_f.html**. Older computing humanists will recall Susan Hockey's book SNOBOL Programming for the Humanities, published by

Solaris 2.5/2.6 Freeware
http://smc.vnet.net/solaris_2.5.html

This site offers ready to install versions of a wide range of public domain software for Solaris 2.5/2.6. The software ranges from C/C++ compilers (gcc) and Emacs to the TeX typesetting package.

Tcl/Tk Information
http://www.tcltk.com/consortium

The Tcl (tool command language) programming language originated with Dr. John Ousterhout while he was teaching at the University of California at Berkeley. The language has continued to evolve while Dr. Ousterhout moved to Sun Microsystems and ultimately to his own company, Scriptics **http://www.scriptics.com**. Both Tcl and its X-Windows extension Tk remain free for downloading over the Web. Tcl scripts are used in a number of web applications and notably in the DynaWeb software from Inso Corporation that serves the SELA website. The HTML pages that are delivered from SELA are dynamically constructed from SGML encoded texts using Tcl scripts.

TeX User's Group
http://www.tug.org

The TeX typesetting language was written by Donald Knuth and is freely available over the Web. Its primary users have been computer scientists and others in the "hard" sciences but it offers a range of typesetting abilities that every humanist should envy. TeX fonts are available for many languages including Klingon. This site offers links to many resources on the Web for TeX and further information on current developments in TeX.

VRML Consortium
http://www.vrml.org

The VRML Consortium was formed to promote VRML (Virtual Reality Modeling Language) as a standard for 3D multimedia and virtual worlds on the Internet. This site focuses on developing this standard with links to technical information on specification, working groups and recommended practices. It also maintains listings of mailing lists, web sites, FAQs and VRML Gems (short articles on particularly useful techniques for the use of VRML).

VRML Repository
http://www.sdsc.edu/vrml

The VRML Repository is the most comprehensive archive available for all aspects of VRML. The San Diego Supercomputer Center (SDSC) maintains this archive as a service to the VRML community of developers. The main page offers access to authoring and browsing tools, software development resources, objects, sounds and textures, and documentation on VRML. Many of the programs at this site are freely available as a service to the user community and scholars who use them to prepare VRML worlds should consider that generosity when creating access policies for their projects.

Unix System Administrator's Resources
http://www.stokely.com/unix.sysadm.resources/index.html

This site is included in this resource listing because serious work on the web or in computing humanities rapidly outstrips desktop computing resources. While most scholars are not interested in the technical aspects of Unix administration, this site can be most helpful to scholars who are learning Unix in the context of using Unix based programs for other purposes. The site covers all flavors of Unix and has links to extensive listings of software for Unix platforms.

W3C
http://w3c.org

The W3C site is the definitive site for anyone interested in current developments in web technology. W3C is an international consortium that promotes the evolution of the web and prepares standards to insure its interoperability. W3C standards, recommendations, proposals, technical reports and other documentation can be accessed at this site. The W3C has also released several software packages to serve as test beds for proposals and standards such as Jigsaw (a server written entirely in Jave) and Amaya (a browser/authoring tool).

WebCoder.com
http://www.webcoder.com/index_real.html

The WebCoder site offers a good selection of materials on both JavaScript and Dynamic HTML. The main page has links to demonstrations, reference materials, and how-to pages on particular techniques. The how-to section covers such topics as CSS (cascading style sheets), the document object model (DOM) and other topics of interest to users seeking more information on Dynamic HTML.

Web Resources
www.cio.com/WebMaster/wm_notes.html

Web Resources is a very complete collection of resources for beginning to expert webmasters. The main page offers links to sections on Graphics, HTML Information, Plug Ins, Programming, Search Engines, Site Management and Technologies.

WebReference.com
http://webreference.com

WebReference is an extremely useful site for experienced webmasters who want to remain current on the latest developments in web technology. The home page has links to several other major web technology sites and an expert section that includes links to topics such as: 3D/VRML Design, DHTML, E-Commerce, HTML, Internet and JavaScript.

XML Info
http://www.xmlinfo.com/

James Tauber of the Electronic New Testament Project mentioned in the Web resource section developed this site on the emerging XML standard. The site organizes links into the following categories: General Information, Specifications, Drafts and Proposals, XLink: The Extensible Linking Language, XSL: The Extensible Style Language, How People are Using XML, Books, Online Papers, Conferences, Seminars and Workshops, Courses, Developer Notes, Discussion Forums, Example XML Documents and Entities. This site covers some of the same topics at the XML/SGML site of Robin Cover but more tightly focused on the XML standard.

XML/SGML
http://www.oasis-open.org/cover/

Robin Cover maintains this website which focuses on all aspects of XML/SGML and related standards. Most requests for information, software and vendor information on XML or SGML discussion lists can be answered by visiting this site. Scholars interested in the academic use of SGML and its derivatives should visit the site often to remain current on the latest proposals and software releases.

Xerox Research
http://www.xerox.com/discoveries.html

The Research page at the Xerox site offers access to the Xerox research centers around the world. Some of the projects offer software for downloading such as the Arabic Morphological Parser noted above in the web resources section.

Subject Index

Art

Asian Religions

Bahai

Bible

Books

Electronic Texts, Collections/Indices

Feminist Perspectives

Greek

Hebrew

1882

Black Bird

18

STORY AND ART BY
KANOKO SAKURAKOUJI

CONTENTS

CHARACTERS

TADANOBU KUZUNOHA
Close childhood friend of Kyo's. Current leader of Kitsune clan.

AYAME
Wife of Sagami, who is a member of the Eight Daitengu.

SHO USUI
Kyo's older brother and ex-member of the Eig Daitengu. He is also kn as Sojo. His attempted c failed and he later die a duel against Kyo.

KYO USUI
Leader of the Tengu clan and Misao's first love.

MISAO HARADA
The Senka Maiden, bride of prophecy.

THE EIGHT DAITENGU
Kyo's bodyguards. Their names designate their official posts.

WE WILL...

...PROTECT YOU.

BUZEN

ZENKI

SAGAMI

HOKI

TARO

SABURO

JIRO

STORY THUS FAR
Misao can see spirits and demons, and her childhood sweetheart Kyo has been protecting her since she was little.

"Someday, I'll come for you, I promise."
Kyo reappears the day before Misao's 16th birthday to tell her, "Your 16th birthday marks 'open season' on you." She is the Senka Maiden, and if a demon drinks her blood, he is granted a long life. If he eats her flesh, he gains eternal youth. And if he makes her his bride, his clan will prosper...And Kyo is a *tengu*, a crow demon, with his sights firmly set on her.

Kyo avoided sleeping with Misao because he knew that sex with a demon is somehow dangerous for the Senka Maiden, but when poison nearly killed him, he finally gave in and took Misao.

Now that Kyo's powers have no equal, his older brother Sho, presumed dead, reappears. After a brutal battle, Kyo finally defeats Sho. With his last breath, Sho ominously predicts that Kyo will end up killing Misao.

Not long after, Misao's pregnancy comes to light. The *Senka Roku*, record of the fate of the previous Senka Maiden, is still missing. But a surviving Nue clan member tells them that "the Senka Maiden will die the instant her baby is born"!

Despite Kyo's arguments, Misao is determined to continue with her pregnancy, and Kyo has been desperately seeking some way to save her. But now the baby's due date is imminent...!

Black Bird

MOM SAW...

...KYO FLYING.

Hello, Sakurakouji here. We've finally come to the last volume of *Black Bird*.

I JUST GOT HOME.

OH, MOM...

Here's a little "thank you"

You didn't have to...

IT WAS SERIOUS ENOUGH.

PLEASE, COME IN.

IT WASN'T THAT SERIOUS, THEY JUST NEEDED TO CHECK ME OUT.

IF YOU'D TOLD US, I WOULD'VE COME TO PICK YOU UP.

YOU'VE BEEN DISCHARGED?

PAT

THIS IS SUCH A LARGE MANSION...

IF YOU LOOK AT IT WITH A CRITICAL EYE...

...THERE ARE A LOT OF THINGS THAT SEEM OUT OF PLACE.

THE WINDOWS ARE WIDE OPEN IN MID-WINTER, BUT IT ISN'T COLD.

YOUNG PRODIGIES.

MYSTERIOUS BOARDER, SUPPOSEDLY AN UNDERLING.

May we eat the cake that Taro baked?

Jiro, this isn't the time or place for that!

Lord Kyo, may I ask you a question?

YOUNG LORD ACTING LIKE A BIG SHOT.

Particle Physics

TADOKORO... ISN'T THAT THE SAME NAME AS THE CHIEF CABINET SECRETARY?

THE LADY.

...REALIZED THAT KYO AND THE OTHERS AREN'T HUMAN.

MOM MUST'VE...

YOU'RE GOING SHOPPING WITH MISAO TODAY, AREN'T YOU?

She's getting ready.

YES...

SHE SAID YOU HAVEN'T BOUGHT EVERYTHING YOU NEED FOR THE BABY.

OH...

HELLO.

WE NEED A RIDE.

Bring the car around, will you?

That's her mom for you.

I'll get ready.

SHOULD I...

...GO SHOPPING WITH YOU TOO?

OF COURSE.

BEFORE YOU KNOW IT...

WELL...

...SHE'LL START KNITTING SOCKS AND THINGS FOR HIM.

SHE'S ON HER THIRD PAIR.

That's the way she is.

Already.

14

MISAO...

ARE YOU TIRED?

WE'RE BACK...

MISAO... ALL THIS STUFF.

Where should I put it?

PARKING THE CAR.

OH, WHERE'S LORD KYO?

WELCOME HOME.

THE OINTMENT THEY PRESCRIBED AT THE HOSPITAL IS WORKING.

OH, THAT'S GOOD!

YES...

WHAT?

THE CUT ON YOUR FACE LOOKS A LOT BETTER.

WHY DON'T YOU COME IN, MOM?

Oh...

THANKS.

I'LL MAKE YOU SOME TEA!

32

I HAVE TO TELL HER...

...THE TRUTH ABOUT KYO...

...BEFORE SHE TELLS ME THAT SHE KNOWS.

MOM...

IF NOT FOR KYO...

...IT WOULD'VE BEEN MORE THAN JUST A SCAR. I MIGHT NOT BE HERE AT ALL...

I THANK GOD.

TO THINK, I HAVE A SON-IN-LAW WHO CAME TO SAVE ME, HIS FACE ALL DRAWN WITH WORRY.

"JUST AS WE SUSPECTED, YOUR MOM KNOWS."

Black Bird

I CAN'T SIT LIKE THIS FOR VERY LONG...

This is tough...

WHEW...

GASP!

FLING

DON'T LOOK!

HA HA, TOO LATE.

AH!

Found it! ♡

That's my underwear drawer.

YOUR INVESTIGATIVE SKILLS, OR NOSINESS...

...KNOWS NO BOUNDS!!

THERE ISN'T A SINGLE THING ABOUT YOU THAT I'LL LEAVE UNCOVERED. ♡

YOU'RE NOT GOOD AT HIDING IT...

...SO I FIND IT EASILY. I'VE READ MOST OF IT BY NOW.

YOU!

ACTUALLY, IT'S OKAY...

THERE ARE THINGS THAT I CAN'T SEEM TO SAY OUT LOUD.

IT'S HARD TO FIND THE WORDS WHEN I'M SPEAKING.

I HOPE IF I WRITE IT DOWN, I'LL BE ABLE TO CONVEY EVEN A FRACTION OF WHAT I FEEL.

Come help me, Mommy!♥

Hey!

I'M JUST A KID...

...SO I CAN'T BATHE BY MYSELF!

AH...

...HE MOVED AGAIN.

HE PROBABLY FEELS NICE AND WARM.

LITTLE SOH MOVES AROUND A LOT WHEN I'M IN THE BATH.

I
KNOW.

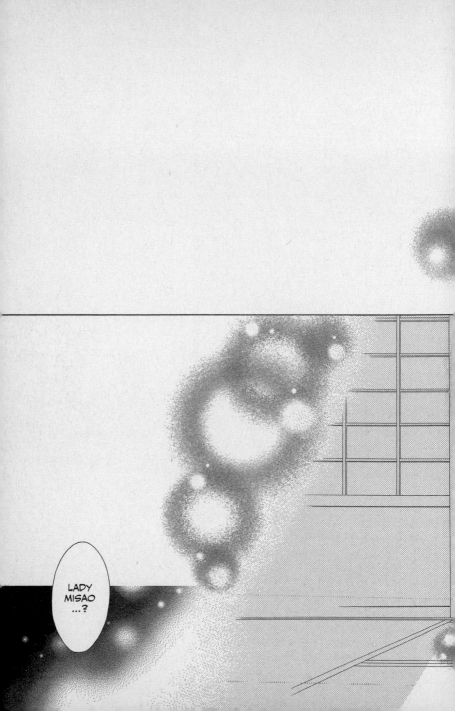

LADY
MISAO
...?

KYO...

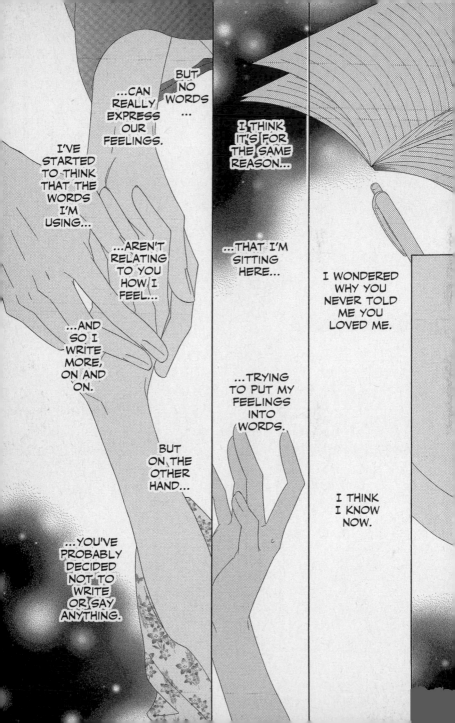

YOU'VE PUT YOUR LIFE ON THE LINE IN ORDER TO LOVE ME.

I CAN FEEL IT.

I UNDERSTAND THAT.

BUT YOU, KYO...

...HAVE ALWAYS LET YOUR ACTIONS SPEAK FOR YOU.

I LOVE YOU SO MUCH.
THANK YOU.
I HOPE THAT MY LIFE...
...WILL LET YOU SEE HOW I TRULY FEEL.

Black Bird

80

WHY IS EVERYONE GLOOMY?

THIS IS SUPPOSED TO BE A HAPPY TIME.

THUD

I...

...READ SO MANY BOOKS.

I SEARCHED...

RUSTLE

"JIRO, JIRO, HAVE A CANDY."

JUST A LITTLE WHILE AGO...

...LADY MISAO WAS LAUGHING AS USUAL.

...BUT I COULDN'T FIND IT...

"THIS IS REALLY GOOD..."

LADY MISAO...

TARO...

...A WAY TO KEEP HER ALIVE.

EVERY-ONE...

...LOVES HER...!

...WAS SO CAREFUL WITH THE FOOD HE PREPARED FOR HER.

TARO...

I SEARCHED SO HARD!

...AND

...DID EVERYTHING THEY COULD.

WHY WASN'T THAT ENOUGH?

THEY COULD...

...ONLY WATCH.

WELL, THAT'S...

...true, I suppose.

FATHER LIKES MOTHER BETTER THAN ME.

THAT'S A LIE!

...HEH.

IN LORD KYO'S HEART...

...NO ONE IS MORE PRECIOUS THAN LADY MISAO.

...IN THE ROOM WHERE THE ONLY SOUNDS WERE THE NEWBORN'S CRIES...

THAT DAY...

...LADY MISAO LAY STILL...

...KISSED HER LIPS.

...AND LORD KYO GENTLY...

...HIS KISS GOODBYE.

EVERYONE WAS SURE IT WAS...

LORD KYO...!

WE WERE FILLED WITH SADNESS...

...AT HIS KISS THAT WENT ON AND ON.

NO ONE THOUGHT THERE MIGHT BE...

...ANOTHER REASON FOR IT.

THE FIRST TO NOTICE...

...WAS THE DOCTOR.

SHE HAS A PULSE.

IS HE...

...USING...

...HIS KISS...

...

IT'S VERY FAINT, BUT—

...LORD KYO?

SHE'S NOT GONE.

NO
ONE...

HE
CONTINUED
...

...COULD
SAY
THEM.

...THROUGH-
OUT THE
FOLLOWING
DAY...

...AND
INTO
THE
NIGHT.

I HAVE
TO KEEP
MYSELF
BUSY...

TARO FEELS THE SAME WAY.

SLICE

SLICE

I BROUGHT IT, TARO.

THANKS.

THIS IS THE CANDY LADY MISAO GAVE US.

OH...

OH, THAT'S...

...LADY MISAO'S CANDY.

"THIS IS DELICIOUS!"

SHE SAID THEY'RE HER FAVORITES NOW.

I just had one.

SO MANY LEFT...

I MUST BELIEVE...

I MUST SUPPORT...

...LORD KYO'S CONVICTION.

"KICK HER RIDICULOUS FATE TO HELL!"

"DON'T GIVE UP."

"HELP HER UNTIL YOU REACH YOUR LIMIT."

"TILL THE VERY END..."

"...KEEP TRYING."

DOZE

...THE WIND HAS DIED DOWN.

Oh!

PLIP

NEVER BEFORE...

...AND NEVER AFTER...

...HAVE WE SEEN LORD KYO CRY.

...THAT HE WAS NEVER SURE UNTIL THE END.

Senka and Misao Preservation possible?

AND THAT BROUGHT TO MIND THE NOTE THAT SHO HAD JOTTED DOWN.

HE HAD BEEN TALKING ABOUT "PRESERVING" ENERGY.

THE STORY SHE TOLD HIM, JUST BEFORE GIVING BIRTH, ABOUT THE TOTAL AMOUNT OF HAPPINESS...

...REMINDED HIM OF THE LAW OF ENERGY CONSERVATION.

HE HAD CURED LADY MISAO OF A COLD ONCE, IN THE SAME WAY.

BUT PERHAPS IT SHOULD BE CALLED "DEPOSITS."

SO THE TRUTH IS, BY RETURNING THE ENERGY, HE WAS ABLE TO BRING HER BACK TO LIFE.

...BY VARIOUS MEANS.

IN OTHER WORDS, THE SENKA MAIDEN GIVES HER HUSBAND HER UNLIMITED ENERGY...

IT MADE SENSE WHEN WE THOUGHT ABOUT IT LATER, BUT...

So well conceived.

THE MORE SHE IS LOVED BY HER HUSBAND, THE MORE ENERGY SHE HAS TO DEPOSIT WITH HIM, AND SO SHE DOES MORE TO ATTRACT HIM.

...AT THE TIME...

...WE COULD ONLY SEE IT AS A MIRACLE.

SHE'S ABLE TO WALK NOW, DUE TO INTENSE PHYSICAL THERAPY.

IT MAY HAVE BEEN AN AFTEREFFECT OF BEING IN A COMA, BUT...

...SINCE THEN, LADY MISAO HAS HAD TROUBLE WALKING.

ARE YOU ALL RIGHT?

THUD

MOTHER!

Oh!

WAAAH!

I'm sorry!

YOU! SOH!

I'VE TOLD YOU NOT TO JUMP ON MISAO!!

LEAVE ME ALONE.

DO YOU REALIZE YOU'LL LOOK EVEN WORSE BALD?

IT'S PAST TIME FOR YOU TO SHAVE YOUR HEAD, YOU CORRUPT PRIEST.

ZENKI IS UNDERGOING TRAINING IN ORDER TO BECOME HEAD OF THE HIYOKUIN ORPHANAGE.

BUZEN LEFT THE VILLAGE AFTER BEING ASSIGNED TO A POST IN THE COUNTRY.

NOW THAT THE THREE OF US ARE ALL ATTENDING TO LORD SOH...

SOME-TIMES, I FEEL NOSTALGIC...

...FOR THOSE DAYS WHEN WE ALL...

OH.

HOKI!

...ONLY SAGAMI AND HOKI...

...PROTECTED LORD KYO'S LIFE TOGETHER...

AM I THE LAST HERE?

...ATTEND TO LORD KYO.

SHE ASKS FOR LOVE...

LORD KYO SAID THAT THE SENKA MAIDEN IS...

...AND CONTINUES TO LIVE WITH DEMONS PROTECTING HER.

...A BEING THAT IS ALWAYS ASKING FOR LOVE.

THE MIRACLE OF THE DAYS SPENT BY THESE TWO.

THE MIRACLE CREATED BY...

...THE UNORTHODOX DEMON WHO LOVED THE SENKA MAIDEN.

IT'S FOR THE DEMON...

...THAT I WRITE THIS DOWN...

THMP

for the demon who will one day love a future Senka Maiden that I write this and preserve this record.

Jiro Usui

Usui Clan
Senka Roku

...WHO WILL ONE DAY LOVE A FUTURE SENKA MAIDEN...

...AND PRESERVE THIS RECORD.

BLACK BIRD THE END

Black Bird

...STILL FEELS THE AFTER-EFFECTS.

KYO...

I AM FINE.

KYO.

SEEING ME SLEEPING...

...BRINGS BACK BAD MEMORIES.

I AM ALIVE...

I AM ALIVE.

PLEASE...

...DON'T TELL HIM...

HIS SECONDS...

...ARE READY.

THANKS.

STARE

Really?

He's not satisfied with just mother's milk.

HE REALLY IS A DEMON, ISN'T HE?

SOH DRINKS SO MUCH...

...MY BREASTS ARE GOING TO SHRIVEL UP.

139

...I LOST MY SENKA MAIDEN POWERS.

ONCE SOH WAS BORN...

...I CAN'T GIVE HIM ENERGY ANY-MORE...

EVEN IF KYO IS TIRED...

GOOD NIGHT.

I WONDER...

...IF ALL I CAN DO IS GIVE HIM MORE PAIN.

CAN'T I EVER BE HIS SWEET LITTLE BRIDE AGAIN...?

I HAVEN'T WASHED MY FACE TODAY.

OH...

Before I knew it...

SOH HAS BEEN FUSSING ALL MORNING...

HUH?

BUT IT'S NEARLY NOON.

144

LORD SOH ISN'T THE ONLY ONE ENAMORED BY HIM.

HIS WINGS ARE AS GLORIOUS AS EVER...

IT'S A LITTLE UNFAIR...

YOU SAY THAT, LADY MISAO...

KYO HAS ONLY THE GOOD TIMES.

...BUT YOU'RE REALLY HAPPY ABOUT IT, AREN'T YOU?

THAT LORD KYO TAKES SUCH GOOD CARE OF LORD SOH...

HOKI AND I ARE GOING TO SEE HORSES!

CLOTHES?

ARE YOU GOING SOME-WHERE?

OH, THAT SOUNDS NICE.

I'D LIKE TO GO TOO.

Hurray!

...SO I THOUGHT I'D TAKE HIM TO A RANCH.

HE'S NEVER RIDDEN A HORSE...

MOTHER...

PLEASE GET MY CLOTHES...

KYO...

PLEASE FORGIVE HIM...

I'm fine, I'm fine.

WOBBLE

ANOTHER SUMMER...

WHY ARE YOU POUTING?

IF YOU KEEP YELLING, SOH WILL WAKE UP.

YOU KNOW VERY WELL WHY!

I HEARD...

...THAT AN ATTENDANT IS USUALLY ASSIGNED AROUND AGE TEN.

IT CAN'T BE HELPED.

...

THAT'S HOW POWERFUL SOH IS.

IT'S TOO EARLY...

...HE'S ONLY FIVE.

168

WE WILL
CONTINUE
TO LIVE...

...OUR
LIVES
AS WE
ARE.

LIFE ✿ THE END ✿ PUBLISHED IN THE MARCH 2013 ISSUE OF BETSUCOMI

DATE

HUH?

WHERE? WHERE?!

THERE'S A REALLY HANDSOME GUY OVER THERE... ♡

STARE

WHAT ARE YOU LOOKING AT?

I WANT
TO FALL
IN LOVE,
TOO!

OH...

YEAH...

DATE * THE END * PUBLISHED IN THE EARLY FALL 2012 ISSUE OF *DELUXE BETSUCOMI*

CAST

STUDIO

→ 13:00 Camera rehearsal

→ 17:00 Taping

19:00 Break

Black Bird drama series filming schedule

TIME	SCENE #	LOCATION	Misao	Kyo	Sagami	Buzen	Hoki	Zenki	Taro, Jiro, Saburo
	⑧13	Mansion	○	○	○	○	○	○	○
	⑧21	School							
	⑧14		○	○					

PLEASE GET TO THE STUDIO.

OH! MISS MISAO...

?

?

182

WHO DO YOU THINK I AM?

I'M SORRY!

HOW COULD WE MAKE A POPULAR CHILD ACTING PRODIGY WAIT!

SO THE TRIPLETS ARE PLAYED BY ONE PERSON...

SHOCK

LADY MISAO...

What a genius!

Wow

OH...

MISAO!

YANK

AH... ALL RIGHT.

WE'RE GOING TO SHOOT THE SABURO SCENE FIRST.

MR. TARO...

TWIRL☆

GRIIN

186

CAST ＊ THE END ＊ PUBLISHED IN WINTER 2012 ISSUE OF DELUXE BETSUCOMI

From now on, we're in charge.

Heh... You're so green.

Good job!

Hoki changed a lot, but not as much as Saburo...

Not all of my characters are here, but it would please me to no end if you would picture them all in some deep mountain village or other, living happily to this day.

Black Bird has safely come to an end. I'm fortunate that this series went on for so long, and that I was able to draw everything that I wanted to. I have nothing but gratitude for all those who supported me throughout.

He has a girl-friend now.

Tsubaki and Ryu aren't twins. They're a year apart in age.

Misao's dad quit working at the college and is now a writer.

SPECIAL THANKS

EDITORS: Y, S, H

ASSISTANTS: Yuka Yuka, Gussan, Meira, Akane, Kazuyo, Hara, and everyone who came to help. And finally, Negishi and Nagisa ♥ ♥ ♥ An auspicious day, 2013

In lieu of a thank you gift, I've drawn a final illustration inside of the back cover. It was actually the most often requested theme... "Dressing up as a woman." Please accept my sincere gratitude!

桜小路かのこ
Kanako Sakurakouji

Kanoko Sakurakouji was born in downtown Tokyo, and her hobbies include reading, watching plays, traveling and shopping. Her debut title, *Raibu ga Hanetara*, ran in *Bessatsu Shojo Comic* (currently called *Bestucomi*) in 2000, and her 2004 *Bestucomi* title *Backstage Prince* was serialized in VIZ Media's *Shojo Beat* magazine. She won the 54th Shogakukan Manga Award for *Black Bird*.

BLACK BIRD
VOL. 18
Shojo Beat Edition

Story and Art by KANOKO SAKURAKOUJI

BLACK BIRD Vol. 18
by Kanoko SAKURAKOUJI
© 2007 Kanoko SAKURAKOUJI
All rights reserved.
Original Japanese edition published by SHOGAKUKAN.
English translation rights in the United States of America, Canada, the United
Kingdom and Ireland arranged with SHOGAKUKAN.

TRANSLATION JN Productions
TOUCH-UP ART & LETTERING Gia Cam Luc, Latty Luc
DESIGN Amy Martin
EDITOR Pancha Diaz

The stories, characters and incidents mentioned
in this publication are entirely fictional.

Printed in the U.S.A.

Published by VIZ Media, LLC
P.O. Box 77010
San Francisco, CA 94107

10 9 8 7 6 5 4 3 2 1
First printing, March 2014

www.shojobeat.com   www.viz.com

Change Your Perspective–Get **BIG**

From Yuu Watase,
the creator of *Absolute Boyfriend*,
Alice 19th, *Ceres: Celestial Legend*,
Fushigi Yûgi: Genbu Kaiden, and *Imadoki*!

Relive Miaka's journey to a
fictional past with the new
VIZBIG Edition of *Fushigi Yûgi!*
Each features:

- Three volumes in one
- Color artwork
- Larger trim size
- New content
- Exclusive cover designs

See why *Bigger is Better*–
start your VIZBIG collection today!

Absolute Boyfriend

BY YUU WATASE

Only $8.99

Rejected way too many times by good-looking (and unattainable) guys, shy Riiko Izawa goes online and signs up for a free trial of a mysterious Nightly Lover "figure." The very next day, a cute naked guy is delivered to her door, and he wants to be her boyfriend! What gives? And...what's the catch?

MANGA SERIES ON SALE NOW

We Were There

By Yuki Obata
Also known as the award-winning series *Bokura ga Ita*

Get to the Bottom of a Broken Heart

It's love at first sight when Nanami Takahashi falls for Motoharu Yano, the most popular boy in her new class. But he's still grieving his girlfriend who died the year before. Can Nanami break through the wall that surrounds Motoharu's heart?

Find out in *We Were There*— manga series on sale now!

SURPRISE

You may be reading
the wrong way!

It's true: In keeping with the original
Japanese comic format, this book reads
from right to left—so action, sound
effects, and word balloons are completely
reversed. This preserves the orientation
of the original artwork—plus, it's fun!
Check out the diagram shown here to
get the hang of things, and then turn to
the other side of the book to get started!

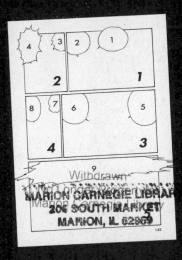